MANAGING
PERFORMANCE
STRESS

MANAGING
PERFORMANCE
STRESS

MODELS AND METHODS

DAVID PARGMAN

Routledge
Taylor & Francis Group
New York   London

Routledge is an imprint of the
Taylor & Francis Group, an informa business

Published in 2006 by
Routledge
Taylor & Francis Group
270 Madison Avenue
New York, NY 10016

Published in Great Britain by
Routledge
Taylor & Francis Group
2 Park Square
Milton Park, Abingdon
Oxon OX14 4RN

Printed in the United States of America on acid-free paper
10 9 8 7 6 5 4 3 2 1

International Standard Book Number-10: 0-415-95252-2 (Hardcover) 0-415-95253-0 (Softcover)
International Standard Book Number-13: 978-0-415-95252-1 (Hardcover) 978-0-415-95253-8 (Softcover)

informa

Taylor & Francis Group
is the Academic Division of Informa plc.

Visit the Taylor & Francis Web site at
http://www.taylorandfrancis.com

and the Routledge Web site at
http://www.routledge-ny.com

To the memory of *my* recently deceased mother,
Mildred Pargman,
and to the next generation — my grandchildren: Sydney, Max,
Macy, and Manny Pargman.

CONTENTS

PREFACE

This is a book about performance and stress. Although initially directed at athletes, it ultimately developed into a text for musicians, dancers, or for that matter, any person who exhibits motor skills in front of or in a competitive way against others. Those who teach, train, or coach performers should also find this book helpful.

Stress exerts a very substantial influence on performance, usually of an undesirable nature. Its effects are undifferentiated, so that its physiological and cognitive consequences cut across a broad array of performance types. By this I mean that the emotional response (e.g., feeling of weakness) that disables the concert violinist before he walks onstage is no different from the unsettling, wracking nervousness felt by the Olympic hurdler lacing up track shoes in the locker room before jogging into the stadium. Stressors make no distinctions among their targets. If they are interpreted as threatening, they will activate similar responses in all who perform or compete. Evidently, there is much of a threatening nature associated with performance and the evaluative process that typically goes along with it. It makes little difference if you are kicking a soccer ball, swinging from a high bar, or plucking the strings of a harp. In terms of stress reaction, the same models and theories explain why you are responding stressfully, and how your reaction will affect performance.

I suspect that if a motive for writing this book had to be identified, the most prominent would relate to a graduate course I teach at my university. Entitled "Arousal and Performance in Sport," the course first deals with various theoretical explanations of stress and anxiety, their causal factors, and their effects upon behavior in sports. A section on performance follows, in which basic principles of motor learning are reviewed; and finally the course deals with the control of stress and anxiety reactions. Although originally organized for the benefit of sports-oriented graduate students, the course soon began to attract people from other performance domains.

I am, so to speak, the founding father of this course at my university and, at the time of this writing, have been teaching it for more than 30 years. However, no single text is available that covers the material I deal with in a sequence and overall manner with which I feel comfortable. Therefore, I have been using an assortment of readings in other books and pertinent articles. My students and I have gotten by, but I have not been entirely pleased. It eventually became clear that a comprehensive reference in which the basic content material of the course would be included under one cover was necessary. After teaching the course for a few years, I decided to write this book. Its Table of Contents parallels the direction and emphases taken in my class.

However, upon searching for more deeply rooted reasons for writing this book, I realize that yet another authentic motive exists. As is the case with many motivations for adult behavior, certain childhood and early adulthood memories still reverberate in my awareness. I have not been able to disengage from certain of them and I believe that they play some part in stimulating me to plan and write this book.

I vividly remember, even though some 50 years have passed, the extreme horror I felt as a ninth grader on the morning of the day on which I was to perform an after-school saxophone solo with piano accompaniment. The performance was scheduled for 3:30 p.m. All day, I remained victimized by a previously unknown but awesome anxiety. I was unable to concentrate on schoolwork. I was ravaged by insecurity, fear, weakness, nausea, and a compelling desire to somehow escape from the commitment.

My mother and paternal grandmother were present at the concert. I remember searching the audience for their faces as soon as I walked unsteadily onto the auditorium stage. I planted my music stand, opened the music book to the selection, "La Cinquantaine" ("The Golden Wedding"), by Gabriel T. Marie, and scanned the audience. I located them. They smiled pridefully and my heart sank even more deeply in my chest.

Despite being well prepared for the concert (my father was my saxophone teacher), I performed poorly. In midperformance, I lost my place. Fortunately Mrs. Kessler, the accompanist, was able to follow my desperate meanderings. She improvised magnificently as I wandered recklessly all over the piece searching for a convenient but logical resolution. Her face revealed surprise and disappointment, which she communicated to me in no uncertain terms the following morning in school.

No one in the audience (with the obvious exception of Mrs. Kessler) seemed aware of my failure to re-create the piece as originally written. No one seemed aware of my struggle. When the performance reached its ersatz conclusion, signaled by a chord of finality on Mrs. Kessler's piano, the audience produced a tumultuous applause. It fairly overwhelmed me. I was a reasonably popular student and my many friends in the assembly responded to me as a buddy, as a basketball player and a nice guy, rather than as a musician. I was glad that my father was not in the audience.

I shall never forget this first experience with performance stress. I know now that it was entirely unnecessary. I should have been the beneficiary of some sort of preparation, some form of conditioning that would have enabled me to deal effectively with the anxiety and stress of performance, or prevent it from occurring at all. It would not have been so difficult to have someone at least talk to me about my feelings. Anyone who knew me reasonably well should have been able to see my plight all through that difficult day.

Today I enjoy performing, speaking, or exhibiting in front of groups. I have learned to be able to do this. But I shudder to think about the countless numbers who never escaped from the trauma of performance-related stress. And I believe my eagerness to somehow reach out to such sufferers is a part of my commitment to this book.

A second memory of near debilitation because of performance stress and anxiety related to membership on my college cross-country team. Already in my late teens and twentieth year of life, I endured untold and powerful anxiety about the Saturday morning meets. Friday was always a day off from training — as my coach would say, "a day for physical rest and mental preparation for tomorrow's meet." But no one ever attempted to teach me or my teammates how to do this, and so Fridays and early Saturday mornings were unforgettably painful. I recall praying for torrential rain or an unrelenting storm that would cause cancellation of the meet. I fantasized terrible occurrences that would permit me gracefully and excusably to scratch from the competition. None ever materialized, and I invariably was left to deal with my "outrageous fortune" alone. In the late fifties, sport psychology was unheard of, and the physical aspect of performance preparation was all coaches and teachers were usually able to deal with.

The chapters of this book were written for mentors of today's performers and perhaps for the performers themselves. To its readers I say, learn about stress. Appreciate its force and influence. This book tries to provide the opportunity to do this in a way analogous to the approach taken by the dog owner whose neighbor's child is frightened of his dog. The pet owner approaches the child benevolently and says, "Give me your hand. Come and touch this animal. He won't hurt you if you get to know him. Come learn what he's like."

The idea is to understand stress so you can deal with it — so it won't hurt you.

David Pargman
Tallahassee, Florida

ACKNOWLEDGMENTS

Gratitude is extended to the many students, performers, and mentors of performers who have attended my classes, workshops, and lectures over the years. They have helped me immeasurably in the development of the ideas and methods incorporated in this book. Special thanks is also offered to my graduate assistant, Kimberlee Bethany, whose assistance was unfailing and invaluable in many ways during the manuscript's preparation.

1

WHAT IS STRESS?

LEARNING OBJECTIVES

After reading this chapter, you should be able to:

- Define *arousal, activation, stressor, stress, homeostasis, burnout, eustress, fear,* and *anxiety*
- Differentiate between arousal and stress, and stress and anxiety
- List potential factors leading to burnout
- Identify symptoms of burnout
- Discuss Smith's model of athletic burnout
- Contrast cognitive and somatic anxiety
- Describe the inverted-U hypothesis, drive theory, and catastrophe theory
- Understand the individual zone of optimal functioning

IMPORTANT TERMS

- Arousal metabolic rate
- Stress
- Stressor
- Anxiety
- Eustress
- Distress

- Burnout
- Fear
- Inverted-U hypothesis
- Drive theory
- Catastrophe theory

1.1 INTRODUCTION

I am seated at a small table in the cafeteria of one of our nation's largest and busiest airports. Part of my two-hour wait for a connecting flight is being spent here. I have already glanced at the newspaper's headlines, taken a walk through colorful lobbies and malls, and visited the men's room. A light snack seems like a good time-killing activity.

I'm en route to a professional conference where considerable attention will be devoted to stress in relation to physical performance. And so I crumble salty crackers into a bowl of surprisingly delicious vegetable soup and feel excitement at the prospect of spending time with colleagues, friends, and professional acquaintances whom I haven't seen in a long time.

As I watch hundreds of travelers stream by on the concourse abutting my table, I think eagerly of the forthcoming conference. I also begin to think about stress and arousal. But my attention tends to shift to the battalion of travelers parading in front of me. I begin to wonder about the degrees to which these strangers are presently experiencing stress. I examine their faces as they hustle by. Because they are on parade and I am seated in the reviewing stand, I enjoy immunity from embarrassment. I do not feel self-conscious about my staring and ogling. My naive subjects move rapidly, unaware of my analytical stare. Many seem tired, others troubled. Some are apparently deep in thought — engrossed in private dilemmas, working their way through problems, predicaments, and puzzles.

Some of my subjects are walking so fast that they appear almost to be jogging. They are late. Why? Why are they late? What are the consequences of their lateness? Anxiety and stress are now paramount in my mind. I seem to see it everywhere. In a flash of introspection I realize that it may just be my present concern with this very chapter that influences my perceptions.

What common thread runs through the anxiety and arousal reactions of so many of my parading subjects? Is it that they have all *learned* to respond to certain stimuli in stressed ways? Or are other persons whom they have just left, will soon meet, or are thinking about responsible for their furrowed brows, grimaces, and other observable signs of stress? Is it anxiety about the hour or moment and what it holds in particular or is it the passing of time in general that is stressful to them? Perhaps their personalities dispose them to behave in the ways I observe. I speculate that beneath their fashionable suits and dresses, many of my subjects are experiencing physiological reactions to stress.

What ghosts and fears beleaguer my subjects as they hurry by my table? What skeletons jangle in their closets? Perhaps their present stress reactions are functions of experiences they encountered years and years ago. As they walk, do long forgotten memories bubble up into their consciousness? Maybe confrontation with those thoughts initiates their stress reactions.

I eat more soup and crackers and feel confident about the need for the chapter I'm presently working on: What Is Stress?

Stress is currently receiving a tremendous amount of attention in the popular, as well as scientific, literature. It is being indicted as a causal factor in such varied maladies as mental illness, cancer, cardiovascular disease, and even the common cold. In our enthusiasm for informal discussion of stress ramifications, we tend to use certain words very loosely. A special vocabulary of terms such as *arousal, burnout, anxiety, fear,* and *eustress* has consequently developed. Our purpose in this chapter is to establish more precise meanings for these terms and to review the concepts underlying their application.

1.2 AROUSAL OR ACTIVATION

An organism must be minimally activated or aroused if it is to be considered alive and alert to the stimuli in its environment. There are different ways to determine degree of activation. Physiological measures (which will be discussed later in this chapter) may be taken, or the organism's overt behavior may be used as a basis for evaluation. For example, activation levels may be determined in terms of frequency or degree of movement. However, not all movement is apparent or observable to the naked eye. Another way of determining degree of arousal is to record personal perceptions from the subject himself. An individual is usually able to report heightened arousal even though its cause(s) may be unclear.

Essentially, *arousal* refers to the extent to which all organs and systems in the body are "cranked up" and functioning. The speed with which the essential, life-sustaining processes occur is referred to as the *metabolic rate*. In a very activated organism, metabolism is high, particularly with regard to gross measures such as heart and respiratory rates. With regard to any specific activity, there is an activation level that yields best results for each of us.

1.3 STRESSORS

Stimuli that are construed as negative, harmful, or unpleasant are known as *stressors*. But there is much room for individual interpretation as to what is actually harmful or unpleasant. One person's stressor may be another person's pleasure. The attachment of meaning to stimuli (perception) is a very personal endeavor. The bountifulness of these environmental stressors tends to complicate matters even more. They are as plentiful as the leaves in my yard in the fall season. Their number defies calculation.

Some events may be safely considered to be universally stressful or unstressful in certain contexts. For instance, while hunting in the woods or firing a round at a shooting range, the sounds of gunshots would probably not cause a stress reaction in most of us. But hearing the very same sounds in our living room at 3 a.m. certainly would. A high school teacher who stands and speaks before classes of 25 to 35 students, four or five periods each day, might not consider a request to address a group of local businessmen at an evening meeting as potentially stressful. Speaking in front of an audience is something with which the veteran teacher is comfortable. However, a dentist, accustomed to dealing professionally with people on a one-to-one basis, might find such an assignment stress provoking.

Whether stimuli are, or are not, interpreted as stressors depends upon your previous experiences (personal history) and the context (physical and social) in which they are generated.

Although appearing in sundry forms and magnitudes, stressors may be conveniently classified into six broad categories: *social, physical, chemical/biochemical, bacterial, climactic,* and *physical/environmental*. Chapter 3 contains a discussion of these categories.

1.4 STRESS AS DIFFERENTIATED FROM AROUSAL

Although we may use the terms *arousal* and *activation* synonymously, careful distinction should be made between stress and anxiety. And the terms *stress* and *anxiety* should be distinguished from arousal and activation. Stress reactions are often arousing mentally and physiologically, but the converse is not true. Heightened arousal is not necessarily, causally related to stress.

At this point, a definition of stress is needed. However, establishing a unanimously acceptable understanding of this concept is problematic. Authorities adopt divergent views, and theoretical perspectives about the origins and underlying dynamics of stress vary considerably. A very helpful historical overview of the term's etiology and a description of its metamorphosis into its current applications and meanings are provided by Richard Lazarus (1993), one of the most well known scholar-researchers in the area of stress and emotions. He traces usage of the word *stress* from the 17th-century focus upon man-made structures such as bridges and the loads they were expected to carry, to its contemporary psychological applications.

1.5 A DEFINITION OF STRESS

For the time being, consider the following definition: *Stress is an unsettling reaction to external and internal factors.* Your reactions to environmental stimuli may be positive or negative, supportive or destructive. When your physiology is altered and your various systems and their particular biochemistry become "charged," the causal stimuli are referred to as stressors. Lazarus (1993) believes that appraisal of the stimuli in relation to perceived personal resources to deal with them and the thoughts subsequently inspired create feelings (affective consequences) that are the real culprits that generate stress. His approach, therefore, is psychological (motivational/emotional) — in contrast, for example, to the more physiological emphasis of Hans Selye (1976), whose ideas we will discuss later.

Unless you have learned to control your sympathetic (fight or flight) and autonomic (involuntary) responses, stress reactions are usually arousing. They are also disruptive of homeostasis (the very delicate state of the body's fluid and biochemical balance, a term coined by the physiologist Walter Cannon in the 1930s). Essentially this approach is the one taken by Selye (1976), perhaps the most renowned of all stress researchers. According to Selye, stress is a reaction to any stimulus that results in the disruption of homeostasis. In a nutshell, stress is typically viewed as having negative consequences and being undesirable. This is the way in which stress is commonly viewed. However, I will continue to suggest throughout this book that this may not be the case. Stress responses may have redeeming consequences.

1.5.1 Eustress

Some authorities use the terms *eustress* and *distress* to distinguish between "good" and "bad" stress reactions. Witness the dramatic physiological upheaval that accompanies sexual orgasm. Homeostasis is momentarily lost, many hormonal responses are at a peak, and vital signs are enormously exaggerated (e.g., heart rate, blood pressure, stroke volume, respiratory rate and depth). And so stress reactivity prevails — but the experience is usually accompanied by feelings of exhilaration, pleasure, thrill, and enjoyment. Stress — yes, but in particular, *eustress*.

1.6 WHAT IS BURNOUT?

Another term that deserves a place in our discussion is *burnout*. The term originally appeared in Freudenberger's (1983) discussion of workers or employees having feelings of failure and exhaustion due to excessive demands on their energy, with insufficient rewards for the effort. Burnout has been applied to sports behavior, and numerous definitions of the term are available. In their review of the literature concerning burnout in sports, Dale and Weinberg (1990) observed: "Many definitions of burnout have been suggested but as of yet, there is not one definition that is commonly agreed upon" (p.68). A common element in burnout is the perception that personal resources are inadequate to satisfy the demands of a task or situation. This is exemplified by the athlete who expresses the following attitude: "I'll never make the nationals. I try and try, I break my buns in practice, but I can't seem to make any progress. The other competitors seem to be consistently better — stronger, more skillful."

But demand overload may not be the exclusive culprit. Burnout may also result from work- or performance-related conditions in which personal resources greatly exceed demands. When the challenge is beneath capability level and personal resources are not tapped sufficiently, the consequence may be boredom. Burnout is typically manifested physically, psychologically, and behaviorally. Loss of motivation and decreased self-esteem are also common outcomes. Other physical symptoms include exhaustion, colds that linger, frequent headaches, gastrointestinal disturbance, weight loss, sleeplessness, and shortness of breath. Psychological symptoms entail mood shifts, irritability, increased levels of depression, loss of caring for people, cynical attitude, increased frustration, feelings of helplessness, and increased risk taking (e.g., smoking, alcohol and drug abuse). Behavioral symptoms often include work-performance deterioration and absenteeism (from work, rehearsal, team practice, etc.) (Freudenberger, 1983; Maslach, Schaufeli, & Leiter, 2002).

1.6.1 Burnout: A Reaction to Stress

Smith (1986) describes burnout as a stress reaction: "Its most notable feature is a psychological, emotional and at times a physical withdrawal from a formerly pursued and enjoyable activity" (p.37). In this context, burnout is quite relevant to sports, as well as to dance and musical training, since it is often associated with dropping out or withdrawing from participation. Excessive pressure to succeed, lack of progress, insufficient fun, and frequent failure are factors that contribute to burnout. On a simple level, burnout may also be viewed as a condition produced by working too hard for too long in a high-pressure situation accompanied by an ongoing loss of idealism, energy, and purpose (Cherniss, 1980). Burnout is more job or performance related than is depression. An athlete who trains at high levels of intensity throughout the calendar year with little or no deviation in the nature of his workouts is a good candidate for burnout. The same would be true of musicians and dancers who "overdo" for extended periods of time. Unrelenting touring and concertizing may sap the energy and vitality of the performer and deprive her of pleasure and satisfaction.

Burnout may also be described in nontechnical terms as physical and emotional exhaustion, loss of interest, low self-esteem, and low performance levels. In effect, the condition is characterized by an inability to cope with exigencies of a particular situation (Freudenberger, 1983). Additional symptoms may also be present; Feigley (1984) identified fatigue, increased irritability, loss of enthusiasm, minor body aches, and eating disorders as elements of burnout.

Henschen (1998) described experiences that athletes endure before burnout occurs, including the so-called performance slump, where nothing seems to go right. Accompanying this are loss of self-confidence in performance ability and self-defeating attempts to compensate and work harder. All of these responses may occur in coaches as well, particularly during certain times of the season (e.g., during playoffs and recruitment) (Kelley, 1994; Kelley & Gill, 1993; Martin, Kelley, & Eklund, 1999).

1.6.2 Measuring Burnout

Although a number of tools are available to measure burnout, perhaps the most popular is the Maslach Burnout Inventory (Maslach & Jackson, 1981). The instrument includes three categories, each of which is associated with a burnout factor. These factors — emotional exhaustion, depersonalization, and personal accomplishment — are considered on a continuum from low to high.

The sports domain offers frequent opportunities for burnout because it is a spawning ground for numerous and powerful stressors on and off the playing field. Burnout need not necessarily accrue from intense athletic participation. Additional potential sources of stress include demanding social relations (getting along with disliked team members or coaches), severe (or at least unpleasant) climatic conditions, physical trauma and associated pain or discomfort associated with injury, time constraints, and everything related to pursuit of the "win" ethic. The sports domain seems to be ideal for the incubation of burnout; however, a very well developed body of research literature testifies to burnout's development and presence in almost all job and career areas. It is certainly present in all performance areas where training, competition, or evaluated exhibition of skills is of essence.

Burnout may cause many youth athletes to leave sports prior to achieving their competitive potential (Nash, 1987). However, some participants may disengage from sports for reasons unrelated to burnout (Gould, 1993). Leaving one sport (dropping out) and entering another may have little or nothing to do with any of the sources of stress listed above. Sometimes children attempt to explore alternatives to their present activities and leave a sport in order to participate in another. These children, therefore, are not experiencing burnout. As expressed by Feigley (1984), "It is ironic that these quiet, concerned, energetic, perfectionists demonstrate characteristics that coaches most prefer" (p.110). When the performance of such children falls short of their goals, they may work even harder, much to the satisfaction of coaches and parents who view them as exemplary participants. Or they may quit.

1.6.3 Smith's Model of Athletic Burnout

What is necessary in seeking to understand performance-related burnout is an underlying theory that identifies its causal factors. To really be useful the theory should also explain how these factors might interrelate, and moreover, how they are linked to burnout itself. In providing a theoretical framework for burnout, Smith (1986) is among the very few who have gone beyond empirical approaches and attempted to provide a conceptual model (grounded in social exchange theory) that clarifies its nature, causes, and consequences.

According to this model, burnout is a consequence of stress-induced costs and too much prolonged stress. An activity that once provided satisfaction becomes so stressful that withdrawal is an attractive alternative. Smith (1986) cites related symptoms such as low energy, chronic fatigue, and increased susceptibility to illness. Also identified are exhaustion during the day, poor sleep at night, depression, helplessness, and anger. With regard to sports behavior in particular, Smith describes decreased efficiency and inconsistent performance as observable signs of burnout. His model depicts the "parallel relationships assumed to exist among situational, cognitive, physiological and behavioral components of stress and burnout" (p.40). Burnout is the consequence of their interrelations. This model could also be applied in helpful ways to performance areas other than sports.

Smith (1986) emphasizes *cognitive appraisal* processes (consistent with the conceptualization of stress by Lazarus, mentioned earlier), that is, the evaluative thoughts held by a performer relative to his or her readiness to meet a particular challenge. According to Smith, the athlete's or performer's emotions are contingent upon perceptions of the situation, its demands, evaluation of available personal resources for satisfying these demands, and an understanding of the personal consequences involved in not meeting them. When one's ability to meet task demands is misjudged because of low self-confidence or irrelevant or incorrect beliefs about the importance of meeting these demands, the stress response is activated. It is therefore important for performers to have realistic views of these abilities and to be able to identify their competency range for different tasks. In addition, these elements interact with motivational and personality variables. Therefore, people with different personality profiles are likely to respond in various ways to the very same stressors; some are inclined to burnout, others are not.

1.7 FEAR

Your level of arousal — the speed with which the little factories in each of your body cells are functioning, and the rate at which your major organs such as the heart and lungs are operating — is influenced by numerous factors, many of which have perceptual/cognitive bases. Some arousal responses are determined autonomically or involuntarily. Others are initiated by the interpretations you make of stimuli in the physical environment. Emotions, or "feeling tones," influence general activation levels. When you are angry, your heart beats faster and your breathing rate increases. The same thing happens when you are overwhelmed (for instance, with news of a death or tragedy in the family). In fact, as the saying goes, you can *feel* the reaction "in the pit of your stomach."

One emotion frequently experienced by performers is *fear.* Fear involves the perception of a stimulus as being harmful to well-being. To wit, it's dangerous. Fear is stressful and usually generates dramatic physiological responses.

Fear involves the conceptualization of a clear and rational source of danger. For example, you are fearful about the well-being of your friend lying critically ill in the hospital. Or, since you are very much aware that you have failed to learn a complex dismount from the flying rings, you are fearful of falling and being injured. Similarly, you may fear being bitten by a large and ferocious-looking dog that chases you during a morning jog. In each of these examples, the emotion of fear is logically based. However, this is not the case with anxiety.

1.7.1 Anxiety

Anxiety may be viewed as a form of fear, but fear with a high degree of subjectivity. In contrast, fear itself is rational. The dog chasing you and the illness with which your friend must contend are real and concrete. However, stimuli that provoke anxiety responses are vague and poorly defined.

A case in point would be the "jitters," the strong sense of uneasiness we feel immediately before going on stage or while approaching the starting line of a ski or road race. Something is bothering us, but we're not sure what it is. We are upset and physiologically activated. We know that we are well prepared. We have practiced regularly and diligently for an appropriate period of time leading up to the event. Our skills and physical capacities are adequate for the challenge, yet we are worried. Why are we worried? We can't seem to put our finger on it. This is anxiety. It's a feeling of, "Must I go through with this, and can I really do this?" Mentors, teachers, and coaches try to intervene with supportive comments, but usually to little avail — "Come on, you can do it" or "What are you worried about?" This is precisely the nature of anxiety. We don't have a good understanding of why we are worried, but we are worried. The parent attempting to comfort a young child in the dentist's waiting room is challenged by the little one's irrationality and finds it extremely difficult to lead his son or daughter through an anxiety escape route: "Sweetheart, there's nothing to worry about. Dr. Smith won't hurt you. He's only going to x-ray and clean your teeth. Why are you so upset?" The nervous child responding to the entire context of environmental stimuli with weak objectivity and increased physiological arousal is experiencing anxiety.

1.7.1.1 The Multidimensionality Approach   The multidimensionality conceptualization of anxiety (often referred to as multidimensional theory) posits two kinds of anxiety: *cognitive anxiety* and *somatic anxiety* (Martens, Vealey, & Burton, 1990). Cognitive anxiety is accompanied by symptoms such as concentration difficulty, worry, and insomnia. Somatic anxiety is accompanied by symptoms such as headaches, nausea, and rapid heart rate. While such distinction can facilitate discussion of anxiety, it is unlikely that these responses are really very different in most individuals. That is, most of us react anxiously both cognitively as well as somatically.

1.8 AROUSAL AND PERFORMANCE: THE INVERTED-U HYPOTHESIS

A number of theories that attempt to clarify the relationship between arousal and performance are available. We now turn to a few that are relatively well known.

The *inverted-U hypothesis,* developed from very old research by Yerkes and Dodson (1908), suggests that the relationship between arousal and correct response (habit) is nonlinear; that is, as arousal increases, correctness of response does not change in lockstep. According to this hypothesis, beyond a certain point of arousal, performance is expected to deteriorate. A stabilization or leveling off of the relationship between arousal and desirable performance occurs at the so-called optimal level.

The curve that represents this relationship hypothesizes a plateau at which optimal performance is expected to occur. The term *optimal level of arousal hypothesis* is often used synonymously with inverted-U hypothesis, which is derived from a graphic portrayal of the curvilinear relationship between performance and arousal. Figure 1.1 demonstrates this relationship. The left side of the curve indicates that the variables of arousal and performance are strongly correlated in a positive manner. As one increases, so does the other. But the right side of the curve portrays an equally strong negative relationship; performance deteriorates as arousal is increased. The trick is to identify the "optimal" level of arousal for each performer, for each task. For instance, this level would be different for typing at a computer keyboard, where accuracy is highly valued, compared with competing in power lifting, where brute strength is paramount.

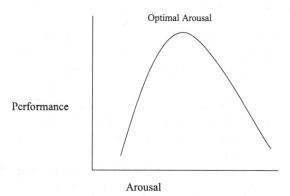

Figure 1.1 The Inverted U represents the relationship between arousal and performance.

1.8.1 Drive Theory

Drive theory posits a linear or direct relationship between arousal and performance. As one variable increases or decreases, so does the other. In juxtaposing drive theory and the inverted-U hypothesis, Landers (1980) observed that in a situation where a subject's drive is high on a well-learned task, drive theory predicts that the quality of performance will be high; whereas the inverted-U approach hypothesizes that the quality of the performance will be low. Landers suggests the need to appreciate the difference between the two hypotheses, since they offer different implications for teaching and coaching practice. For instance, according to the inverted-U hypothesis, too much arousal is capable of causing a decrease in performance, whereas drive theory predicts a continual improvement in performance as drive increases. However, Landers also points out that the inverted-U hypothesis does not explain the relationship between arousal and performance but only describes its curvilinear nature. In recent years, drive theory has lost a good deal of its original support and has been replaced by more supportable theories.

1.8.2 Catastrophe Theory

With sports performers in mind, Hardy and Parfitt (1991) offered an interesting alternative to the inverted-U hypothesis. Their *catastrophe theory* predicts that increases in arousal will account for optimal performance (as predicted by the inverted-U model). However, once an athlete's arousal exceeds this preferred point, his performance decline is very marked. Athletes do not regroup after this catastrophic drop-off. The inverted-U hypothesis predicts a more gradual or symmetrical decline in performance.

All performers should be aware of their level of arousal. More importantly, it is beneficial for the performers to be able to modify the degree to which they permit themselves to be aroused in accordance with particular tasks that must be executed. For example, a higher level of activation would be appropriate in wrestling than in shuffleboard. This arousal control is not easy to do and requires training. Arousal may be fine-tuned with techniques such as biofeedback training, muscle relaxation training, and breathing control. These techniques are to be acquired and, like any other skill, must be properly taught, patiently learned, and adequately practiced. They will be described in Chapters 10, 11, and 12.

Unquestionably, some researchers are critical of the optimal arousal or inverted-U approach. For instance, approximately 30 years ago, Baddeley (1972) faulted this hypothesis because it accounts for a wide variety of results, as long as they do not have to be predicted in advance. And even earlier, Naatanen (1969) criticized the relationship between activation and performance and observed that performance is related to particular features of various experimental research designs. Martens (1974) portrayed the inverted-U hypothesis as sort of an after-the-fact notion, or, to employ research jargon, a "post-hoc analysis" rather than something that might necessarily occur. Fazey and Hardy (1988), Neiss (1988), and Weinberg (1990) have also criticized the conceptual basis and utility of this hypothesis.

Perhaps Welford's (1973) remarks best summarize the negative criticism. He cites as problematic: (1) the matter of actually locating the so-called optimal point, (2) why it differs from task to task, and (3) what indeed occurs when this point is excluded. All of these critics who registered their concerns decades ago (i.e., Baddeley [1972], Martens [1974], Naatanen [1969], and Welford [1973]) were concerned about ambiguity surrounding the optimal arousal approach. On the other hand, this model is accepted by many psychologists today, and since the early 1980s, it has served as the basis for numerous intervention programs (Bunker & Rotella, 1980; Cooke, 1982; Landers, 1980). So, although well known and often discussed in textbooks dealing with the psychology of physical activity, the inverted-U hypothesis is by no means definitive.

1.8.3 Individual Zone of Optimal Functioning

It is difficult to assess arousal or its fluctuations during performance, particularly in contact sports. Difficult, but not impossible. The same is true with regard to musical performance. Some researchers, as well as performers themselves, employ heart rate monitors in order to learn about heart rhythmicity during performance. The pace with which the heart functions provides a rough indication of overall physiological activation. By knowing the heart rate, performers may use various techniques to adjust it appropriately. When jogging regularly in an effort to achieve a high level of aerobic fitness, it is helpful to know if a prescribed heart rate is being sustained. With this in mind, a monitor is strapped to the chest, so that it beeps when heart rate exceeds or goes below the required range. However, such methods may not be practical to employ when certain tasks are performed competitively or exhibitionally (e.g., contact and combative sports, operatic performance). Therefore, various self-report scales and physiological measurements can be administered and taken during convenient breaks in performances, but this tends to inhibit the validity of results. Hanin (1989, 1997) in his work with athletes advocates the use of retrospective assessment of anxiety levels, whereby the performer is asked to look back at a good or poor showing and recollect her state of arousal. Hanin reports high correlations between actual and recalled state anxiety. He recommends using the athlete's averaged state anxiety score on the Spielberger State–Trait Anxiety Inventory (STAI) plus or minus four points in order to define an *individual zone of optimal functioning* (IZOF) (Chapter 8) rather than only one optimal level of state anxiety. This approach may be effective in designing arousal management training programs for athletes. It is a practical approach in determining where an athlete's arousal level should be prior to performance. Although his research has been conducted primarily with athletes, Hanin's findings and recommended actions may easily be applied to performers in other domains.

1.9 SUMMARY

Words such as *arousal, activation, fear, anxiety,* and *burnout* are frequently used in very loosely defined ways. In order to appreciate the full connotation of the term *stress,* these words should be clarified and distinctions among them established. This is what was attempted in this chapter. The notions of burnout and the relationship between stress and performance are approached via three well-known theoretical constructs: the inverted-U hypothesis, catastrophe theory, and the individual zone of optimal functioning.

Categories of common stressors and appropriate examples were also provided with emphasis upon the individual nature of stress reactivity. Among the categories of stressors considered were social, chemical, climatic, and psychological.

2

SIGNS OF STRESS: DIFFERENT PERSPECTIVES

LEARNING OBJECTIVES

After reading this chapter, you should be able to:

- Name and elaborate upon the three stages of the general adaptation syndrome (GAS)
- Provide an original performance-related example that follows the three stages of GAS
- Define bracing and its potential effect upon performance
- Describe the measure known as galvanic skin response
- Discuss how stress may influence sweating, breathing, heart rate, pulse rate, skin coloring, blood pressure, and cholesterol levels
- Understand how stress may be related to health conditions such as ulcers and diabetes

IMPORTANT TERMS

- GAS
- Homeostasis
- Muscular tension
- Pulse
- Blood pressure
- Sphygmomanometer

2.1 GENERAL ADAPTATION SYNDROME

What do performers in the grip of a stress reaction look like? What outward symptoms do they evince while in the throes of performance-related anxiety? And what internal upheaval is transpiring? These are questions addressed in this chapter.

The work of Hans Selye (1982), the patriarch and certainly among the most well known of all stress researchers, addresses these questions. Selye's conceptualization of a syndrome of adaptive physiological responses to stress clearly contributes to the objectives of this chapter. His work spans more than 60 years of research into the stress phenomenon.

Essentially, Selye suggests that irrespective of the agent that causes an increased demand upon the body (this is the way in which he defines stress), the very same kind of stress response is elicited. This reaction is the essential element in his model. The stressor is irrelevant. His insight into the stress response is heavily (if not exclusively) physiological.

In the next chapter, social, physical, chemical, bacterial, climatic, and psychological stressors will be discussed. Examples of each are given. What Selye has continually maintained is that in response to any or each of these, the organism experiences a three-stage syndrome (a collection of symptoms that occur together), which he calls the general adaptation syndrome (GAS). These stages are as follows (see Figure 2.1):

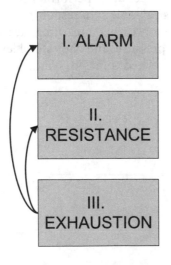

"Uh Oh! – A Problem!"

Stressor Visits.

"Everything is OK."

Adaptation to the upheaval of Stage I. A counterbalancing of stressor effects.

"Can't hold the line much longer."

Adaptive abilities fade. But if Stage III doesn't linger too long, the body may revert to either Stage I or II.

Figure 2.1 General Adaptation Syndrome.

1. *Alarm reaction*, wherein the body's defense mechanisms are rallied to oppose the influence of the stressor. This stage represents a sort of "wow, look what's happening here" effect, in preparation for a vital defensive stance.
2. *Resistance* follows if the agent initiating the alarm reaction is not so severe as to cause the death of the organism. If the organism survives the alarm-reaction stage, it enters the stage of resistance, wherein countless hormonal and chemical changes are activated in order to preserve or regain a necessary state of delicate biochemical and fluid balance. For a period of time, then, the body actually adapts to the harmful effects of the stressor. It is able to mobilize forces that adequately counterbalance the noxious effects of the stressor. But after a while, if the adaptive ability is lost, the organism may enter the third stage of GAS.
3. *Exhaustion.* This stage is begun when the strength of the demand upon the body has been maintained and applied for any appreciable duration. The body's ability to adapt within this three-stage syndrome is not indefinite. The adaptation capacity eventually wears out. Very serious organic damage or even death may be the consequence if stress continues at severe levels. But if the stage of exhaustion is reasonably short-lived and the stressors are removed during rest (e.g., sleep), a large portion of previous levels of resistance may be restored.

In considering Selye's stages of adaptation, Lazarus (1993) characterizes stages 1 and 2 as being analogous to the psychological *coping* mechanisms he himself describes. Here the organism is mobilizing its resources (in this case, physiological and biochemical) to countermand the effects of the pernicious stressor.

Physiological consequences of the battle, or as Selye calls them, "chemical scars," may accumulate. Over the years this process results in a sort of wearing away that contributes to aging. However, this third stage is not necessarily always achieved. Most stressors initiate only first- and second-stage GAS activity. Selye (1982) describes the specific chemical mechanisms of these adaptive responses in detail, but they are too complex to offer here.

Dobson (1982) provides an excellent overview of fairly intricate physiological and psychological responses to stress that interested readers might advantageously pursue. However, some background in human physiology is probably necessary if you intend to read Dobson's material.

Let us now recapitulate the above sequence in terms of a common physical performance experience probably known and understood by most of us — swimming. You begin to swim, and after a while, the demands placed upon your muscles and cardiovascular system become stressful. You develop an awareness of this (alarm reaction) as your breathing begins to be labored and your arms increasingly difficult to lift and move. After a while, your body makes a series of physiological adjustments, and you are able to deal with the stress (resistance). But this does not last indefinitely, and if your swim is not terminated, fatigue eventually overwhelms you (exhaustion). You may ultimately succumb to exhaustion and drown, or if rescued, require medical treatment and hospitalization. Upon being medically discharged, you are rejuvenated and no longer exhausted, but the experience may have taken a serious physical toll, leaving chemical scars from the trauma of the experience.

A good way of summarizing the contents of the above few paragraphs is to observe that any demand made upon the body that elicits the GAS may be considered a stressor. And illness, in some way, shape, or form, is the inevitable outcome.

2.2 HOMEOSTASIS

A very precise balance of biochemical contents in body fluids must be constantly maintained for good health to persist. Even minute shifts in the biochemistry of your blood or cellular fluids may cause serious health problems or even death. Intricate sensing and feedback mechanisms regulate the production and composition of the *enzymes* (proteins produced within an organism, capable of accelerating a particular chemical reaction) and *hormones* (excitatory chemicals secreted by glands of the body and transported by the blood to other cells or organs) that control the composition of body fluids. The term *homeostasis* — from the Greek, "same position" — refers to the balances of these enzymes, hormones, and other body fluids. The eminent physiologist Walter Cannon (1932) is credited with first applying this word.

According to Selye (who, incidentally, is not alone in describing the importance of these mechanisms), the nervous and circulatory systems are responsible for transmitting alarm signals indicating that proper balance of cellular fluid chemistry is in jeopardy. This in turn leads to modification of fluid production and chemical composition. Environmental stressors serve as these alarm signals. Thus, as previously noted, Selye defines a stressor as any agent that evokes responses designed to counteract tendencies to disturb homeostasis.

2.3 THE MUSCULATURE

Muscle function is also responsive to stress and anxiety stimuli. And since the musculature is vital to the kinds of performance central to the concerns of this book, it would be of benefit to overview its role and certain of its anatomical aspects. Over 400 muscles in the human body are involved in movement. These are known as *skeletal muscles*, since most of them are attached by *tendons* to bones. Your bicep muscles (biceps brachii) are a good example. They are connected to both the upper arm and the forearm. When the biceps contract, the forearm is drawn toward the upper arm. Muscles themselves are constructed of bundles laid out side by side, comprising long muscle fibers.

Skeletal muscles are of various shapes and sizes that correspond to the type of function they perform. Some muscles are flat and wide; others are full-bellied in their middle portions and tapered at both ends. Usually, skeletal muscles respond to voluntary stimuli of the nervous system. They contract on demand and are therefore also referred to as *voluntary muscles*. The precise chemical episodes that account for the mechanics of muscle fiber contraction are unclear.

There are other types of muscles in the body as well: cardiac muscles and smooth muscles. The heart comprises the former kind of muscle, and the lining of the digestive system, for example, the latter kind. Sometimes, muscle tissue is stimulated to contract by chemical messages rather than by nervous stimulation. The movement with which we are concerned is accounted for mostly by skeletal muscle.

The amount of muscle fiber in your body — for instance, in your thigh or arm — is genetically determined. Males have more muscle mass than females. While the quantity of muscle fibers is constant, the thickness and chemical ingredients of the fibers may be increased with resistance training. This is also true for the blood vessels and connective tissue (tendons and ligaments) that surround the muscle fibers. Regular contraction of skeletal muscle against periodically increased resistance will yield a thicker, firmer, and larger muscle. When the diameter of muscle fiber increases, more numerous blood capillaries are generated and connective tissue thickens. This would result in strength improvement.

2.3.1 Slow-Twitch and Fast-Twitch Fibers

There are two types of skeletal muscle tissues, in terms of their role in permitting movement. Some fibers predominate in long-term or endurance activities (slow twitch) and others in short-term or speedy activities (fast twitch). A typical skeletal muscle contains both kinds of fibers. Heredity may provide an abundance of one type of fiber, thereby improving performance in certain kinds of movements and performances. For example, a high percentage of slow-twitch fibers are found in the leg muscles of champion distance runners, whereas champion sprinters have a very high percentage of fast-twitch fibers. This suggests that determining the relative percentages of slow- and fast-twitch fibers within a trainee's muscles might help the teacher or coach understand potential performance capabilities and specialty areas. However, particularly at low levels of performance ability, other factors such as motivation, self-confidence, discipline, and intelligence may override the advantages and disadvantages of slow- and fast-twitch fibers.

2.3.2 Fuel for Muscular Contraction

Skeletal muscle requires energy in chemical form, in order to contract. Muscle tissue actually contains pockets of energy provided by adenosine triphosphate, or ATP. This material eventually breaks down when conditions are right, and yields most of the energy for brief muscular contraction. However, when the energy demands are very prolonged, such as in a long dance performance or an extended swim or run, the body must have a reserve of fuel available for the energy-hungry muscles. In this case, special dietary considerations become important.

Exercise physiologists are scientists who study phenomena such as energy metabolism and fuel reserves in relation to work or exercise. A good reference for expanding your understanding of the chemistry of muscular contraction is Powers and Howley (2001).

2.3.3 Muscular Tension

The many reactions to stress that may inhibit physical performance include increased tension in the large skeletal muscles. These muscle groups are always in a state of moderate contraction, which allows maintenance of the upright body position. It is this natural, moderate, and unrelenting tension in the body's back and neck muscles that enables you to oppose the powerful force of gravity and maintain an erect posture. If these muscles no longer receive the stimulation to sustain their tension (or *tonus*), you collapse and fall to the floor unconsciously. This is the case when the central nervous system is temporarily traumatized by a punch to the jaw, where a collection of nerves involved in this relay mechanism is located. You are knocked out.

However, this necessary muscular tension can become highly exaggerated as part of the stress reaction. When this occurs, certain muscle groups become noticeably "tight." In particular, the muscles of the shoulders and neck (the trapezius and sternocleidomastoid muscles) experience increased tension due to stress. This tension is noticeable not only to you, but also to someone who touches the area or offers massage in a helpful effort to relieve the tightness. The term *bracing* is used to refer to this stress-related muscular tension, which is not usually associated with positive effects. We would be hard-pressed to identify a motor skill whose performance is benefited by bracing. Most physical performance skills suffer some degree of impairment as a consequence of stress-induced muscular tension. Fine-motor skills, which are dependent upon accuracy and delicate movements (e.g., archery, performance on many musical instruments), are particularly impaired by bracing. Moreover, individuals in whom back muscles are tensed excessively over prolonged periods of time due to stress may be prone to backache.

2.3.3.1 Tension Headaches　　Another consequence of increased muscular tension is *headache*. According to one authority on the subject (Dobson, 1982), muscle tension is responsible for more than half of all chronic tension headaches. Tense muscles require a certain amount of oxygen, and when blood flow fails to keep pace with oxygen demand, the blood vessels expand and produce a tension headache. As any sufferer knows, it is not difficult to pinpoint the source of the headache, because the pain stems directly from the tight muscles. Muscle tension may be attributed to any number of factors, but the principal reason is emotional stress. Anyone who is regularly experiencing tension as part of his daily life is likely to suffer from chronic tension headaches.

Many causes of different kinds of headaches have been identified. Lest you conclude from Dobson's remarks that muscular tension is an exclusive precipitator of headaches, I suggest that you recognize that other possibilities are likely. Having provided this caveat, permit me to say that stress is assuredly a major contributor.

2.4　SWEATING

The sympathetic nervous system activates all physiological responses and "kicks in" to assist the body in coping with stress. The sympathetic nervous system regulates sweat gland activity. During times of stress, the functioning of this part of the nervous system is increased. And so is sweat gland activity. It is mostly the *eccrine sweat glands,* located in the palms and soles of the feet (glabrous skin), that are stimulated into exaggerated function by psychological stress. Sweaty palms and feet occur irrespective of environmental temperature. Or as physiologists would say, there exist nonthermal "modifiers" of sweating (in humans). On a very cold day, the downhill skier waiting on a mountaintop for the signal "go" may be gripping her poles with perspiration-drenched gloves. A concert pianist bedecked in tuxedo or formal gown may perspire profusely before appearing on stage, as well as while on stage, despite the air-conditioned environment. The "cold sweat" phenomenon is unfortunately well known to many performers, irrespective of their experience on the field, the court, or the stage.

We would expect physical stressors such as friction and heat to induce an increased sweating response. But psychological stress also has a strong influence upon sweating.

The degree to which *palmar sweating* occurs in relation to prevailing psychological stress may be measured by the application of electrodes attached to each side of the hand (one electrode on the top of the hand between the knuckles and the wrist, and another in the center of the palm). The amount of perspiration on the palm determines the extent to which the flow of electricity through the hand is impeded. A device known as a whetstone bridge is located in an apparatus attached to the electrodes. The amount of electricity reaching and passing through the bridge is revealed by a fluctuating needle connected to the bridge. The needle registers the drop in electrical resistance of the skin, which is a function of the amount of palmar sweat. This is known as *galvanic skin response* (GSR). The more palmar wetness, the higher the GSR score. The GSR is an index of general arousal and is used in lie detection procedures along with other measures such as heart rate, skin temperature, and respiratory rate. When significant changes in these parameters occur abruptly, physiological arousal is indicated. It is assumed that this increase in activation is due to speaking untruthfully (telling a lie).

Another method for assessing sweat volume involves the application of a liquid, latex-like material to the fingertip. When this latex-like material hardens, it is peeled off and examined under a microscope or magnifying glass. The dots within a square millimeter of area on the thin rubbery material are representative of individual pores that are open in the fingertip. The more dots, the more open pores; a higher number of open pores indicates a higher anticipated volume of sweat being delivered to the skin.

Excessive sweating may result in a reduction in blood volume and consequently blood pressure, if lost fluid is not replaced. Obviously a meaningful drop in blood pressure may compromise certain kinds of gross-motor performance. Endurance activities therefore require frequent ingestion of fluid.

2.5 RESPIRATORY RESPONSES

One of the first stress reactions that we are able to notice, in others as well as ourselves, is irregular and accelerated breathing. When you are reacting to stress, the amount of carbonic acid in the blood tends to increase. The respiratory center in the brain, located in the *medulla oblongata,* is sensitive to this change. In response, the medulla oblongata emits signals through various nerve tracts that stimulate action of the diaphragm and consequently lung activity. The diaphragm is a flat, sheetlike muscle that forms the floor of the rib cage, or thoracic cavity, in which the lungs are located. When the diaphragm contracts, it moves downward, thereby increasing the volume in the thoracic cavity. As a consequence of decreased pressure, the little air sacs, or alveoli, that compose the lungs expand. When the alveoli expand, environmental air rushes in through the nose and mouth and fills the lungs. When the diaphragm relaxes, moving in an upward direction, the reverse process occurs, causing exhalation.

Muscles between the ribs — the intercostal muscles — are also stimulated by changes in blood chemistry. These muscles play an important role in your breathing rate in that they move the ribs by lifting and rotating them, and thus create changes in thoracic cavity volume. In laboratory experiments in which the respiratory rate of the subject must be determined, electrodes that are sensitive to the electrical discharge (known as electrical potential) emitted by muscles are attached to the intercostals. The frequency of muscular contraction may thus be recorded on a screen that transforms the electrical signal into a bleep or spike.

When your intercostal-muscle function is compromised because of injury or disease, breathing is impeded. A smashing blow to the ribs (and the muscles between them) makes breathing painful and problematic.

Increased breathing depth and rate in response to stress is difficult to camouflage. Altered breathing is usually a dead giveaway that you are emotionally aroused or stressed.

Learning may play a role in respiratory responses to stress. A stimulus that at one time was associated with heightened arousal may still elicit increased breathing even if the possibility of the appearance of the specific stressor is nil. For example, a dancer walking onto a stage where she performed many years ago may presently experience a conditioned respiratory response (rapid breathing), despite the fact that she is no longer expected to dance. Performers may possess *schemas,* or memory packages that contain echoes of past experience. When stimulated by contemporary environmental triggers, they may surface and carry into consciousness all of the stored experiences — including arousal symptoms, such as those associated with breathing.

2.6 CARDIOVASCULAR RESPONSES

During very stressful conditions, it is not unusual for heart rate in some individuals to exceed 200 beats per minute. It is the sympathetic nervous system that basically accounts for cardiac acceleration. Parasympathetic activity is responsible for deceleration and general calming or reduction in arousal. The *vagus nerve* carries messages to the heart from the brain that decrease its rate of beating, and the cardiac center in the brain's medulla controls heartbeat through the emission of nervous signals.

A link between stress and heart disease has been hypothesized, and those reporting high stress levels in their lives also tend to report more chest pain (McCleod et al., 2002). Interestingly, electrocardiogram (EKG) follow-up in the McCleod et al. study revealed that many of the subjects who suffered chest pain did not actually have heart disease, thereby shedding some doubt upon the relationship between these two variables. Despite its controversial nature, the link between stress and heart disease should not be disparaged entirely. Additional research may ultimately resolve the uncertainty.

2.6.1 Pulse

Your pulse rate (roughly 70 beats per minute, depending upon variables such as age and sex) is reflective of heart rate. Under pressure by heart muscle contractions, the blood slams against the walls of blood vessels and travels through the body. Near the skin's surface, the blood movement (pulse) is detectable by gently pressing against certain places of the body with your fingers (e.g., wrist, neck, groin).

Sometimes, the heart beats so rapidly and powerfully in reaction to stress that it is unnecessary to take the pulse to assess cardiac response. When serious stressors that cause dramatic cardiac reactions are present, you can distinctly feel your heart pounding in your chest, or see this action in others.

2.6.2 Blushing

Facial skin color may also fluctuate due to psychological arousal. A fair-skinned person becomes "white with rage" when the small blood vessels in the face receive signals to constrict, because reduced blood flow makes the face look pale. Conversely, if the medulla sends signals to the facial vessels to dilate, it will cause *blushing*. The neural messages instructing facial blood vessels to constrict or dilate depend on the ways in which you interpret environmental stimuli. Since the face remains uncovered in most performers, dramatic changes in its coloration may be indicative of stress and or anxiety response and may be fairly noticeable to the interested observer (of course, this may not be the case with performers wearing makeup or costumes that obliterate the countenance).

2.6.3 Blood Pressure

Blood pressure is another circulatory function that is influenced by stress or anxiety. As it flows, the blood exerts a pressure upon the walls of the arteries. Stress and anxiety tend to cause *systolic* blood pressure to rise. This is the pressure of the blood exerted upon the arterial wall during the contracting phase of the heart. On the other hand, *diastolic* blood pressure prevails continuously (not just during the contraction phase of the heart muscle).

Add 100 to your age in order to determine the approximate appropriate level for your resting systolic blood pressure expressed in terms of millimeters of mercury (mmHg). When blood pressure rises excessively (hypertension), dizziness may occur. Already weakened, small and delicate blood vessels, which may have been weakened through disease or physical trauma, are in jeopardy of bursting. Interestingly, only about 20 percent of all cases of hypertension seem to be related to organic disease or caused by a physical malfunction. The remaining 80 percent of hypertension cases have elusive origins and are very difficult to define. It is likely that of this remaining and very large amount of cases, many are related to stress.

Stress and anxiety produce changes in heart rate, blood circulation, and blood pressure. Prolonged and repeated reactions to stress have also been linked to coronary heart disease (CHD). Approximately 30 years ago, Friedman and Rosenman (1974) observed that heart attacks in men were largely a consequence of work-related stress.

Friedman and Rosenman (1971) have also indicted stress as a contributing factor in the elevation of cholesterol in the blood and in CHD. Cholesterol is a yellowish, fatty substance that is manufactured by the body. It may also be ingested from dietary foods high in cholesterol, such as fattier meat or dairy products. Cholesterol deposits tend to clog arteries, making them hard and ultimately narrowing the bore of the vessels through which blood must travel. Time and time again, researchers have identified cholesterol as a major factor in chronic heart disease. In their 1971 study, Friedman and Rosenman were able to show that as the typical workweek progressed from Monday onward, work-related anxiety and stress increased accordingly, as did levels of blood serum cholesterol. However, much more recent research suggests that lowering blood cholesterol levels may not prevent coronary heart disease (Ravnskov, 1992) and that the previously established connection may have been caused by researcher bias. The jury is still out on this question.

2.7 BIOCHEMICAL AND ENDOCRINOLOGICAL RESPONSES

Many of the physiological responses to stress that we've just discussed have very noticeable characteristics. Rapid heart and breathing rates are easy to notice, as is palmer sweating. Blushing or blanching (turning white) are easily detected by almost anyone in the environment. Even though you may not be able to accurately determine your blood pressure without a *sphygmomanometer* (the cuff, rubber bulb, and gauge apparatus applied to your arm), you may very well be aware of its increase due to signs such as dizziness.

There are other stress reactions, however, that are not apparent. Very subtle changes in functions relating to biochemistry and endocrinology (secretion of hormones and other blood-borne fluids) occur as your body experiences stress reactions. They may wield enormous impact on your physiological status without your immediate awareness. Invariably, their effect becomes obvious all too often in the form of illness. Usually, blood analyses or other medical tests are necessary in order to identify these biochemical responses to stress.

Earlier in this chapter we discussed the term *homeostasis*. We now address this concept in more detail as we consider a few of these biochemical reactions to stress.

2.7.1 Ulcer

Special cells lining the stomach are stimulated to produce gastric juices by a substance known as adrenocorticotropic hormone (ACTH), released by the pituitary gland in the brain. Stress can excessively initiate this response, and stomach acid secretion tends to be increased in response to stress.

Digestive juices, and *pepsinogen* in particular, when increased in acidity and quantity over a prolonged period, may contribute to a peptic ulcer. A peptic ulcer is a lesion, tear, or erosion of the mucous lining of the digestive tract. Research suggests that gastrointestinal weakness is due to heredity, but social and cultural stressors are the factors that alter the production of the biochemicals that have the potential to further damage the gastrointestinal system. Recently, bacterial infection has also been indicted by the medical community as a causal factor in ulcer of the digestive system (Osipenko, Pankova, & Vergazov, 2004).

Therefore, administration of antibiotic drugs would be the treatment of choice.

In the sports world, the term *coach's ulcer* is frequently bandied about in a lighthearted manner as well as in serious contexts. In team sports such as basketball, unrelenting intervention, management, and decision making by the coach over years of very long seasons are the norm. In such long-term stress situations, the stress-induced ulcer may become a reality. Although scientific studies giving credence to this speculation are not yet available, this phenomenon is often speculated to be a vocational liability.

2.7.2 Diabetes Mellitus

Stress interferes with the body's ability to remove carbohydrates, which results in an elevation of the blood's glucose level. Insulin is needed to metabolize blood glucose (sugar, in layman's terms). If the glucose is not metabolized, fat in the blood is not completely broken down and this results in the formation of a number of blood poisons that may cause coma and even death.

Ironically, in diabetic individuals, in whom insulin production is nil or very low, some forms of anxiety and stress have been shown to further reduce blood glucose. Studies by Vandenbergh and Sussman (1967) and Simpson, Mackay, and Cox (1974) have shown this to be the case. These relationships can produce frightening and confusing consequences in individuals who are unaware of their tendencies toward diabetes.

2.8 SUMMARY

This chapter has dealt with the body's reaction to stress. When stress visits, what happens physically? What are its important bodily manifestations? Selye's general adaptation syndrome is a well-known description of three phases of stress reaction. According to Selye, irrespective of the stress (physical trauma, excessive heat or cold in the environment, fear, etc.), all organisms respond stereotypically. Selye's definition of stress emphasizes a loss of homeostasis, or biochemical balance. Stress elicits reactions from the muscular, respiratory, and cardiovascular systems, from mere sweating and blushing to pathologies such as ulcer and diabetes mellitus.

3

SOURCES OF STRESS

LEARNING OBJECTIVES

After reading this chapter, you should be able to:

- Interrelate the terms *stress* and *stressor*
- Describe Freud's definition of anxiety and discuss his views of anxiety causation from a psychoanalytic perspective
- Define displacement, repression, denial, and rationalization
- Identify the primary distinction between psychoanalytic and learning perspectives of stress
- Define modeling and discuss it in relationship to stress from a social learning perspective
- Elaborate upon value dissonance and social change as they relate to stress from a sociological/environmental perspective
- Discuss how personality may interact with stress
- Contrast trait and state anxiety
- Distinguish among social, physical, chemical, bacterial, and climatic stressors

IMPORTANT TERMS

- Defense mechanisms
- Value dissonance

- Personality
- Personality trait

3.1 INTRODUCTION

Now that we have a sense of what stress is, let us turn to the matter of its origins. Where does it come from? Being able to understand this phenomenon and differentiate it from other similar human, psychophysical responses is but one concern. In order to strengthen our understanding of stress, it is important to appreciate its causal factors, that is, the underlying experiences that result in stress response.

As noted previously, the perspective adopted in this book is that stress is a *reactive* experience and that *stressors* are external or internal environmental stimuli that provoke it. However, experts differ with regard to the importance allocated to these stimuli or sources of stress.

3.2 DIFFERENT THEORETICAL APPROACHES

In accordance with their training and background, many theorists approach the challenging question of stress causality from strikingly different directions. Some authorities consider only social factors as being causally related to human stress reactions. Others indict deeply rooted unconscious factors, while learning and reinforcement are paramount in the explanations of other theorists.

In this chapter we will deal with four theoretical perspectives; certainly not the only ones to be found in the stress literature, but perhaps the most prominent. These are: *psychoanalytic orientations, learning orientations, sociological orientations,* and *personological orientations.*

Assuredly we will not be able to resolve the ongoing debates about which approach should prevail. But if we establish as our chapter goal nothing more than the description of these various directions, its accomplishment should be worthwhile. Our purpose now is to review categories of *causes of stress* rather than to discuss consequences of stress. We shall also identify and briefly talk about four other kinds of stressors, namely, physical, chemical and biochemical, bacterial, and climatic. These four are especially paramount in the sports-performance domain, and although present in others, are less viable.

3.2.1 Psychoanalytic Orientations

Ask any group of individuals living in Western society to associate the word *psychoanalysis* with any other term that comes immediately to mind. Without doubt, you will be immediately inundated with a barrage of "Sigmund Freud" responses. This name is very well known throughout the Western world, and Freud enjoys an enviable reputation as the patriarch, founder, popularizer, director, and executive producer of contemporary psychiatry, psychoanalysis, and psychotherapy. This is not to say that his ideas have successfully withstood criticism and challenge. In truth, many of his insights and explanations have been rejected by contemporary scholars and practitioners. But all are indebted to him for his insistence that powerful forces, residing in less than fully conscious levels of awareness, guide, stimulate, and mediate our thinking and behavior. Put very simply, Freud believed that deep-rooted intrapsychic conflict accounts for bottled up *libido* or *drive*, and that this "tension" requires release or *discharge*. These conflicts cause what Freud labeled *traumatic anxiety*. They are somehow related to painful or unpleasant experiences during infancy and birth or are sexual in nature. When triggered, the memory of these experiences causes anxiety.

Freud didn't use the term *stress* to refer to the manifestation of these bottled-up forces but preferred instead the word *anxiety*. We have already commented upon the need to distinguish between these two concepts, and I have argued that they are not exactly the same. But for the sake of convenience, I'll occasionally use them interchangeably in the following discussion.

Freud (1926) viewed anxiety as a signal that acts as a warning about danger in the outside environment that is perceived as real. He called this *signal anxiety*. Other psychoanalytic theorists have clarified, modified, or disagreed with aspects of Freud's interpretations. Some have maintained that Freud's emphasis upon sexuality is excessive. Others argue that harmful or threatening life events that took place in the relatively recent past are deserving of more attention than are memory traces associated with long past experiences. However, despite these differences with Freud, one theme has been retained in many, if not most, of his critics' theoretical approaches to anxiety. Essentially, anxiety is a fear of experiencing some kind of traumatic state.

Such fear may result in a number of psychological responses. When anxiety or stress-initiating stimuli occur, we sometimes choose to deal with them in less than fully conscious ways. Sometimes we utilize indirect approaches to defend against environmental threats, which may be viewed as *coping mechanisms*. Some examples of these coping mechanisms follow in simplified form:

- *Displacement* involves a reduction of feelings and impulses from the probable causes of anxiety to undeserving objects. Rather than take direct responsibility for a particular set of problem-related stimuli in her life, the individual shifts this responsibility elsewhere. The term *scapegoat* is used to refer to the recipient of displaced feelings or blame.

- *Repression* is a defensive mechanism whereby anxiety-provoking stimuli are unconsciously removed from awareness. Amnesia is a dramatic example of this form of anxiety-coping strategy. Problematic ideas and experiences are shunted to lower levels of consciousness so that they are gotten out of the way. They are relegated to a place where they cause no trouble.

- *Denial* involves the rejection of reality that carries threats to emotional well-being. Danger signals or evidence of potentially harmful stimuli are simply and conveniently rejected. For instance, athletes who have been seriously injured on the field of play may deny the seriousness of the situation. Feelings of "this can't happen to me" are employed to defend against noxious agents that would provoke anxiety or stress responses in others.

- *Rationalization* is a defense technique that employs excuses for avoiding stress-causing situations. Not being invited to be a member of an athletic team or not receiving a call-back after an audition for a theatrical role might be anxiety provoking. The individual copes with this stressor by concluding that he or she couldn't have accepted the invitation in the event it had been extended because of the necessity to work after school. Thus, the alleged schedule conflict is used to protect against disappointment caused by rejection. This represents a good example of why the term *defense mechanism* is employed.

The psychoanalytic approach to understanding stress and anxiety continues to be scrutinized and criticized. Yet, many of its aspects continue to be recognized as helpful clarifiers of behavioral disorders.

3.2.2 Learning Orientations

Perhaps the most important distinction between learning or behavioral explanations of stress and the psychoanalytic explanations previously outlined is that the learning/behavioral approach gives primary attention to more recent stress-inducing stimuli. While psychoanalytic theorists emphasize events that have occurred in the distant past, learning theorists consider much more immediate experiences to be paramount. In addition, they consider stress reactions to be learned very much in the same ways as we acquire most any kind of behavior or response. Conditioned association through reinforcement, transfer of learning, and information about the quality of previous responses (feedback) are all examples of learning principles that predict or influence the ways in which we respond to environmental stimuli. The loud bang that you react to casually as you stand on a noisy, inner-city street corner waiting for a bus elicits no alarm response. You recognize it as the sound of a backfiring automobile motor. You've heard noises like that on many mornings and have *learned* to associate them with nonthreatening consequences. However, the same sound stimulus may elicit an entirely different reaction from a person who has only recently returned from active military service. Gunfire, danger, pain, and death are examples of conditioned associations that the military veteran may deal with momentarily. This person has *learned* that these are likely consequences of the loud bang and therefore reacts stressfully.

Psychologically induced stress reactions probably receive more attention from researchers than any other kind. However, they are not easy to isolate, define, understand, and control.

As we noted in Chapter 1, anxiety may be considered a psychological stressor with vague and poorly defined causes. Somehow, anxiety is rooted in an attitude of impending doom, yet the specific source of danger is unclear. Preperformance nervousness (the so-called jitters) is a widespread form of stress. Its origins lie with anxiety about factors such as performance outcomes, as well as overall performance evaluation (both self- and external). Another factor that is likely to contribute to the development of anxiety is the perception that you are lacking in the resources required to satisfy the demands of the task(s) facing you. When you realize that you don't have what it takes to do the job, you become anxious and you react stressfully.

Certain performances are obviously more highly valued than others. An audition for a professional dance position or a tryout for an elite athletic team is likely to figure very prominently in a performer's world. Such exhibitions are therefore apt to generate more intense stress reactions than are informal, recreational, or casual performances done for friends. In very young performers facing dance or instrumental recitals or trying out for youth soccer or football on a formal team, exceedingly high levels of stress might be involved despite the "recreational" nature of the circumstance.

Products of mental activity — such as evaluations of previous performances, comparisons with other performers, and perceptions about the criticality of a forthcoming performance — are all likely to cause psychological stress. Psychological preparation for performance often involves application of mental mechanisms by which an individual attempts to reduce or in some way cope with unwanted stress responses (i.e., those that may adversely affect performance). A good portion of this book is devoted to these mechanisms. Later, you will be introduced to quite a few of them.

Learning theorists, psychoanalytic theorists, and those from other theoretical camps are generally in agreement about the physiological manifestations of stress responses. They all acknowledge that changes in heart rate, breathing rate, sweat production, and hormonal and bio-chemical status are connected with stress reactions (although these changes do not correlate very well among themselves). Theorists differ, however, with regard to the causes of these reactions, and consequently about ways in which to modify stress reactions. Psychoanalytic theorists are inclined to favor strategies that are first aimed at uncovering past experiences recessed in lower levels of awareness. Through catharsis — an uninhibited confrontation with these buried conflicts to "get them out of your system" — undesirable stress reactions may be alleviated.

Learning theorists, on the other hand, are inclined to emphasize modification of the behavioral consequences of stress as a stress management technique. If diarrhea, muscle tremors, or excessive perspiration accompanies certain perceptions about events such as performance, then rather than attempt to understand why these responses occur, the therapist utilizing a behavioral approach would direct remediative efforts toward changing the very behavior itself — the sweating, diarrhea, or muscle tremors. Little concern would be directed toward gaining an understanding of *why* these reactions to performance occur. Some of these behavioral techniques for stress control will be addressed in subsequent chapters of this book.

3.2.2.1 Individual Responses to Stressors We tend to respond to stress in personal or idiosyncratic ways. We do not all tremble, sweat, or breathe heavily to the same degree when reacting to stress stimuli. Some of us experience rather strong urges to urinate; others begin to perspire profusely. The relative strengths or weakness of our physiological systems and subsystems seem to be revealed when we cope with stress. Headache, nausea, and diarrhea are other examples of conditions that may accompany reactions to psychological stress for some but not for others. Perhaps this is due to reinforcement of certain responses that occur unwittingly or unintentionally. Words we may utter when admonishing another do not always jibe with our physical gestures and body language. Thus, the message we believe we are transmitting is not always the same that the learner is receiving.

Through classical conditioning (Pavlov, 1927), individuals may learn to associate certain environmental stimuli with specific physiological responses. Apparently, some physiological responses are more susceptible to conditioning in some of us than in others. This suggests a biological readiness or preference for learning certain pairings (associations) involving stress or anxiety (Driscoll, 2005). Similarly, *avoidance behavior*, a tendency to abandon an environment in which danger or pain is likely, may also be learned. This learning may have a preferential aspect, in that some individuals seem to learn certain avoidance behaviors better than others.

Perhaps these affinities for learning have a Darwinian basis, in that they may be directed toward preserving the species. However enticing this line of thinking may be, it remains highly speculative and unproved. Cognitive functions undoubtedly play an important role in learned reactions to stressors. Thinking and information processing probably modify the Pavlovian conditioning process that underlies acquired response to stressors. Imagination, language, prediction, and observation of stress reactions in others (modeling) are also cognitive variables that are likely to influence learned stress responses.

Operant or *instrumental conditioning*, which typically involves reinforcement of behavior in many different ways, and the use of many different kinds of reinforcers administered through different schedules of reinforcement, may result in learned reactions to stress. The parent who coddles a child when it cries upon seeing the dentist thereby reinforces that particular response, and the dentist's waiting room becomes associated with tears, anxiety, and stress.

3.2.2.2 Modeled Behavior   In their attempts to acquire or teach performance skills, learners as well as teachers rely upon a powerful technique known as *modeling*, or social learning. You've undoubtedly been exposed inadvertently or strategically to its influence. Learners tend to, or are encouraged to, copy from others who perform appropriately or correctly.

In his research and writing, the eminent psychologist Albert Bandura (1977, 2001) extols the importance of observing, integrating, and emulating proper and/or desirable behaviors of others. These models may be real or symbolic, and their reproduction need not occur right away. Future situations may become opportunities for demonstrating modeled roles or actions. Physical or motor skills are not the only behaviors that may serve as models. Attitudes, problem-solving approaches, and appropriate social interactions may also be modeled. In sports, beginning coaches often emulate the working behavior of well-known, successful athletic coaches. Voice and drama teachers *demonstrate* for their students how "it should be done" and thereby use themselves as models. Performers can also learn what not to do through modeling. One is discouraged from replicating an action when others have failed or have been punished for it. Observing a teammate being injured may deter an athlete from repeating an incorrect or unsafe behavior. In other words, performers accomplish a great deal of learning by observing others.

Sometimes, when left to their own devices, performers emulate models that are biomechanically incorrect. Young children need guidance as to which available models are appropriate and which ones put them at risk. Ironically, difficult skills, when executed by experts, may appear to be easy. Naive copiers with inadequate preparation, in whom a skill may be weak or nonexistent, may observe a complex, physically demanding behavior being done with aplomb. When or if they conclude that "it's a piece of cake — I can do that," the consequences may be horrendous. Such was the case a number of years ago when three students at my university stealthily entered our campus circus facilities, where a trapeze, high-wire cable, and other circus paraphernalia were located. They had evidently observed the highly skilled and practiced routines of well-trained acrobats who performed efficiently and accurately (the earmarks of a high degree of motor skill, which we will discuss in more depth in Chapter 5). Regrettably, the totally unprepared and foolish copycats used them as models. This poor model selection resulted in the death of one and severe, permanent injury to the two others. They modeled inappropriately.

By observing well-known and popular performers, we learn which stimuli to respond to stressfully and which to ignore. In addition, the ways in which the stress reaction occurs, that is, how we permit stress to be manifested, may also be modeled. I have often observed youth sports coaches employing dramatic displays of bravado as they stand chest to chest and face to face with umpires and referees in emulation of irate major league managers. What may be acceptable in major league, professional sports may not be appropriate for leaders of children. Impressionable children emulate their teachers and parents as well as peers in regard to loss of temper and anger management.

3.2.3 Social and Environmental Orientations

Still another theoretical direction taken by those attempting to clarify the antecedents of human stress reactions is the *sociological perspective*. Within this orientation, social or interpersonal and environmental conditions receive primary attention. Sources such as job loss, race or gender bias, and occupational or marital stressors are emphasized.

This approach suggests that life's most real or significant stressors relate to the challenges of earning a livelihood, preparing for a career, and securing services essential to one's well-being. All of these experiences involve relationships and interactions with others. They may occur in large or small groups or may exist exclusively on one-to-one bases. The group may be as small as a trio of professional musicians who must perform in unison and rehearse in a cooperative and supportive manner, or as large as an entire society.

Stress reactions involving relations with other individuals fall into this category. For example, you dislike certain members of your community. You know things about their past behavior and attitudes that you find distasteful. Yet, you feel obliged to attend a gathering at which they will be present. You suffer through the event, working hard to reveal none of your displeasure. You try to be congenial, yet you are inwardly very uncomfortable with your situation. When a mutual acquaintance brings one of these persons to you, you stand there feeling very stressed.

Some societies are known to be relatively stressful because of their highly industrialized and competitive nature. Such is the reputation of North American society.

Within the sociological perspective are two factors that deserve consideration as prominent antecedents of stress: (1) dissonance between personal values and the social/economic objectives one feels obliged to pursue and (2) rapid social change.

3.2.3.1 Value Dissonance Social development continues throughout life. It is an ongoing process. As we progress developmentally from one level to another, we are likely to encounter goals, needs, and values that are at variance with one another. You might highly value physical fitness and personal health. Many of us do. You strive to satisfy this value. You are a college-aged student and you exercise regularly and eat reasonably well, but sparingly. Then, in your early or mid-twenties you may find yourself with tie, sport coat, and briefcase battling morning rush hour traffic en route to a recently acquired job. A career has been launched and you've entered a new phase of social development. The gratifying morning jog is now sacrificed or rescheduled to a later time in the day, if it occurs at all. Calorie-laden "two martini" luncheons become requisites for consummation of important business deals. The health and fitness value is insidiously compromised in deference to the goal of professional success.

Sometimes these goals are self-imposed and sometimes they derive from obligations imposed by others or the social system itself.

For example: You are a so-called elderly person and retired. You have three grandchildren, and their parents, your daughter and son-in-law, are divorced. You and your spouse feel obliged to "help out." You take the kids for most of the summer recess from school; you pick up various expenses that the kids incur; you extend yourself physically and emotionally. You know that this is not right — but what can you do? They're your grandkids. You respond stressfully.

Value dissonance may also be a result of cultural differences associated with geographic location in a country as large and expansive as the United States, or immigration from one country to another. Religious convictions and variations associated with ethnicity may also account for disharmony with other societal factions and differences in ways of thinking and acting. The perception that one doesn't fit or that one's belief system is at odds with that of others living in the same community may be a stressor. It is not uncommon for high school, college, and professional athletes to choose not to compete on certain days that their religion has designated as times of rest, introspection, or observance. Christian, Jewish, and Muslim athletes are occasionally challenged in this manner. Some undoubtedly are not conflicted by such demands, and the decision to desist from participation comes easily. For others, the dilemma is stressful. The film *Chariots of Fire* exemplifies such a challenge confronting an Olympic runner who chooses not to compete on Sunday — the Lord's Day — rather than pursue a personal dream of winning a gold medal. The renowned pitcher for the Brooklyn Dodgers Sandy Koufax stayed away from the ballpark on the opening game of the 1965 World Series rather than perform (i.e., work) on the Jewish holy day of Yom Kippur. He was scheduled to pitch. Only these athletes knew to what extent these decisions were stressful. Entertainers are taught to abide by the cliché "The show must go on" — but if and when it does, not all performers participate unfailingly in a stress-free condition.

Power and authority accompany professional advancement, and the mandate to use them may also conflict with personal values. One may feel obliged to treat subordinates in a "tough" manner in order to fulfill the responsibilities of a new professional status. But being "tough" with others may run counter to your preferred behavioral style or long-accustomed manner of relating to others. Or colleagues may now view you differently. For the first time in your life, you encounter people who don't like you, and their number seems to increase as your authority and power increase. Cognizance of such outcomes produces personal conflict that may be stressful. And these conflicts relate to people — to environmental conditions, to social relationships and interactions, to status, to role conflict. The degree to which you are prepared to deal with these sociocultural factors and the psychological disharmony they may generate influences the degree to which you experience distress. The extent and quality of the support received from others (relatives, friends, loved ones) during a time of conflict determine how much stress will be experienced.

3.2.3.2 Social Change   Many types of change in the social environment are stress inducing. And, of course, changes interpreted as having negative consequences are particularly stressful. Change may demand new responsibilities, new ways of dealing with the environment, and new relationships.

Perlin and Leiberman (1979) and Perlin, Menaghan, Lieberman, and Mullan (1981) place all social changes, which they refer to as life events, into one of two categories: *normative events* and *nonnormative events*. Normative events are commonplace and anticipated. Their inevitability is assumed, although the exact time of their occurrence is unknown. Marriage, death of a grandparent, beginning a first job, and birth of a child are examples. Nonnormative events, while also occurring commonly, are not nearly as predictable or scheduled. They include divorce, injury and unexpected illness, premature death of friends or relatives, and broken friendships. Because of their unpredictability, these events or changes are considerably more stressful than the normative kind. However, all kinds of social change alter the conditions or environment in which we live.

Another variable that modifies the strength of stress reactions is the degree to which a particular kind of change is *chronic*. Persistent occurrence of nonnormative or normative events correlates with strength of distress. In some cases, frequently repeated changes in the social environment may produce a tolerance by which a person's negative reactions become decreasingly potent. In contrast, a cumulative effect may also be a consequence, wherein the more recent life events represent comparatively more powerful stressors, any one of which may become, so to speak, the straw that breaks the camel's back.

Lastly, the *rapidity* and *sequence* of the social change influence the extent to which events precipitate stress reactions. It is difficult to develop coping skills, strategies, and adaptive responses when stress stimuli (in this case, change) bombard the senses at high frequency. Performers must disengage from their interpersonal conflicts, attitude dissonances, and similar sociological stressors. When on stage, on the competitive field of play, or when concertizing, failure to do so will enable stress response to interact with elements of performance.

In one way or another, stress will exert its influence. Recall our discussion in Chapter 1 of stress and anxiety-related physiological arousal. We described the relationship between arousal and performance as depicted by the inverted-U hypothesis. Thus, inappropriate increase in arousal may dislodge the performer from the desired "optimal range," thus compromising performance efficiency and accuracy (quality).

3.2.4 Personological Orientations

Another approach to the understanding of stress etiology is through personological considerations. Within this theoretical approach is the assumption that some individuals are more or less vulnerable to stress reactivity because of their personality framework.

Personality suggests a collection of behavioral dispositions that are unique to an individual. Most of us have the same tendencies in our personal package, but their strengths and the ways in which they interact with one another may differ. These distinguishing dispositions toward behavior are known as *traits*. Examples of traits included in some standardized personality inventories are:

- *Introversion,* characterized by shyness and introspection
- *Aggressiveness,* characterized by tendencies toward destructive, hostile, or hurtful behavior
- *Anxiety,* characterized by tendencies to be generally apprehensive, although clearly defined reasons for fear are vague

Today, *personologists* (psychologists who specialize in the study of personality) talk about a *five-factor model* as being preeminent (Digman, 1990; McCrae & Costa, 1997; Smith & Williams, 1992). Included in this model are the dimensions of:

- Neuroticism or emotional stability
- Extroversion
- Openness to experience
- Agreeableness
- Conscientiousness

Although some of the same traits are included in many of the standardized trait personality paper-and-pencil tests, not all personality theorists agree as to their precise meaning. One theorist's interpretation of a particular trait may be quite different from the implications provided by another, although the terms themselves are identical. Some traits are absent from many of these inventories because personologists often disagree about the existence or meaningfulness of some alleged trait. Most personologists maintain that traits are not easily modified and are therefore enduring or long-lasting. Some traits are said to be located superficially in the personality structure and, in contrast to others deemed *core* traits, may be more (relatively speaking) amenable to modification traits. An experience of considerable psychological impact is required for a trait to be significantly altered. According to this line of thinking, adults are likely to carry the very same inclinations toward certain kinds of behavior that they had as young children. Particularly if they are core, or deeply embedded, traits. And it is not very likely that these traits will be abandoned. Sometimes, we may give the impression that our styles of behavior have changed. This may be a consequence of our having learned that it is best not to behave in certain ways. The inclinations, however, are likely to remain. It may require an experienced and trained observer to see that beneath the camouflage and inhibition, the behavioral tendencies still persist. Further, some personality traits counteract the strength of others and are said therefore to "interact" with one another. Consequently, behavior that would reveal the existence of a fairly strong trait may not always be observable. Sometimes, a particular situation will stimulate a trait to manifest itself behaviorally, whereas other environments may stifle it.

Of primary interest here is the extent to which personality and stress reactions are related. Are individuals with certain arrangements, interactions, and strength of traits predisposed to responding stressfully to particular environmental stimuli? The answer to this question seems to be yes. Numerous psychological instruments that measure the strength of an individual's anxiety trait, such as the State–Trait Anxiety Inventory (STAI) (Spielberger, Gorsuch, & Lushene, 1970), correlate very well with responses to stimuli that threaten ego and self-esteem. Stimuli or situations that do not threaten psychological well-being are not nearly as predictable by scores on tests that measure the anxiety trait. This is not to say that stress or anxiety responses are not stimulated by anticipation of physical harm or perception of threat, but only that identification of individuals who would respond this way in relatively greater degrees cannot be identified according to their personality traits.

A brief explanation of Spielberger et al.'s (1970) dual conceptualization of anxiety is appropriate here. Spielberger et al. postulate two kinds of anxiety and devised an instrument for assessing each: (1) *trait anxiety*, which refers to the enduring tendency to respond anxiously to a variety of stimuli and situations and (2) *state anxiety*, which refers to temporary, situation-by-situation anxiety responses. Most of us would probably feel considerable anxiety in the face of a physician's diagnosis of a life-threatening disease. Most of us would feel anxiety as the physician described positive results of a cancer diagnostic test. When we experience elevated anxiety in such special circumstances, according to Spielberger et al., the term *state anxiety* is applied. But some individuals have anxiety that always functions at high levels. They may, therefore, be described as anxiety prone. They tend to respond anxiously to many stimuli that would not typically evoke such reactions from those achieving a lower score on the A (anxiety)-Trait scale of the STAI. Both trait and state anxiety have a number of dimensions, including social evaluation (assessments made about you by others) and physical danger.

Perhaps a sensible direction to take when discussing personological orientations is to conclude that one's traits, interacting with situational stimuli, produce stress and anxiety reactions.

3.3 PHYSICAL STRESSORS

Pain and physical trauma resulting from a fall, blow, or twisted limb are physical stressors for most persons. These kinds of stimuli are common in the sports world. Sports performance, especially at elite levels, is certainly characterized by high risk. If you are involved in competitive sports for a meaningful duration, the likelihood of your sustaining physical injury is high. But sports cannot lay exclusive claim to such stressors. Discomfort associated with a poorly fitting costume or an unduly hard, inflexible stage floor constructed without consideration for the dancers' spinal cords or leg muscles can also cause distress.

3.3.1 Chemical and Biochemical Stressors

In this category would fall adverse reactions to various medicines, foods, or chemicals introduced into the body from external sources. Skin rash, fever, and nausea are examples of *allergically* induced stress reactions. Sometimes the body itself produces chemicals that generate stress responses. Too great a concentration of digestive juices or acids produced by faulty cellular metabolism or central nervous system stimulation may result in biochemical stress (heartburn or indigestion). Even perceptions about environmental happenings may stimulate excessive productions of body chemicals, which in turn cause stress reactions. It appears that many such stress responses are related to genetically determined sensitivities to the chemical ingredients (certain proteins) of specific plants, animal hairs, and foods. Allergic reactions can vary in intensity from fairly mild skin eruptions and sneezing to serious shock (failure in blood circulation) known as *anaphylaxis*.

While in graduate school, I worked during the summer months as head lifeguard and director of aquatic activities at an exclusive country club. The bane of my staff were the children running with reckless abandon around the pool's deck. Playfully they would snap wet towels at one another, squirt streams of water from plastic pistols, and drive us to despair. Their parents' attitude was that it was within the job description of the life-guard staff to baby-sit their unruly and often belligerent children while they golfed, played cards, or otherwise recreated. Throughout the day we blew our whistles, cajoled, threatened, punished, and of course carefully monitored these kids' actions. We were realistically concerned about the numerous kinds of mishaps that could befall them in an area as prone to accident as a large swimming pool.

One little boy was particularly troublesome. We repeatedly chastised him to no avail. He was inveterate in his disobedience. We were vigilant observers of his every move. Needless to say, his behavior kept us on edge. One day, despite our diligence, he fell and scraped his knee while galloping after a cohort. He came to me for first aid, which I administered in conjunction with a lecture and admonishment. I applied a few dabs of bactericidal ointment after cleaning the scraped (certainly nothing more) knee and sent him on his way. A few minutes later I heard a scream of terror being emitted by this boy. He lay supine on the deck. I ran to him as did two of my guards. His face and torso were flush. His hands trembled and he hysterically yelled, "I can't see — I'm blind, I can't see." I picked him up, carried him to the office designated as the first-aid area, and dispatched one of my guards to return with a club member I had seen earlier known to be a physician. When he arrived, he quickly diagnosed the stricken boy's condition as anaphylactic shock — a circulatory disturbance whose consequences could include death. "This kid is reacting to something he's been in contact with very recently — something that is toxic to him. It is causing a dramatic physiological upheaval, and he very likely has compromised vision and a bunch of additional strong symptoms at the moment." In a remarkably calming manner, the physician spoke to the boy and assured him that he would shortly feel better. Some chemical agent was administered by the doctor, and gradually the malady released its hold on the child.

After a while the physician turned to me. "It's important that we find out what he's recently had to eat or drink. Perhaps he's been bitten by an insect or come in contact with one of the chemicals used for pool and deck cleaning." And so we fired question after question at the boy in our attempt to recapitulate everything that had transpired antecedent to the anaphylactic reaction and identify the offending agent.

Finally we hit it — it was one of the ingredients in the bactericidal cream I had administered.

3.3.2 Bacterial Stressors

Bacterial infections may cause local swelling and inflammation, elevated body core temperature (fever), and, if unchecked, tissue destruction. When infection occurs within a body location or part that plays a primary role in the execution of a motor skill, then performance may be undermined. An infected hand will severely inhibit the shooting and dribbling capabilities of a basketball player; an infected (sore) throat may cause a singer to cancel a performance. In addition, in order to combat harmful bacteria that have begun to reproduce and generate substantial amounts of *toxins* (poisons), the body itself produces and circulates certain materials. These chemicals may also stimulate stress responses despite their absolute necessity in counteracting potentially harmful bacterial effects. Lymph nodes may become enlarged as they attempt to filter out dead blood cells and other casualties of the body's warfare against invading bacteria. *Swollen nodes* or *glands,* as they are commonly referred to in the vernacular, can be painful, distracting, and stressful.

3.3.3 Climatic Stressors

Variations in environmental temperature and barometric pressure also affect physical performance. Many athletic events and musical festivals are conducted out of doors, particularly during the summer months. Inclement weather may create adverse performance effects. Performance of fine-motor musical skills, involving, for example, very dexterous finger manipulation (stringed instruments) or changes in embouchure (brass or woodwind instruments) may easily be disturbed by low environmental temperature that may inhibit optimal contraction of skeletal muscle. To the contrary, few performers appreciate hot, humid environments in which perspiration flows profusely, despite the fact that heated muscles typically contract relatively more efficiently than cold ones.

At the behest of the "show must go on" slogan mentioned earlier, certain sports are played almost irrespective of weather conditions. Soccer and football matches are rarely canceled because of inclement weather. Although the performance may indeed proceed, its quality may very well be influenced by the weather, particularly when it brings exaggerated heat or cold. Heat stress is something with which many athletes are forced to contend. Altitude, as well, may become a critical performance factor. Performers would do well to consider these variables in their preparation (training for performance). That is, if you are confident that you will be required to perform in a difficult climate, try to prepare for this eventuality by rehearsing under similar conditions.

3.4 SUMMARY

Four theoretical approaches are employed in this chapter to clarify stress causality: psychoanalytic orientations, learning orientations, sociological orientations, and personological orientations. It may be that more than one must be incorporated into a comprehensive model for understanding sources of stress. Psychoanalytic orientations emphasize stress-engendering stimuli located in relatively lower levels of consciousness; learning orientations argue in favor of stress reaction being a function of acquired responses; sociological orientations look upon variables such as time imperatives (the clock), interactions with other persons in the environment, and value dissonance as causal factors; and personological orientations address psychological attributes or tendencies in cognition and behavior in an effort to clarify stress and anxiety reactions. Modeling is one of the learning orientations and is a powerful force that results in the acquisition of stress responsivity.

Some theoretical approaches maintain, essentially, that stress responses derive from sociological sources, wherein interpersonal actions seem to be stressful stimulations. Other theories emphasize learning in order to clarify the causes of stress reaction. In this theoretical camp, *classical* and *operant conditioning* models are emphasized. Stress reactivity is believed to be an acquired phenomenon.

Psychoanalytic orientations are also discussed in terms of their implications for understanding stress etiology. Concepts such as *intrapsychic conflict*, *signal anxiety*, and *memories of trauma* are related to the development of Freud's *energic* or *discharge* theory of anxiety.

Personological considerations are offered as possible clarifiers of human stress response. Stress reaction within this theoretical approach is viewed as a function of personality strengths and/or vulnerabilities. Enduring dispositions toward behavior — *traits* — are the bases of individual responses to environmental stressors.

Physical stressors include trauma and chemical, biochemical, bacterial, and climatic agents or factors.

4

WHAT IS PERFORMANCE?

LEARNING OBJECTIVES

After reading this chapter, you should be able to:

- Define the terms *self-actualization, flow, peak performance, skill,* and *ability*
- Reflect upon why outside observers are often compelled to criticize performance
- List two kinds of professional critics and their two basic functions
- Distinguish among performance as entertainment, as a cognitive experience, and as a physical experience
- Explain the cognitive information processing model
- Differentiate between each of these terminology pairs: fine- and gross-motor skills, open and closed skills, internally initiated and externally initiated skills, and simple and complex skills
- Contrast discrete, serial, and continual skills

IMPORTANT TERMS

- Performance
- Peak moment
- Peak performance
- Flow

- Information processing
- Gross-motor skill
- Open and closed skills
- Fine motor skill
- Discrete skill
- Serial skill
- Continual skill

4.1 INTRODUCTION

In this chapter performance itself is closely examined in an effort to understand its nature and unique qualities. A number of relevant concepts such as entertainment and criticism are discussed.

4.2 PERFORMANCE AS AN AESTHETIC EXPERIENCE

Behavior on stage or on the playing field is expected to be technically accurate. Often it is not — but the expectation is always in place. Even rank novices are expected to "do it right." Audience members respond to lapses in memory, performance error, and miscalculation with disappointment, displeasure, and perhaps even embarrassment. In most instances, such infractions are simply unacceptable. Only the most generous, empathetic, and compassionate audiences tolerate technical error — exceptions being, of course, audiences composed of fellow students, parents, and relatives of the artists.

But a special or memorable performance goes beyond technical correctness. If a performance is to be evaluated as noteworthy, it must somehow engage its audience by being lovely, interesting, or exciting. Correctness is not enough. We ask more of performers than flawless execution.

The eyes and ears of the beholder of performing art desire and deserve gratification. Audiences want to be satisfied, pleased, stroked, thrilled, and excited. Sophisticated consumers — those of long standing and experience — tend to be comfortable with larger doses of nontraditional performance materials. They are more flexible, more tolerant of innovation, more eager to take different directions, and more prepared to give the avant-garde a chance. But too much dissonance or departure from traditional models is irritating to the ordinary viewer or listener. Performance that deviates too much from tradition is suspect for such an audience.

This is also true in the world of high-level sport, which I consider to be a form of performing art. In this domain, accuracy and correctness are taken for granted. Incorrect and inaccurate performances are associated with the minor leagues or lower levels. Fans demand successful execution of skills, and although they crave victory, they also desire excitement. The diving or leaping catch is more highly valued than the routine play.

But in order for performance to be exceptional, it must transcend correctness. It must have some special quality — it must be enormously pleasing and beautiful and compell an ecstatic response from the audience.

4.2.1 Beauty in Physical Performance

Aesthetic qualities are highly valued in the performing arts. When a physical act or series of movements is executed with excellence — when the response it creates within the viewer is unusually appealing, when it not only yields the expected outcome but strikes very special chords of aesthetic satisfaction — then it is beautiful.

The wide receiver leaping acrobatically to snare a pass in football, the sprinter skimming the hurdle and rhythmically gliding over another and another — these are beautiful to behold, irrespective of the game's or race's outcome. The baseball batter's swing is beautiful because it is smooth and powerful, even though the ball may be missed. Grace and efficiency are components of beauty in sport. In the musical domain, lyricism, modulation, restraint, and interpretation all contribute to beauty. Beauty is a quintessential element of all physical performance. Appearance, body form, costume, and deportment all contribute to the aesthetic quality of performance in the world of dance. Although these qualities may be independent of physical performance itself, they bear upon its overall outcome. These factors help create impressions of beauty. Skilled physical performance is often evaluated in terms of its aesthetic component.

In sports, the slow-motion camera may be used to reveal aesthetic qualities of skilled behavior. A case in point is the televised film clips of professional or collegiate football players executing their skills against a background of recorded music. Here the score of the game is immaterial. The league standing of the team is irrelevant. Nothing matters but the mechanics of the skills cinematically transformed into a time-distorted but comprehensible and pleasing physical performance. The camera glorifies the grace and rhythm of the quarterback's movements and the lofted pass and dancelike airborne gyrations of the receiver. Thus, football may be viewed not only as rugged, violent, and physically abusive, but also as beautiful. Beauty is a redeemer of marginally condoned social activities.

4.2.2 Pleasure and Joy

Not all athletes are elite or professional. Not all performers ply their skills in front of audiences. Performance may be experienced in highly isolated and private ways for the sake of personal satisfaction. This is particularly true of nonelite performers. One dances alone in his room; one sings in the shower (presumably alone); and one rallies a tennis ball against a wall. A musical passage is repeated again and again without anyone else being present, without a request from an external source, simply for the sake of personal pleasure, of satisfaction deriving perhaps from the thrill of interacting with the piano or violin; for the sake of producing sound, tone, and melody in accordance with the prescriptions of a distant or even deceased composer. When we perform for our own satisfaction, we may do so because performance validates our abilities, skills, and vulnerabilities. It reveals what we know and how much we know — how much we have learned.

Performance is an experience in which our bluff is called. Some of us enjoy this bold-faced test; some of us do not. Under certain circumstances, which we may define in personal ways, performance becomes the reason for practice and the motive for commitment and enormous effort. Performance is a looking glass through which the entire self, or many of its parts, may be examined and understood. It is a way of better knowing who we are. We have the capacity to define the parameters of our performance, to impose limitations and restrictions, and to establish criteria for our very own performance success. In these ways, performance may be self-serving as a medium for pursuing self-fulfillment and joy.

Perhaps you know amateur musicians, people who play because they find it relaxing. Are they diligent in maintaining a regular practice schedule? Often they are. A former neighbor of mine was such a person. Often at 1:30 A.M., when his four young boys were asleep, he would sit at his piano and play. I never heard him but was able to see him through his window. I doubt that anyone heard him. He played only for his own satisfaction while his family slumbered. He was a pathologist by profession, but in the wee hours of the morning he performed for himself. He required no criticism from others, no applause, and no comment. He defined good and bad playing according to his very own standards of excellence.

Perhaps you have friends who take dance classes religiously but who certainly do not aspire to professional careers. Perhaps you are such a person. What about those of you who participate in amateur community theatrical productions? Why do you do this? Do you care much about the criticism of others and their reactions to your performance? Perhaps not, and if not, then maybe your motivation emphasizes pleasure and joy. Perhaps these outcomes derive from performing alone, without audiences or without critical reaction from anyone other than yourself.

Later in this book we'll talk about stress and anxiety as it relates to performance. We'll see that certain kinds of performances generate very little or none of these kinds of stress reactions, whereas others seem to cause a great deal of distress. Do you believe that stress deriving from performance done for oneself is, or can be, as great as stress from performing in front of others?

4.3 PEAK MOMENTS

Humanist psychologist Abraham Maslow (1971) has written about *self-actualization,* a defining and exhilarating condition attained when one perceives that one's basic needs in life have been met. The self-actualized individual is no longer in quest of mundane items such as nourishment or an adequate water supply. He is physically safe; his relationship requirements have been successfully addressed; and he is comfortable in the environment in which he operates. He finds his milieu appealing and replete with physical loveliness and admirable elements. Beautiful lakes, trees, sunsets, and mountain ranges are available to him, and he is spiritually fulfilled. He knows happiness. He lives on cloud nine, and cloud nine in Maslovian terms is self-actualization, wherein acceptance of one's adaptive responses to internal and external environmental needs prevails.

More recently, other scientists, such as Csikszentmihalyi (1975) and Jackson and Csikszentmihalyi (1999) have begun writing about such contentment, but with an eye toward physical activity, particularly sports and play experiences. An individual would thus come to know high levels of joy and satisfaction during physical performance, notably when it was smooth, comfortable, and worry-free. Csikszentmihalyi called this pleasing set of feelings *flow.* Flow need not entail outstanding or accurate behavior, but rather tremendously satisfying or joyful behavior that is intrinsically rewarding. This concept may explain my former neighbor's involvement in nocturnal piano playing totally alone and in a private environment.

On the other hand, *peak performance* refers to a remarkable exhibition of skill and ability, such as that of the dancer whose leaps and spins are extraordinarily powerful, explosive, and balletic — more so than she's ever before experienced — or the basketball player who sinks every shot she takes from the floor and knows in her soul that anything she puts up will go in. These are examples of *peak performance.* A peak performance, therefore, is something outstanding, remarkable, and uncommon. Some performers use the term *zone* to refer to this extraordinary condition when everything clicks, all is perfect, and nothing can go wrong. In and of itself, performance is a special form of behavior: It is behavior that incorporates a competitive dimension, that involves a desire for mastery and superiority, and that more often than not is done in the presence of others. Peak performance supersedes these objectives. Peak performance is an *incredible* performance.

4.4 CRITICISM

Sometimes it is difficult to witness another's performance without reacting judgmentally. Often, we are invited to offer critical reaction. Sometimes, discretion dictates that we say nothing. On occasion, we are simply grateful for the opportunity to view or vicariously participate in the performance and we are simply happy to be there and to offer support and encouragement, irrespective of the quality of the performance.

I well remember the fourth-grade band concert one of my sons participated in a number of years ago. He was a delight to behold in his white shirt, blue tie, and trousers (the band's concert uniform). His hair was slicked, his cheeks were flushed, and his fingers drummed rapidly and nervously on the rented metal clarinet resting across his lap. I remember the excitement he radiated as he scanned the audience looking for his parents, and his obvious relief and satisfaction at having found us. My wife and I watched him with pride, and later, we forgave the frightful squeaks and horrendous noises that his group produced. Although admittedly rhythmic, their sounds mercilessly assaulted our senses. At the concert's conclusion, when our son eagerly came to us seeking approval, we permitted our mouths to form smiles rather than well-deserved words of criticism. Technically and musically, the performance was awful. But we acted with restraint and subordinated our impulses to be critical to a higher order. In unison, and intuitively, we parents chose to reinforce and encourage a thrilled and delighted fourth grader.

We often feel obliged to judge a performance after its conclusion. We turn to friend, spouse, or date and speak our critical minds. In essence, we project our expectations, standards, and values onto what transpired on stage or field. If too much discrepancy exists between our expectations and actual occurrence, our reaction is negative. We carry models in our minds when we enter the theater or ballpark. We expect actual performance and the idealized model to be congruent.

We are not required to do this. When tickets are purchased for a show, game, or recital, no obligation to be critical is imposed by the box office. No space is provided on the ticket for critical remarks or evaluation. Yet we feel a responsibility to offer it. Why? Perhaps the answer lies in the human tendency (the strength of which varies in each of us) to assert, control, and exercise power. Criticism provides for satisfaction of such needs. By judging the performance of others, we momentarily give our self-esteem a boost. We become involved in the performance and enter a vicarious relationship with the performer. In so doing, we appoint ourselves judge and jury and preside over the performer's tribunal. If we are reasonably well versed in the performance area, we are able to criticize within a framework of intellectual honesty. If we are naive about the area and presume to criticize, we do so audaciously.

Somehow, we are driven to provide criticism, and comparing critical reactions is a popular and friendly way of spending time after the performance. One shares reactions with others. Discussions develop and arguments often follow. We seem to revel in these kinds of experiences. Ironically, the performer hears none of it. Although pretty much aware of the strengths and weaknesses of his presentation, he seeks reaction from a limited number of individuals: the coach, the teacher, the fellow performer, the professional critic.

Most performers acknowledge the efforts of mentors who fulfill instructional roles. Feedback from such persons is obviously welcome. The teacher/coach has helped develop strategies for the performer. The coach removes obstacles to successful performance. The teacher clears error, ignorance, and similar artifacts and debris from the path to success. The teacher/coach is a silent partner all throughout preparation for performance. She understands the nuances of the performance and is in excellent position to offer critical reaction.

Additionally, the performer himself makes attributions about the performance outcomes and their causes. As performers, we therefore tend to be self-evaluative. We ask, "How come I did so well?" or "How could I have possibly played so poorly?" We also are inclined to provide our own answers; we do not simply raise such questions rhetorically. Moreover, the answers we generate guide and shape the way in which we approach future performances that are similar. The conceptual area that deals with such evaluative thoughts is known as *attribution theory*; about which we will have more to say later.

A *co-performer* also has valuable insight, since he or she interacts with the execution of the performer's skills. Team members, other actors in the play, and other members of a musical ensemble may insightfully criticize a colleague's performance or the quality of the entire group's achievements. Co-performers feel and appreciate the impact and character of the performance, for they have just experienced it in a very meaningful and direct way.

4.4.1 The Professional Critic

From the Greek word *kritikos*, which means "able to discuss," comes the English word *critic*. Professional "discussants" are evaluators who are duty bound to analyze selected exhibitions in the performing arts and sports. As a rule they do this with conviction, passion, and seriousness of purpose. On occasion they do it with insight, authority, and sensitivity. In a sense, the critic represents all viewers of the performance, all audience members, and the entire public. His evaluations inform us of the performance's acceptability, vulnerabilities, and strengths, and thus his role may be justified.

As Walter Sorrell (1965) poignantly suggested in his article "To Be a Critic," criticism is a secondary art, in that it depends on a creative act preceding it. Sorrell suggests that a piece of criticism may indeed be a greater artistic product than the performance it professes to criticize.

If we accept the professional critics' reactions as authoritative, then we are obliged to compare our reactions to a performance with his. The professional critic, therefore, establishes a standard. He determines what is good and bad, exciting and dull, tasteful and plebeian. In so doing, he encourages or discourages others to attend subsequent performances. He has already seen it and is now eager to let you know what chance you have of enjoying or profiting from it. Many potential ticket buyers depend upon his analyses and predictions. Undoubtedly, many of us hesitate to enter a theater or performance arena without critical support for the production, or assurance by the critic of its high quality.

A critic fulfills two basic functions: clarification and evaluation, both of which derive from her personal experience with the performance, as well as the ways in which it has been internalized. The critic explains and reviews the performance and offers an assessment.

There are two kinds of professional critics: one is a former participant in the performance area itself; the other is typically a newspaper writer or journalist, assigned to report a particular performance—e.g., a sports journalist whose medium is newspaper, radio, or television. Usually, the former participant lays claim to greater insight into the performance than does the journalist.

Not surprisingly, the so-called critic's choice is fallible. On occasion, audiences find poorly rated performances to be significant, effective, and valuable. Disparaging professional-critical evaluation may be vigorously rejected by the public. When this happens too frequently, the professional critic's reputation and job are placed in jeopardy.

Do we really need and benefit from professional criticism? Take a moment now to reflect upon the most recent vocal, instrumental, dance, or sports performance you've heard or seen. Can you recall your reactions? Were they favorable? Were you satisfied or pleased? How did they jibe with the critical responses of the expert reporting in the news media? Did the two reactions match? If they did not, were you disappointed? Were you glad you experienced the performance despite the critic's reaction?

4.5 PERFORMANCE AS ENTERTAINMENT

A performer assumes a number of responsibilities, one of which is entertainment. Performances are designed to be amusing, diverting, and pleasurable. When they serve such purposes, they constitute entertainment. Those who offer such performances are entertainers. However, occasionally behavior not intended to be entertainment is interpreted as such by others.

Entertainment is evaluated not only with reference to having achieved its amusing, diversionary, or pleasure-generating potential, but also in terms of its innate skillfulness, artistry, cunning, or craft. If it is without such trappings, its audience is disappointed and reacts negatively. Such is the nature of entertainment, or as the saying goes, "That's entertainment."

In a sense, we are all entertainers at times. In some psychological way, we are gratified when we are able to amuse others. Somehow, knowing that we have helped others divert their attention to light-hearted and pleasurable subjects fulfills us. Those who do this very well may become professional entertainers.

Professional entertainers contrive to gratify others, usually through the medium of music, dance, comedy, or other derivative modes of communication. We commonly use the term *artist* to refer to entertainers (although not typically to athletes) who are consummate in their performances and who have honed their skills to very high levels.

4.5.1 *The Athlete as Entertainer*

To make my point about the athlete as entertainer, let me use a scenario that although having taken place a very long time ago, is nonetheless helpful.

Years ago, I organized and taught a graduate-level course at a major university, entitled Sport in American Society. Among the topics we treated was racism in relation to sports. At the time, a neighbor of mine was Reggie Smith, who was a center fielder for the Boston Red Sox, of the American League in major league baseball. The class met in the evening during the fall semester (off-season for baseball players), and on one occasion I invited Mr. Smith to attend a session, participate in discussion, and contribute a personal perspective to the class's study of the topic. He came, he listened, and he spoke. He was a very effective participant, in that he was able to share a wealth of illuminating personal athletic experiences. Reggie Smith is black, and his insight into the topic being treated was therefore keen.

Among the issues that surfaced during the evening were the so-called gestures of political and social dissent on behalf of two black track athletes at the 1968 Olympic Games in Mexico City. Victorious in his event, John Carlos stood atop the platform reserved for gold medalists. Tommy Smith, who had won the bronze medal in the same event, stood adjacent to him. When the American flag was unfurled and hoisted and the national anthem of the United States played, both athletes raised black-gloved clenched fists overhead and held them there for the duration of the "Star-Spangled Banner." Thousands of spectators watched in confusion from the stands, as did many millions of television viewers around the world. Later, the act was interpreted as a statement of revolution. Two black men had lodged a protest against white America. They had spoken out against racism by using a gesture (the raised clenched fist), which symbolized part of the turbulence and discontent of the tumultuous 1960s in the United States and other countries.

Reggie Smith was asked by class members to comment upon the appropriateness of this demonstration at the Olympiad. Much to the surprise of many of my students, he expressed disapproval of what had happened. His response is worth paraphrasing here, though more than 30 years have elapsed since he expressed himself. His viewpoint has relevance to our present discussion of performance as entertainment.

Smith had, and undoubtedly still has, a good deal of pride in being black. Evidently, he endured a considerable amount of psychological abuse during his ascendancy to athletic stardom. On numerous occasions he was the victim of racial epithets and vitriolic slurs as he tended his portion of turf in the Red Sox outfield. In certain ballparks, bottles and trash had also been thrown at him, thereby making him vulnerable to injury as well as insult.

But never in all his years in minor and major league baseball did he publicly demur. He felt that he was an entertainer — a professional. His job was to perform for the pleasure of paying customers. Therefore, center field in Fenway Park (where the Red Sox played) was not a proper forum for expressing sociopolitical points of view. Those, he maintained, would be reserved for times, places, and situations where he was not under the influence of his professional mandate to entertain. In Smith's view, professional athletes are professional entertainers. As entertainers, they are obliged to subjugate personal beliefs and causes to a higher goal — performance excellence. Perhaps this is also true of nonprofessional entertainers.

In a more contemporary vein are the questionable escapades and antics, both in and out of the ring, of American boxer Mike Tyson. Whether prizefighting is or is not an acceptable exemplification of sports is arguable (I believe that it's not). However, it is difficult to deny that professional boxers (as well as wrestlers, for that matter) are entertainers; and at the elite levels, they are very well known and very well paid entertainers. Yet, Tyson's deportment in the ring and his history of alleged physical and verbal abuse among friends, acquaintances, and his spouse suggest an inclination for antisocial outbursts. In a word, Tyson is, or was (in his prime), a highly competent fighter but not a nice guy. While certainly not condoning his deviant and often vicious out-of-the ring shenanigans, some observers maintain that entertainers like Tyson are under no obligation to be wholesome role models for others, particularly children. Furthermore, they argue that Tyson's personal life is his own business and that although perhaps not a person whose company we might covet, it is his boxing acumen — his valued success as an entertainer — that should be paramount in our assessment of his place in society. In other words, behavior on the stage, court, or field or in the boxing ring should be distinguished from nonperforming behavior. The entertainer's commitment is to performance excellence and nothing else.

4.6 PERFORMANCE AS A COGNITIVE EXPERIENCE

Our next chapter, Chapter 5, is devoted to *skilled behavior*, and there we will examine the components, as well as the strategies, commonly used for skill acquisition. But we now turn briefly to an essential aspect of skill learning, namely *cognition*.

Mental processes that involve thinking, reasoning, understanding, and making choices, especially when related to problem solving, are known as *cognitive* experiences. The act of simply recalling a previously stored memory would involve minimal cognitive function. Sometimes, high-order cognition works in relation to something random, as in the case of a card player who makes a judgment after recalling what cards other players have previously thrown. Physical acts in sports, music, and dance include important cognitive elements.

Different theories attempt to explain what happens neurologically when a motor skill is performed. Some approaches suggest that a programmed response is stored within the neuromuscular system (due to learning and practice) and that when the appropriate "button" is pressed (the stimulus), the act is automatically executed. Other theories argue that the formation of a mental picture, image, or model is imperative before a learner can execute a motor skill reasonably well. The learner conceptualizes the act and tries to duplicate it.

At any rate, playing a musical passage; executing a series of whirls, twirls, and leaps on the dance stage; or selecting a receiver to whom to pass in a football game are all examples of problems that performers must solve. Performers therefore reflect upon, ponder, and consider available information prior to or sometimes during physical performance. The degree to which they complete these processes is, more often than not, a critical determinant of the performance's outcome.

Sometimes, when the skills are particularly highly organized and complex, the performer may be encouraged to reduce cognition. "Don't think so much — just let it happen" is what some coaches advise. In this instance, the teacher or coach is suggesting that cognition may be an inhibitor of excellent performance. A series of twists and somersaults off the diving board may very well be executed so rapidly that the performer has no time to ponder, reason, or reflect while in midair. Cognitive mechanisms may have been in full swing prior to mounting the board or while the diver stood still for a few seconds after ascending the ladder. In such a case, the actual performance was, in all likelihood, executed in a programmed or prepackaged fashion. Once the performer leaves the board, the dive "automatically" unfolds — providing it had been well learned.

Cognitive processes play vital roles in physical performance — so much so that it is precisely the ability to reason, understand, and deal with previously acquired knowledge brought to bear in current situations that may distinguish superior from mediocre performers. Often, playing positions and assignments in sports, as well as certain roles in theatrical or dance productions, are assigned to performers with keen cognitive abilities. An example would be the quarterback position in football or the outfielder brought in to the game in the last inning of a baseball game because of his well-developed defensive skills (he's not likely to make any "stupid errors").

4.6.1 Information Processing

Information processing is a popular term currently employed by learning psychologists to explain the way in which we construct and use knowledge. Think for a moment about the enormous amount of information we tuck away in our brains. Think about our frequent need to pull up this information so that problems may be solved, objects and people identified, or facts recalled. A helpful model is available that illustrates how we may actually accomplish these things. It's called the *cognitive information processing model,* and although not all theorists consider it to be definitive, I believe it to be helpful here. It works like this. Stimuli from the environment (external as well as internal) enter the central nervous system via highly specialized organs of sensation, such as the eyes, ears, and nose, which funnel these stimuli to the brain. The first stop for the incoming stimuli is a hypothesized center known as the *sensory register.* Here, the material remains very, very briefly — perhaps much less than a second — before it is moved to the next temporary depository, the *short-term memory,* or *working memory.* It is in this place that meaning is attached to the smells, sounds, or visual images originally funneled in by the organs of sensation. These sensations interact with memories of prior experiences brought up from *long-term memory* into short-term memory. It is speculated that material remains in short-term memory for about 15 to 20 seconds.

According to the cognitive information processing model, whatever we have experienced in our personal histories, whatever we've seen, done, or felt, is stored permanently in long-term memory. Although we have access to this depository, we sometimes are unable to retrieve these past experiences, facts, or memories. We therefore claim that we "can't remember" or "don't know." The efficiency, strength, and orderliness with which we deposit the experiences in long-term memory dictate the ease with which we can eventually bring them up. To complicate matters a little, certain experiences occurring during our attempts to recall or deposit information may inhibit these functions. An example would be our attempt to access something already committed to memory when someone is speaking to us. Our attempt at recall is inhibited by the need to process incoming stimuli.

Mentors, coaches, and teachers should, therefore, present instructional materials to their performers in a manner that enables smooth, efficient, and powerful storage of information. The images used by instructors, the memory tricks (*mnemonic devices*) employed, and the characteristics of the content itself must be selected with an eye toward efficient information processing. Care should also be given to providing a performance environment that provides for minimal amounts of inhibition in recall or retrieval.

4.7 PERFORMANCE AS A PHYSICAL EXPERIENCE

In order to appreciate the physical side of performance, it is necessary to understand the functional and structural characteristics of the bones and muscles. Together, these organs enable movement to occur. The skeletal and muscular systems, respectively, represent the levers and cables that account for throwing, kicking, leaping, picking the strings of a banjo, or pirouetting. Therefore, let us now briefly review their major features.

Physical performance (at least the kind of performance we are referring to in this book) typically suggests movement. Movement involves changing the position of body parts or the location of the body itself in space (locomotion). Either or both happen when limbs move. Limbs move when muscles shorten or lengthen. Arms and legs are limbs. They are moved by muscles, which in turn are stimulated to contract by nerves.

Dysfunctional muscles or a defective skeletal framework does not permit efficient movement; sometimes, it does not permit any movement at all. Moreover, if the bones are properly aligned and articulated at joints and the muscles that move them are sound but no innervations (nervous impulses) are provided to stimulate their contraction, movement will not occur.

When muscles that control breathing are dysfunctional, air cannot be properly inhaled or exhaled. Hence, the wind or brass musician cannot play, and the singer cannot sing. If muscles of the forearm or hand do not flex or contract properly, the performances of the keyboard musician and the percussionist are compromised. Muscular well-being is essential to movement, and movement is a requirement of performance.

4.7.1 The Skeletal System

The skeleton is a collection of bones. The skeletal frameworks of many different vertebrates (animals with backbones) that do not appear to have much in common (e.g., birds, rodents, man) are, in fact, remarkably similar in design. There is a long vertebral column of short bone segments to which the skull is attached at one end (the skull encases and protects the brain).

Holes in each of the vertebrae are aligned to form a tube through which passes the *spinal cord*. The spinal cord leads from the brain and generates numerous branches of nerves that serve organs and systems (a group of organs with common purposes) throughout the body.

Limbs are attached to the skeleton at two girdles, *the pectoral* and *the pelvic,* which are wide and flattened bones. We commonly refer to these girdles as the breast or chest area and the pelvis, respectively. In humans, the arms are attached to the pectoral girdle and the legs to the pelvic girdle. *Joints* are locations on the skeletal frame where bones connect and movement occurs. Joints have lubricating tissues that provide a slippery fluid designed to facilitate motion. Thick fibrous *ligaments* keep the joints from pulling apart. The design of the joint permits various forms of movement. For example, the hip joint, where the upper leg connects with the pelvic girdle, allows for quite a different range of motion than does the ankle or elbow joints (where upper arms and forearms meet). Some joints bend in only one direction, others in many. Movement at the shoulder and hip joints is fairly free and rotational. These are known as *ball and socket* joints. Movement occurs in only one place at the knee and elbow, where the joints are said to be *hingelike*. Function varies with regard to the dimensions and shape of the bone and the joints where bones articulate.

The human vertebral column consists of 24 *vertebrae* and two larger pieces at the bottom: the *sacrum* and the *coccyx*. Pads or disks that assist in shock absorption prevent the vertebrae from coming in contact with one another. Unfortunately, these pads may be damaged or "ruptured." When this happens, considerable discomfort or pain results, which may severely inhibit movement.

Ribs are long, curved bones that attach to the vertebrae and arch around forming a cage in which the heart and lungs are located. Most of the ribs attach to the sternum, or breastbone, on the front (ventral side) of the body.

4.7.2 Motor Skill

It is difficult to evaluate or even consider performance without utilizing the term *skill*. Although used in a variety of ways, we apply this term here to suggest a motor act that is performed with grace, efficiency, and accuracy. In this sense, *skill* refers to a learned movement or pattern of movements that have been honed and polished through repeated trials, under favorable conditions (practice). Strolling leisurely and aimlessly on the beach involves the motor skill of walking. Toddlers, with the help of parents or others, *learn* to walk. Walking on a balance beam (a piece of gymnastics equipment) or a circus high wire is also an example of the same fundamental skill, namely, walking. However, it represents a more complex and difficult form of walking. All sorts of readiness (coordination, muscular strength, self-confidence, etc.) are prerequisite to learning balance-beam and high-wire walking. The typical toddler would not be prepared to acquire this form of the walking skill.

The word *ability* is used to describe a capacity that underlies a number of common motor acts. For example, tossing a beanbag (overhand), pitching a curve in baseball, and passing a football are distinctly different skills. But they all depend upon the motor ability of throwing. The frequency and accuracy with which a skill is practiced, as well as the psychological framework in which it is repeated, will determine the strength with which it is ultimately learned. As you'll observe in forthcoming chapters, psychological stress can influence both skill performance and learning. Later in this book, we'll have more to say about the relationship between stress and skilled performance.

The goal of all performers is to acquire necessary skills thoroughly and securely. Skills that are deeply embedded in the nervous system are more likely to be completed with high degrees of correctness, even in adverse circumstances.

4.7.3 Different Kinds of Skills

There are a number of ways in which skills may be classified for purposes of performance analysis. Sometimes, one classification scheme is both logical and helpful; and at other times, its use is burdensome and inappropriate. Don't feel obliged to fit any or all motor skills neatly into one of these categories. Sometimes, it's best to use more than one of the following to describe a skill.

4.7.3.1 Fine- and Gross-Motor Skills   Movements that depend upon small-muscle activity and emphasize accuracy are said to be *fine-motor skills*. *Neuromuscular control* and *dexterity* are also good terms for describing these kinds of skills. The left-hand effort of a right-handed violinist is intricate and deft. It is therefore an example of a fine-motor skill. Additionally, fine-motor skills usually involve a relatively small number of muscles.

In contrast are learned motor acts involving comparatively more and larger skeletal muscles. These movements tend to be less complex. The actions of the violinist's right hand and arm, the javelin throw, and a somersault on the trampoline are examples of *gross-motor skills*. Many groups of large muscles are activated for these skills. A continuum with *gross* and *fine* situated respectively at either end is a helpful, sensible framework for presenting these ideas. Figure 4.1 represents these continua. This kind of arrangement suggests that a motor skill need not be classified as exclusively gross or fine, but rather that it may fall somewhere along the continuum.

4.7.3.2 Open and Closed Skills   Skills may also be classified according to their degree of dynamic change in the midst of execution. Some skills vary with regard to directionality or the force with which they are performed from second to second or moment to moment. Environmental stimuli apparently trigger variable reactions. The performer changes one or more aspects of skill execution in response to

Gross   Fine

Tackling in football---Playing a trill on the piano

Banging cymbals (in the orchestra)------------------------------Firing a pistol at a target

Shot putting-- Executing a short golf putt

Figure 4.1 Continuum for fine and gross motor skills.

cues from others or from the physical environment itself. The hockey player, skating down-ice while controlling the puck, alters his speed, changes direction, or may transfer linear motion into vertical motion (i.e., he jumps). He may stop abruptly, start again, and spin in a 180-degree turn — all in accordance with the behavior of opposing defensemen, as well as his own teammates. Thus, the hockey player executes many *open skills* — open because they are amenable to modification in midstream.

Closed motor skills, on the other hand, are characterized by an absence of such variability. In fact, if they do vary to a considerable degree, they are deemed incorrect or inaccurate. The golfer's swing, for example, must be carried out according to an original neuromuscular plan. Since the position of the golf ball is fixed, no deviation in this plan or change in swing mechanics is appropriate as it is addressed by the club.

4.7.3.3 Discrete, Serial, and Continual Motor Skills   Skills may also be classified as *discrete, serial,* or *continual.* Dart throwing exemplifies a discrete skill. Such skills terminate quickly and are composed of movements that are only loosely connected or not critically dependent upon one another. The dart thrower moves the throwing arm to the rear, then forward (sharply and rapidly), releases the dart, and follows through. The skill execution is completed in fairly short order. A single vertical leap by a dancer is also an example of a discrete skill, although more gross than is dart throwing.

Skills that comprise movements done in a highly prescribed sequence are known as *serial* skills. Playing an arpeggio on the piano is an example. If movements are done in improper sequence, the passage will be incorrect. Therefore, each part is more critically related to antecedent or subsequent parts than is the case in discrete skills. Another way of viewing a serial skill is by considering it to consist of a number of connected discrete skills.

A *continual* skill is repeated over and over, with no apparent pause between parts. The whole is then immediately "replayed." Cycling and swimming are examples of continual skills. A very elongated roll on the snare drum (such as the percussionist in a circus band is sometimes required to play) is another example. Once learned, continual skills are resistant to forgetting, even over periods of many years. It is speculated that this is so because of the incalculable number of repetitions that were invested in their learning. In other words, a tremendous amount of physical practice goes into the learning of continual motor skills. Evidently, there is more learning than occurs with discrete or serial skills.

Once again, a continuum is appropriate as a framework for presenting discrete, serial, and continual motor skills. Often, a skill belongs somewhere between these designations.

4.7.3.4 Internally and Externally Initiated and Paced Skills

The baseball pitcher begins his windup volitionally (when he is ready). So does the server in volleyball and tennis. However, the baseball batter and service receiver await the pleasure of the pitcher and server. In the former cases, the skills are *internally initiated*. In the latter cases, the skills are said to be *externally initiated*. Members of the orchestra's violin section await their conductor's downbeat. Performance of their skills is therefore stimulated from an external source. On the other hand, the violin virtuoso playing without orchestral accompaniment initiates the first note of the sonata internally. The terms *internally paced* and *externally paced* refer to the speed or rhythm of the skill execution, that is, its pace, irrespective of its beginning.

4.7.3.5 Complex and Simple Motor Skills

Sometimes it is helpful to classify skills according to their degree of complexity. Skills with many components and with very little or no latitude for variation in performance are said to be *complex*. Many patterns and steps in advanced levels of folk dancing are intricate and difficult to perform. They are high in skill complexity. Their structure is highly defined and they typically require much practice before they can be executed reasonably well. A conceptualization (forming a picture in the mind's eye) of what the correctly performed skill looks like is also helpful. It's not likely that one can simply watch a demonstration of complex motor skills and immediately follow suit.

Experts disagree as to the best ways of teaching complex skills. Some advocate the skill's breakdown into component parts, each of which is to be presented and practiced separately. Ultimately, when the skill's segments are learned, they are assembled into a *whole*, which is then practiced. Probably, highly complex skills are best taught to beginning learners in a *part*, or segmented, fashion.

On the other hand, *simple* skills can most likely be efficiently acquired by presenting them in whole or complete form. Rolling a tennis ball on the floor (just rolling the ball, not trying to strike an object or putting it into a target or a hole) is an example of a simple motor skill. The learner whose neuromuscular mechanisms are functioning properly would be expected to repeat this task after simply observing its demonstration. In fact, many gross-motor skills of low complexity are efficiently learned (with few practice trials) by modeling or copying a good demonstration.

Through reading this past section, you are becoming familiar with motor performance from a physical perspective. You have been introduced to terminology that should make discussing, classifying, and understanding motor skills easier. Let us now turn to matters that concern the *acquisition* of skills. In the next chapter, you will read about processes that underlie *motor learning*. Many texts and a virtually incalculable number of research articles have addressed this broad topic. We'll deal with this voluminous material in synopsized form and begin by discussing the experience of learning itself. Then we'll overview the human nervous system, wherein learning actually takes place. Lastly, we'll address conditions necessary for optimal (best) learning to occur. (A good book to consult for more detailed description of the topics and subtopics that we can deal with only superficially here is Magill, 2003.)

All of these matters bear very directly upon stress and arousal, which we are committed to investigate rather thoroughly in later chapters of this book.

4.8 SUMMARY

The aesthetic aspects of performance and the idea of beauty (in terms of exhibitionistic performance) were examined in this chapter. A performance is deemed beautiful when it transcends ordinary expectations or minimal requirements for correctness or accuracy. It must evoke feelings of pleasure among viewers. It must be creative, graceful, skillful, and appropriate. Above all, it must be appealing to its audience.

Pleasurable and joyful dimensions of performance from the performer's point of view are best understood in terms of *flow*, or a sense of sublime competence in the task. Although performers are generally aware of "how they did" in any given outing, they still value feedback from teachers, coaches, and mentors. Professional critics lend legitimacy to public evaluations of performances.

Motor aspects of performance include many classifications: fine- and gross-motor; open and closed; discrete, serial, and continual; internally and externally initiated; complex and simple.

5

SKILLED BEHAVIOR

LEARNING OBJECTIVES

After reading this chapter, you should be able to:

- Describe the nervous system, including specification of the central, peripheral, and autonomic nervous systems
- Define the terms *memory, information processing, feedback, kinesthesis, knowledge of results, transfer of learning, practice,* and *mental practice*
- Briefly explain operant conditioning and the role of reinforcement in learning
- Identify the characteristics of knowledge of results that are most conducive to learning
- Understand transfer of motoric, cognitive, and affective skills as effective for learning
- Distinguish between massed and distributed practice, and part and whole practice

IMPORTANT TERMS

- Synapse
- Autonomic nervous system
- Feedback

- Knowledge of results
- Motor program
- Operant conditioning
- Practice
- Part–whole practice
- Massed practice
- Mental practice

5.1 INTRODUCTION

So much of our daily behavior is learned that if we were to miracu-lously delete this experience from our lives, we would be left with little more than innate behavioral responses to environmental stimuli. We wouldn't have the capacity to think, solve problems at a high level, or benefit from previous experiences. We might be motivated to escape from aversive elements in our surroundings and act in other reflexive ways, but without learning and the behavior it generates, there would be little else in our lives. We could execute movements for which we have been genetically programmed for millennia, but beyond these kinds of responses, our days would be "boring." Even pursuit of basic drives such as hunger, thirst, and sex require the use of acquired social, physical, and cognitive skills.

Our basic values are learned; so are our social taboos (i.e., those things that we are not supposed to do), our manners, and our cultural customs, or mores. Those who learn well or have an affinity for learn-ing are socially rewarded. Good school grades, preferred jobs, promo-tions and attractive careers typically await the proficient learner. A popular view is that fast or efficient learners are intelligent or bright. Slow learners, or those whose attempts at learning are problematic, are often singled out for special attention in school. Sometimes, there is prejudice against those labeled as slow learners.

Among other things, learning means acquiring skills. The extent to which a skill has been learned can be determined only through its eventual performance. The two experiences, learning and per-formance, are symbiotically intertwined. A dance student would be extremely hard-pressed to validate the learning of the pirouette other than through its actual performance. With regard to motor skills (which typically involve observable movement of some sort), there is an additional important dimension, although one that may not be as important in intellectual or social skills acquisition. This dimension is *retention*. The actor who memorizes lines of a play is not expected to be able to recall these sequences of words beyond the duration of the play.

The same is true for the student who learns geometric theorems or the names of the cranial nerves or the correct declension of an irregular Spanish verb for the purposes of a final exam. However, with regard to the motor domain, skill retention is expected. The musician is forever obliged to retain and recall at will the correct fingering for a particular note on her instrument. The football quarterback, once having learned to throw a swift and accurate spiral pass, must never forget throughout his playing career the various sequences of movement (motor pattern) that yields this skill. Although each game over a period of years provides new challenges and problems, the mechanics of the pass remain fixed and dare not be forgotten.

In this chapter, we will discuss various features that are essential to your understanding of how learning occurs.

5.2 THE NERVOUS SYSTEM

A collection of body organs working together for the purpose of achieving a physiological goal comprise a *system*. The human nervous system, which consists of the brain, the spinal cord, and the peripheral nerves, controls bodily activities such as muscular action. Thus, the nervous system plays a vital role in the performance of motor skills. Motor skills are acquired through nervous system function.

The nervous system may be thought of in terms of two separate portions: the *sensory portion* and the *motor portion*. The brain processes information about change in environmental conditions (stimuli) that is brought to it by the sensory mechanisms. As discussed in Chapter 4, special organs of sensation such as the eyes and ears collect and analyze stimuli and forward them to the brain via peripheral nerves. Branches of the spinal cord bring nervous messages to the cord itself (encased in the bony spinal column), which then transmits them to the brain. The brain and spinal cord are known collectively as the *central nervous system*.

In the brain, the stimuli are interpreted, and appropriate muscular responses (movements) are selected. This processing of information occurs in many different specialized brain centers. Exactly how this happens is still highly speculative, although neuroscientists are making significant advances in the quest to map brain centers specifically associated with certain functions (including information processing). Findings from brain-mapping research indicate that processes of high-order thinking are located in the prefrontal area of the cerebral cortex, directly behind the forehead and extending to approximately the ears. It is currently believed that long-term memories are stored in the *hippocampus,* part of a brain section known as the *limbic system,* and are recruited or brought forth so that we may solve problems, make computations, and *think.* This is what the brain does in an operational or functional sense; and this function is referred to with the term *mind.* Another way to refer to the prefrontal part of the cerebral cortex is with the expression *the brain's executive (or command) center.* Specific reasoning functions are associated with localized activity within the prefrontal areas.

Today, most scientists agree that no single seat of authority exclusively regulates thought, cognitive function, and ability. Rather, current conventional wisdom holds that control of these functions is dispersed throughout this so-called executive area (also known as *Broca's area,* after the French anatomist who first identified it). Various circuits in different locations contribute to information processing and may substitute for one another in the event that one is temporarily or permanently disabled. The brain is constantly distributing and redistributing, analyzing and assessing information throughout its enormous array of networks.

After stimuli are interpreted, nervous messages are communicated to the skeletal muscles, which in turn move limbs. The messages travel from the brain down the spinal cord and through peripheral nerves that communicate with muscles and other organs. These nervous transmissions occur from one nerve cell to another (at locations called *synapses*), which together form long links of *nerves.* The messages themselves are partly electrical and partly chemical.

5.2.1 Brain Plasticity

The brain continues to reorganize itself, make new neural connections, and perhaps even acquire new neurons (nerve cells) well into adulthood — all of which provide promise that old dogs can indeed learn new tricks, although the brain loses some of its plasticity in later life. The least plastic part of the brain, the amygdala, is that which is associated with emotions. The ways in which we respond emotionally are probably learned at both conscious and nonconscious levels and are also heavily influenced by genetically determined predispositions. In other words, we may *learn* to feel fear when confronted by a coiled snake, or control our anger when offended by another person. However, the tendencies to experience fear and anger are hereditarily ingrained in us for protection of the species. For more than 40 years the work of Paul Ekman (1993), has focused on the emotional reactions that are expressed in facial expressions. In establishing the cross-cultural meaning of certain expressions (such as fear, anger, surprise, and joy, which are all expressed facially in the same way irrespective of culture), Ekman's work has given credibility to a notion originally espoused by the eminent Charles Darwin (1859).

5.2.2 The Autonomic Nervous System

The *autonomic nervous system* is part of the motor portion of the nervous system. It basically innervates (gives nervous commands to) smooth-muscle tissue. Many of the internal organs such as the stomach, urinary bladder, and blood vessels are lined with sheets of smooth muscle. This muscle is "instructed" to contract or relax by different autonomic nerves. The autonomic nervous system has two divisions: the *sympathetic nervous system* and the *parasympathetic nervous system*. Chains of sympathetic nerve fibers lie on either side of the spinal column and prepare the body for fight or flight. The sympathetic apparatus functions dramatically during stress or emergency. It stimulates heart function, causes the release of additional fuel for muscular activity (glycogen) into the blood, and provokes dilation of the tiny air sacs in the lungs. Put simply, the sympathetic nervous system carries arousing or activating signals.

By contrast, the parasympathetic division of the autonomic nervous system, whose fibers lie just above or below the sympathetic system, delivers orders to organs of just the opposite kind. Relaxation, slowing down of the heart rate, and reduction in sweat gland activity are all examples of parasympathetic activation. Most organs, glands, and muscles have both sympathetic and parasympathetic connections. *Cardiac,* or heart, muscle (muscle tissue that is intermediate between smooth and skeletal muscle) is also innervated by the autonomic nervous system.

5.3 INFORMATION PROCESSING

Knowledge about environmental events is called information. Information reaches the brain and is stored there, sometimes over surprisingly long periods of time (years) and sometimes very briefly (seconds). Some of this deposited material is eventually retrieved or somehow encouraged to surface into consciousness. Information is stored in *memory,* an abstract entity that serves the purpose of a warehouse or a repository. If the memory involves observable movement, such as in the case of motor skill execution, we use the term *motor memory.*

Information processing is the term used to refer to the deposition of information in memory, the retrieval of information from memory, and the enactment of a movement in response to a stimulus. (A good book to consult for a more detailed discussion of how information is processed and the factors that limit its storage and retrieval is Schmidt & Lee, 1999.)

What we store in our memories, and how well we store and retrieve it, varies with the psychological conditions prevailing at the time of storage, as well as the stimulus for retrieval. Teachers and coaches should try to manipulate these conditions by creating and shaping environments that maximize learning and performance.

Later in this book, we'll have a lot to say about arousal and stress in relation to information processing. In fact, one of the book's thrusts deals with ways to manage the responses and conditions that cause arousal and stress in order to facilitate performance.

5.4 FEEDBACK AND KNOWLEDGE OF RESULTS

As skills are performed, the brain receives information about performance effectiveness. Nerves attached to muscles and various sensors serving many organs and systems of the body provide feedback to the brain about the quality of the skill execution. The term *feedback* refers to internal (within the body) sources of information.

When the information deals with the position of the body or its parts in space, we use the term *kinesthesis*. Information that does not derive from visual processes is said to reach us kinesthetically. For example, you know that you are holding up two fingers behind your back even though you can't see your hand. Kinesthesis provides this awareness.

Sometimes, information is provided by other persons. For example, the teacher or coach responds with, "Now you've got it!" or "That's pretty good, but bend your left elbow a little more." The orchestra conductor uses gestures to signal the percussionist who is playing too loudly or the soprano who is singing too softly. We call this *knowledge of results,* or KR. Sometimes, information about the quality of skill execution may reach the performer because the task is *self-reporting.* This is the case in basketball shooting. You know when the ball goes through the hoop. You can see it and you don't need another observer or an intricate internal sensing mechanism to let you know about the shot's outcome, because your visual powers suffice. Sometimes, KR is provided by machines such as video replay or motion pictures.

The ways in which we execute motor skills are influenced by the information reaching our brain during performance. We can correct and modify important aspects of performance in midstream. We can adjust limb angles, position of the head, length of stride, or pressure on the mouthpiece of a trumpet, all in accordance with information about the performance that reaches our consciousness kinesthetically, visually, auditorily, or through input provided by observers.

On occasion, an intricate skill must be performed so quickly that no time is available for feedback or KR. Even kinesthetically derived information cannot be handled by the nervous system rapidly enough in order to correct or modify performance in these situations. Certain series of movements in tumbling, gymnastics, figure skating, and diving fall into this category. While in midair, the diver cannot process information coming to her brain from sensors in the skeletal muscles fast enough to do anything. The entire sequence of twisting, turning, and somersaulting occurs over a period of seconds. Therefore, in such a case, nervous impulses coming from the organs have virtually no impact upon performance, and feedback is ineffective. The entire set of signals that control the skill execution evidently come directly from the brain or spinal cord, where they are stored. Messages go directly to the key skeletal muscles, with virtually no accommodation of feedback or KR. Thus, an intricate dive from the three-meter board is said to be programmed. A *motor program* contains messages about the proper sequence of muscle contractions, as well as their force.

Teachers and coaches who organize and direct learning and performance experiences also have an opportunity to construct and modify the environments in which these activities occur. Indeed, their obligation is to facilitate learning and performance by shaping the environment into a design that encourages learning.

The learning process is a complex phenomenon that has been studied by a host of theorists, all of whom feel that their individual models best clarify the ways in which it proceeds. In order for a coach or teacher to justify his instructional strategies or manipulations of the physical or social learning environment, a rationale for such interventions is necessary. In other words, teacher- or coach-inspired programs for skill acquisition should be based upon theoretical foundations. Intuitive teaching methods based upon successful past experience are not to be denied; however, optimal approaches incorporate theory. Let us now consider a few of these so-called theoretical factors.

5.5 OPERANT CONDITIONING

Operant conditioning is a theoretical framework that involves environmental structuring or restructuring. The renowned B. F. Skinner (1963) of Harvard University emphasized *reinforcement* of desired behaviors as well as those that come close to or are introductory to the ultimate behavioral goal. Skinner and other *behaviorists* believe that as long as the learner is able to associate reinforcement with behavior that is preferred, the likelihood of it being repeated is strengthened. Behaviorists wait patiently for a learner to volitionally (whenever the learner is ready) move or perform a desired or preferred act, or one that approximates it. Then this action is reinforced with something that the subject interprets as rewarding (e.g., words, gesture, preferred food, physical contact). In this way, the learner "acts" or "operates" on the environment. Hence, the origin of the term *operant conditioning*. According to Skinner, through the utilization of the basic principles of this theory, any organism may be conditioned (taught) to acquire any skill.

Other theories emphasize different dimensions of physiology, psychology, biochemistry, or heredity to explain skill acquisition and behavior. Here we have only dealt superficially with Skinner's model in an attempt to exemplify a learning theory that could support coaching/teaching methodological decisions. Rushall and Siedentop (1972) demonstrate how principles of behaviorism may be specifically applied to the teaching of motor skills. These applications take the form of so-called operant techniques, also popularly referred to as *behavior modification techniques*. They emphasize the control of behavior through reinforcement.

Irrespective of the many different directions taken by learning theorists, a number of factors seem to be generally accepted as basic to efficient skill acquisition: namely, KR, transfer of learning, and practice.

5.5.1 Knowledge of Results

At this point, it is necessary to add the dimension of KR *accuracy* to what we've previously discussed. The accuracy of KR influences learning and ultimately performance, particularly in the early phases of learning. Generally, the more accurate the information about performance that is provided, the better the learning. However, KR that is too precise may confuse the learner and inhibit performance. In addition, there is some evidence to suggest that inhibition to skill acquisition can result if the KR delay is *too short*.

Curiously, the immediacy of KR (how quickly it is provided after the performance) has not been clearly shown to affect learning in humans. In some animal learning studies, however, this variable does seem to be important.

5.5.2 Transfer of Learning

Previously acquired skills may influence the acquisition of new skills. The notion of transfer suggests that there is profit in generalizing from skills that have been previously practiced to attempts to acquire new skills. For example, saxophone-playing skills are probably more easily acquired by the experienced clarinetist than by someone who has trained as a string bass player. The task of breathing in coordination with fingering of the keys is very similar in many reed and woodwind instruments, and much of the fingering itself is similar.

In the domain of sports, the somersault done by the diver is strongly analogous to that executed by the trampolinist (that is, while in the air). Conceptually and strategically, soccer and ice hockey overlap tremendously. One team defends one goal and the other team defends the other goal, and the idea for both teams is to get the ball or puck into the opponent's net. Athletes in soccer, field and ice hockey, and water polo all share these objectives.

However, elements of skilled performance may also be transferred from one skill to another in an undesirable way. A case in point is the nearly straight-arm forehand in tennis, which often is incorrectly transferred to badminton. In badminton, there is considerably more emphasis placed upon a bent wrist than in tennis. Tennis instructors can usually identify beginning students who have played a good deal of badminton because their tendency to "wrist" the ball is a giveaway.

Two important points about transfer of learning deserve consideration. With regard to skill acquisition, there is much profit to be found in using an old skill as a reference for learning a new one. In fact, the more alike the two skills are, the greater the opportunity for transfer. Learners should be encouraged to seek and identify opportunities for learning transfer. But, the skills need not always be motoric just because the performer is functioning in the motor domain. Athletes, musicians, and dancers must develop cognitive skills in addition to motor skills if they are to perform effectively. An understanding of defensive and offensive strategy, different zones, and coverage schemes must be thoroughly understood and *learned* by the team sports athlete, particularly at high levels of competition. These things may be accomplished in a classroom-like setting with chalkboard or distributed printed materials (such as the football playbook). The musician copes with a complex score and must understand the effect the composer or conductor is seeking. In fact, merely reading a musical score involves visual-cognitive skills. Sight-reading involves several skills, including motor control and different mental skills. In dance, similar requirements must be coped with.

In the performance of motor skills, there is considerable opportunity for capitalizing on the transfer of those skills that have been previously learned, as well as those that are cognitive in nature (reasoning and thinking). The latter kinds of skills, as well as intellectual ones such as those used to memorize a score or a piece of choreography, are not of paramount concern in this chapter, but we would be remiss if we did not at least refer to them.

Actors are called upon to emote in various ways, frequently on very short notice. That is, they must quickly show or "turn on" happiness, horror, remorse, etc. They must learn to develop skill in the *affective domain* (having to do with feelings and emotions). "Method acting" is an approach to developing such skills by requiring that the actor bring to mind feelings associated with previous real-life experiences that have caused anger, sorrow, jubilation, and associated reactions such as tears or laughter. By thinking of such past responses at a time when crying, laughing, or any other form of emoting is necessary for performance, the actor re-creates the desired behavior. This is another form of transfer.

Learners usually do not appreciate the frequent opportunities for transference of skills available to them. They need to be encouraged to apply this technique. Learners, especially beginning skill learners, must be conditioned to ask a series of questions during the early phases of learning, such as "Where have I seen these elements before?" "How did I solve this problem before?" and "In what way(s) did I move when previously confronted with this kind of challenge, and was that response effective?" These past experiences reside in the long-term memory system referred to in Chapter 4. The teacher, coach, or mentor must provide stimuli that encourage the movement of these past experiences into short-term, or *working*, memory.

Many of the motor abilities previously mentioned are transferable conceptually, as well as mechanically, from one skill to another. Usually, though, some form of modification is necessary for a particular skill. Throwing, for example, has many transferable aspects, from football to baseball to softball to javelin throwing, but there are differences in each type of throwing. In certain instances, the same is true of kicking in soccer and football. Performers must be motivated to seek out opportunities for transfer of learning. In this respect, the teacher or coach has an important role to play.

5.5.3 Practice

On occasion, we're all given to quoting and accepting clichés. But these time-honored statements, although familiar to the ear, do not necessarily contain truth or wisdom.

One cliché bandied about frequently, but clearly without substantiation, is "practice makes perfect." Certainly, practice is essential to efficient learning, but by no means does it guarantee performance perfection. Take a moment to calculate the number of years you have been writing your name in script (signature). Perhaps 10 to 15 years, and in some cases, even more. Yet your handwriting is far from perfect, despite the thousands of times you have practiced it.

In order for practice to be effective in strengthening skill acquisition, it must be conducted under certain conditions. We now turn briefly to a review of these conditions and some controversial questions they raise relating to practice.

First, we need to define the term *practice,* since it is often used in a loose, nonscientific context which may be confusing and even irrelevant to the way in which we shall actually apply it here.

One campus athlete to another: "Can you give me a lift home after *practice?*"

Coach to team member: "Where were you yesterday? Why weren't you at *practice?*"

In these contexts, *practice* refers to a rather broad and time-consuming experience that may incorporate a wide range of cognitive, affective, and physical experiences. In fact, however, in the world of sports, some of the physical experiences may have little to do with skill learning and much to do with muscular strength and cardiorespiratory endurance training. The time spent with the coaching staff dealing with problems relating to a specific forthcoming athletic event is commonly known as *practice*. Incidentally, the very same meaning is implied by the term *rehearsal* in the domains of dance, music, and drama. Sometimes *rehearsal* brings to mind a full complement of actors, dancers, or musicians, whereas only one of these persons working alone (memorizing lines from a script or a solo musical passage) is said to be "practicing." Thus, *practice* in a non-technical or nonmotor learning context suggests a block of time wherein activities pertinent to performance are conducted (regardless of whether these activities are related to the learning itself).

In this book, the term *practice* is used in a more restricted way. We define practice as *trial-by-trial repetition of a task*. A task is a skill, such as a prescribed movement pattern, a gymnastic stunt, etc. The first practice variable to be considered is *number of repetitions*. How many practice trials should be performed for optimal skill learning? Clearly, the answer depends upon the nature of the skill itself, as well as upon certain characteristics of the learner. Therefore, in order to answer this question it is necessary to have information about (1) the task's complexity and degree of organization (more specifically, the location of the task on the fine- to gross-motor skill continuum and the degree to which it is open or closed), and (2) the familiarity of the learner with the task's demands (the degree to which the learner has already experienced the task, and the ways in which this experience has occurred).

5.5.3.1 Massed Versus Distributed Practice
Yet another issue relating to practice is the *massed versus distributed* question, in which concern is directed toward practice schedules or the blocks of trials in which practice occurs. Should the repetitions be done in blocks of trials separated by periods of rest, or should all repetitions be executed one after the other, with no intervening rest? Figure 5.1 illustrates the two schedules.

In both models, the number of trials is the same. The rest between trials need not be "flat-on-your-back" rest; it can involve merely a change in activity, as would be the case of the musician who stops practicing one musical piece (or section of a piece) and moves on to another. In the world of sports, a rest interval could mean switching from a fast-break drill in basketball to foul shooting, or changing from starts off the blocks to flip turns in the swimming pool. In the practice setting, rest suggests diversion.

Researchers are often divided about which schedule produces comparatively better learning. In some studies, massed schedules yield superior results, usually when learners are advanced and motivation is high. On the other hand, when the learners are beginners, distributed schedules seem to work best. This may be due to the fact that beginners practicing a motor skill become fatigued earlier than advanced skill learners and profit more from rest. Additionally, some studies report no meaningful differences between the two schedules.

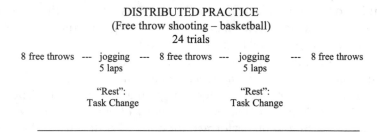

DISTRIBUTED PRACTICE
(Free throw shooting – basketball)
24 trials

8 free throws --- jogging --- 8 free throws --- jogging --- 8 free throws
5 laps 5 laps

"Rest": "Rest":
Task Change Task Change

MASSED PRACTICE
(Free throw shooting – basketball)
24 trails

24 consecutively taken free throws.
No task change.

Figure 5.1 Massed versus distributed practice schedules.

5.5.3.2 Part Versus Whole Practice An additional practice variable is the part–whole question. There are two alternate ways of presenting a skill for practice purposes: (1) the skill broken down into its component parts, and (2) the skill presented in its entirety. An example of component-part presentation is a tennis backhand stroke that is taught "by the number system":

> Stand with feet shoulder-width apart; right hand gripping the handle of the racket; left hand loosely holding the racket's neck between forefinger and thumb. Body weight is shifting forward, knees are bent, and feet are pointed straight ahead. This is the correct starting position. Now, at the count of *one*, pivot on the ball of the left foot so that it is pointed out — and simultaneously, cross over with the right leg so that the right foot is now a stride ahead of the left. Also, bring the racket across your body so that your right elbow is approximately above your right knee. Ready, *one!* Good. Now, back to the starting position. Let's try this once again. Ready, *one* — and back to the starting position. Again, *one* and back to the starting position. Okay, now at the count of *one*, when you bring your arm across your body, bend your elbow; keep your head up; bend the right knee and be sure that the face of the racket head is pointed toward the direction of the net.

An example of the "whole" method as applied to the teaching of the backhand tennis stroke would be as follows:

> Can everyone see me? Good. Now watch [instructor demonstrates all movements of the tennis backhand sequence]. Now we'll all try it. First spread out — give yourself plenty of room. Whenever you're ready, try it. I'll walk among you and see how you're doing.

Which model produces the best learning and performance outcomes? Once again, the answer seems to depend upon the nature of the task. Little attention or information processing is required in skills that are low on the complexity dimension. Therefore, the *whole* model would be a good choice for skills of low complexity (few components) and high organization (the parts are critically related). *Part* practice would produce best results when the skill is high in complexity and low in organization. A flip turn in the swimming pool has few but integrally related parts and would therefore be best practiced by the whole method. However, a rapidly executed modern-dance pattern might be suited for the part method of practice, because it is high in complexity but low in organization, that is, it has many loosely connected components.

5.5.3.3 Mental Practice   By no means the most important of all the practice issues, mental practice is certainly among the most intriguing. It suggests that trial-by-trial repetition of a motor skill can occur in the mind's eye of the performer. Our ability to conceptualize ideas and images is virtually limitless. What constitutes nothing less than a remarkable observation is that by practicing motor skills mentally, one can actually enhance physical performance; a number of studies have verified this phenomenon (Feltz, Landers, & Becker, 1988).

Just imagine that you are sitting in your favorite rocker or armchair at home. You conjure a vision (with eyes closed) of the stage upon which you intend to dance; the mound and home plate from which and to which, respectively, you will pitch; or the podium upon which you will face your orchestra and conduct. Comfortably nestled in your seat, you execute your dance, athletic, or musical action. Over and over again, you repeat the leap, the windup, the pitch and follow through, or the dramatic sweep of the baton through the space in front of you. You repeat the series of movements with appropriate form and no errors, performing accurately, gracefully, and efficiently in your mind's eye. This is mental practice.

In a later chapter, we'll discuss a similar experience called mental imagery. We'll see how it can be used to manage undesired reactions to stress. For the time being, let us limit our concern to mental practice and draw an important conclusion from the available research findings: Mental practice in combination with physical practice produces a higher degree of skill learning than does physical practice or mental practice alone.

It seems clear that *physical* practice is irrefutably a necessary experience for skill acquisition and performance improvement, but mental practice also helps. Why? There is some speculation that muscle fibers that would be contracted during skill performance are also innervated during mental practice and that therefore some form of movement (albeit unobservable) is actually going on. As you can imagine, methodologically sound and well-controlled research is difficult to conduct in the area of mental practice. Researchers are handicapped in their efforts to assess what subjects are practicing mentally or how correctly the practice is proceeding.

5.6 SUMMARY

Basic concepts underlying skill acquisition focus on learning and retention and the central, peripheral, and autonomic components of the nervous system.

Information processing is defined in terms of motor memory, motor control, motor program, and motor learning. Feedback is a procedure by which evaluation information about task-related behavior is provided to the performer. It is one of the conditions for learning, which also include kinesthesis, knowledge of results, transfer of learning, and practice.

6

ASSESSMENT AND EVALUATION OF PERFORMANCE

LEARNING OBJECTIVES

After reading this chapter, you should be able to:

- Define evaluation and recognize its role in eliciting performance anxiety
- Differentiate among measurement, evaluation, and assessment
- Define the terms *social facilitation, audience effect,* and *coaction*
- Discuss research findings related to performance and the presence of others, including the interaction of variables such as task difficulty and advance notice
- Define the term *goal* and identify the characteristics of goals that lead to optimal performance
- Understand the various ways in which goal setting may influence performance

IMPORTANT TERMS

- Evaluation
- Assessment
- Measurement

- Social facilitation
- Cognition
- Goal setting

6.1 INTRODUCTION

Performance is a special kind of behavior. It involves *evaluation*, which means that not only are the actions of the performer on display, but her behavior is being observed and judgment is being made about the quality of the performance. Evaluation, therefore, is a distinguishing characteristic of performance. The performer exhibits his wares — his abilities and skills — and audience members react judgmentally. By clapping, booing, yelling, stamping their feet, whistling, or their very silence, audiences express their reactions to what has transpired on the stage or sporting field.

These issues were briefly discussed in Chapter 4, but what is worth repeating here is that this dimension of performance — evaluation — is what may actually account for performance anxiety and the physiological arousal that invariably accompanies it. This, then, is the focus of the present chapter. Among other things, we will highlight distinctions between and among processes such as evaluation, measurement, and assessment.

6.2 EVALUATION

Awareness of present or impending evaluation is what may cause the emergence of a vaguely defined, highly subjective, and often irrational form of fear that plays havoc with information processing and skill acquisition. And when a performer's attentional focus is directed toward what others may be thinking, her observable performance may be compromised.

Let's pause now and differentiate the term *evaluation* from other words that are frequently used synonymously or in conjunction with it, namely *measurement* and *assessment*. *Measurement* involves procedures such as determining dimensions (length, width, height) or the frequency of occurrences of an act. When we measure, we accumulate quantitative data, which may also include the frequency with which error has occurred. *Assessment* emphasizes the determination of individual or group needs and discrepancies between needs and available resources. When we *assess,* we examine attitudes and perhaps skills, but we do so in ways that do not necessarily utilize traditional paper-and-pencil tests. Qualitative approaches such as interviewing, self-reporting, and observing behavior are typically employed for assessment. Measurement tends to be a more formal and concrete approach than assessment. Measurement involves observations of a descriptive nature, such as things to be accomplished in order to achieve an important goal. For example, the determination that 53 percent of marching-band members had been studying music for more than 5 years is a type of measurement.

In contrast, evaluation produces judgmental conclusions such as: "There are not enough members in the band with formal musical experience," "Our pitching staff lacks depth. If two of our starters are injured, we'll be in deep trouble," or "Our field-goal kicker can't hit anything beyond 35 yards with consistency" (based upon an assessment made by reviewing all attempted kicks during the last two seasons of play). Evaluation takes us beyond counting and number crunching. We can establish a useful perspective about the three terms *measurement, assessment,* and *evaluation* by using the simple continuum presented in Figure 6.1. Measurement anchors one end and assessment the other, with the location of evaluation being somewhere in between, overarching and subsuming the other two.

6.2.1 Evaluation and Anxiety: The Connection

Many performers experience preperformance worry or doubt about a pending competition, recital, or concert. Often, the worry is overbearing in spite of encouragement by co-performers, acquaintances, mentors, teachers, and coaches. Supporters may say, "Just get up and do it — don't worry about it! There's no way you'll lose — you're well prepared — you're good, you're better than the other guy" or "You know the material, you'll be great." But usually such encouragement is to no avail. The well-known symptoms of anxiety discussed in Chapter 2 surface and prevail. Among them are the frequent urge to urinate, excessive perspiration, the sensation of heart *palpitations,* unquenchable thirst and dryness of the mouth, and the perception of overall weakness (particularly in the knees).

What underlies such reactions? A compelling speculation is that the imminent prospect of evaluation forces the emergence of self-generated and very poignant questions such as: "Do I have what it takes to do

Evaluation

Measurement..Assessment

Figure 6.1 Meassurement assessement Continuum.

this job?" "Do I possess the resources to meet the demands of the present task?" "Can I do this?" This kind of daunting introspection may, in and of itself, provoke insecurity and doubt. These doubts, in turn, are accompanied by an emotional shift and heightened levels of arousal, as well as an abandonment of the physiological balances that we discussed previously (i.e., homeostasis). The sympathetic nervous system is engaged and the athlete prepares for battle, or as Cannon put it years ago, for "fight or flight." But she's worried. She's got the pregame jitters; she's anxious. Figure 6.2 portrays these links in a proposed model that applies just as well to musicians, actors, dancers, and performers of all persuasions as it does to athletes. Once again, the core element of the model is evaluation. If evaluation produces doubt about the presence of personal resources required to do the job, the consequence is likely to be a hefty dose of anxiety.

6.2.2 Evaluation by Others

The explanation of the term *performance* that I've provided brings to mind skill execution in the presence of others. Performance is behavior that involves exhibition. In some way, the performer puts on a show in front of, or for the benefit of, others.

Observers of performance such as parents, fans, friends, acquaintances, directors, judges, and coaches, not only sit in the aisles, stands, and bleachers, but also sit in judgment of the exhibition. Because

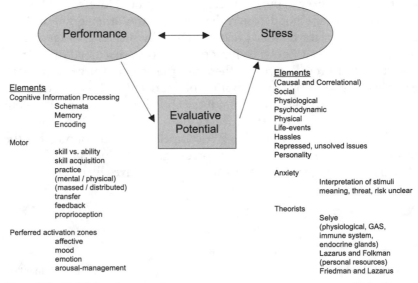

Figure 6.2   Model of performance stress.

the performer is aware of their presence he may display his skill and creative or interpretive acumen for their benefit. Audiences judge what they see and hear and respond or provide feedback, sometimes with immediacy, sometimes with a delay of days. Dancers, actors, and musicians are entertainers, and so are athletes. They all realize that what they do on stage or on the field of play will, in some way and at some time, be evaluated. This awareness may generate concern and worry (anxiety). Evaluation by others, or the implication that others might or will stand in judgment of your performance, gives rise to stress and anxiety responses. In Chapter 7, we will talk about another form of evaluation — self-evaluation, which is, in effect, a judgment of your own ability to perform adequately that you conduct prior to actual performance. This preperformance evaluation typically gives rise to the question "Am I smart enough, fast enough, strong enough to meet the demands of the task before me?" The answer is a measure of *self-efficacy*.

6.3 SOCIAL FACILITATION

The performance of others in the environment and their behavior are believed to influence the quality of performance. And since performers more often than not execute their skills in front of others, what follows is a section devoted to the effects exerted upon the performer by those in the environment — those who are seated in the concert hall, bleachers, and stands, as well as those who share the field of play, stage, or orchestra pit with the performer. The expressions *social facilitation* (Carron, 1980; Cotrell, 1972; Iso-Ahola & Hatfield, 1986; Zajonc, 1965, 1980) and *audience effects* (Cratty, 1981) both refer to the influence and behavior of other persons on the conduct of performance. Cox (1993) has suggested a distinction between these terms, in that "social facilitation" brings to mind performer/audience interaction, while "audience effects" indicates a noninteractive influence of the audience upon the performance. However, these terms are used interchangeably by most researchers (e.g., Borden, 1980; Green, 1980; Iso-Ahola & Hatfield, 1986; Wankel, 1984; Zajonc, 1980).

The expression *social facilitation* was first applied by Allport (1924), who defined it as "an increase of response merely from the sight or sounds of others making the same movement" (p.262). Zajonc (1965) later broadened the concept and designated it "coaction." Zajonc's definition has been accepted by most contemporary scholars. In its popular application, social facilitation refers to performance changes — improvements as well as decrements — that are due to the presence of others in the environment. About 30 years ago, social facilitation was identified as the fundamental concern of researchers in the area of social psychology (McCullagh & Landers, 1975; Weiss & Miller, 1971). A voluminous body of research findings focused upon social facilitation are available in the sports psychology literature. A sample of reported findings follows.

Some results in the literature contradict Zajonc's hypothesis of performance change due to the presence of others. These contradictions are explained as being due to the employment of different research methods (Bond & Titus, 1983). Landers and McCullagh (1976), although generally supportive of an audience-induced arousal effect, identified two situations that are exceptions: (1) The presence of a calm companion when the audience is initially encountered and (2) a companion's interference with a subject's reception of aversive stimuli. Both mitigate audience-induced arousal effects. In other words, having the support of a fellow performer who provides a model of serenity and control countermands the tendency toward arousal.

Most of what the literature offers about social facilitation and performance is sports related. Sports has a heavy physical orientation that distinguishes it from other performance types. And although much of the reported studies are quite old, their vintage should not necessarily deter us from clarifying the relationship between others in the performance environment and increases in arousal associated with performance. Rather, it is quite different from other human experiences because of its physical demands.

The first known experiment in social physiology was set in a sports environment. Triplett's (1897) study dealt with the effects of coactors on cycling performance. He found that the presence of others facilitated motor performance, and he concluded that "the bodily presence of another contestant participating simultaneously in the race serves to liberate latent energy not ordinarily available" (p. 533).

6.3.1 Mere Presence

Most of the early social facilitation studies were stimulated by Zajonc's (1965) drive theory explanation, and therefore a majority of the research dealing with audience effects on motor performance were conducted after 1965. Singer (1965) was the first to examine the influence of spectators on motor behavior (which encompasses sports but is not restricted to it). He compared performance on a balance task in athletes and nonathletes under an audience condition. Contrary to his expectation, Singer observed that nonathlete subjects performed significantly better in front of spectators than in front of athletes. He therefore concluded that audience effects on sports behavior might be event specific and nontransferable. In other words, simply because an athlete experiences heightened activation in the presence of spectators watching him compete on the tennis court doesn't mean that he will react similarly when performing in a basketball game. In reviewing Singer's study, Iso-Ahola and Hatfield (1986) suggested that athletes might experience greater evaluation apprehension than nonathletes, because they frequently perform motor tasks in front of others. Moreover, athletes may feel a higher expectation to perform well in motor tasks.

With reference to Singer's early study, balance is only one aspect of physical activity, and its contribution to performance is variable from sport to sport and task to task. Whether or not its relation to evaluation apprehension is similar to other performance variables is not known. Wankel (1975) also tested the effect of the presence of others on balancing performance. Although two evaluative peers were used as spectators, no interactions were found between audience and motor performance. Wankel speculated that the audience condition in his study was not powerful enough to affect the performance. In line with this observation is the problematic issue of laboratory studies in comparison with field studies. In the real world of sports, audience members more often than not comprise much larger numbers than are typically employed in laboratory investigations. Football stadiums, for example, can boast capacities of 80,000 to 100,000 spectators, and soccer games in many European and South American countries frequently accommodate well over 100,000 raucous fans. Many laboratory studies refer to 2 or 3 others in the environment as "the audience." Such differences in audience size make the transferability of laboratory findings to real-world competitive environments suspect.

6.3.2 Coaction

The effects of coaction (others performing the same task at the same time) on reaction time (RT) and movement time (MT) — two critical components of dance and sports in particular — have also been earmarked by researchers. Some old research findings are available that shed light on coaction. Carron and Bennett (1976) and Wankel (1972) examined this kind of social facilitation, but their findings did not support Zajonc's (1965) model. The coaction condition was expected to produce increased drive, which in turn would facilitate production of the dominant or well-learned responses. However, results from these studies revealed no interaction among coaction, RT, and MT. Therefore, Wankel (1972) hypothesized that rivalry, coaction, and audience influence affect motivation and thus alter RT and MT. Once again, no supportive evidence for this hypothesis was found. Because Wankel did not find any elevation of physiological arousal in the coaction condition, he concluded that the presence of a coactor might not affect cognitively based drive (activation related to thinking and problem solving).

Haas and Roberts (1975) investigated effects of evaluative others on a complex motor task. Their results support Zajonc's (1965) work, in that subjects learning a mirror tracing task were significantly inhibited by the presence of an evaluative audience. Subjects who have already learned the task were significantly facilitated in their performance by spectators who were involved in evaluation. Mere presence (audience members do nothing, but they are present in the environment) as well as evaluation apprehension were also investigated by Haas and Roberts. They concluded that since subjects who perform in front of a blindfolded audience execute the mirror tracing task significantly better than those in the alone condition, Zajonc's (1965) "mere presence" hypothesis is sustainable. That is, mere presence of an audience is sufficiently arousing for social facilitation to occur, but evaluation by the audience may be too arousing and thus interfere with performance.

Social facilitation effects have been examined in field situations infrequently. In two unusual studies, Obermeier, Landers, and Easter (1983) assessed the influence of coaction on performance of both animals and humans. In their first study, the running speed of greyhound racing dogs was measured under two conditions: alone and coaction. The dogs ran significantly faster in the coaction condition than in the alone condition. Their second experiment examined the effects of coaction on a 400-meter dash in human subjects. The results supported social facilitation theory in that subjects ran significantly faster in the coaction than in the alone condition. Interestingly, however, subjects in the alone condition ran more evenly paced trials than those who ran with coactors.

6.3.3 Task Difficulty

MacCracken and Stadulis (1985) investigated the effects of alone, coaction, and spectator conditions on easy and difficult dynamic balancing performance in children. Their findings indicate that the presence of five spectators produced increments in performance for subjects who were of comparatively higher skill and decrements in performance for subjects of lower skill levels. MacCracken and Stadulis also found significant differences among higher-skill subjects performing a difficult task (walking on a balance beam) in three conditions: alone, coaction, and spectator. When subjects of higher skill performed a difficult task, they did so significantly better under the spectator condition. The coaction and alone conditions yielded the next best results, respectively.

6.3.4 Advance Notice

An additional and interesting dimension of social facilitation is what is known as *advance notice*. Paulus, Shannon, Wilson, and Boone (1972) found that when male subjects in introductory gymnastic classes were told in advance that they would be observed, their performance suffered significantly. This result was further examined in a study by Paulus and Cornelius (1974), where a gymnastics performance was observed under three conditions: alone, presence of spectators with advance notice, and presence of spectators without advance notice. Higher-skilled subjects showed greater decrements in performance than less-skilled subjects in both spectator conditions. This effect was greater in the advance-notice condition than in the no-notice condition. Considering the previous study (Paulus et al., 1972), Paulus and Cornelius (1974) suggested that although the two investigations support what Cotrell, Wack, Sekerak, and Little (1968) called the evaluation apprehension hypothesis, the inverted-U hypothesis rather than drive theory (both of which were discussed in Chapter 1) may account for the social facilitation effect, especially in complex motor performance. The inverted-U hypothesis and drive theory attempt to clarify motivation for behavior from physiological arousal perspectives. The inverted-U hypothesis postulates a curvilinear relationship (i.e., two variables have a positive relationship up until a certain point when the relationship changes direction) between arousal and performance; and drive theory indicates a linear or direct relationship (*linearity* here refers to the variables continuing their relationship unchanged).

So what may we conclude about social facilitation? In summary, Zajonc's (1965) theory has been widely studied in motor behavior contexts. A majority of the laboratory and field studies support the theory's efficacy; however, each athlete's perceptions relative to audience characteristics may mediate audience effects. As suggested by Wankel (1984), most competitive athletes prefer to perform in front of audiences, but their individual cognitions about audience attributes should be taken into consideration by coaches and sports psychology consultants. Failure to incorporate cognitive and other individual psychological variables into experimental designs has been a serious shortcoming of much of the social facilitation research and accounts for a good portion of the inconsistent findings reported in the literature.

Performers other than athletes may also experience changes in physiological arousal in response to the presence and behavior of coactors and others in their environment. Performing in an ensemble setting may diffuse the perception of burden of responsibility in individual dancers, musicians, and actors. Unlike athletes, they at times are not competing, but cooperating. Shared responsibility may reduce the onus.

6.4 PERFORMANCE CRITERIA AND GOALS

Those who evaluate performance may do so insightfully or naively. Figure skating and gymnastics judges at elite levels such as the Olympic Games are expected to know their stuff. Years of personal competitive experience and significant background in judging are implicit in their professed preparedness for work at the Olympic level. In addition to years of apprenticeship, judges are expected to demonstrate their readiness to function as experts by passing written tests of their sport-specific knowledge. They are also observed by examiners who gauge their efficiency and effectiveness as judges in actual competition. Professional baseball scouts employed by major league teams search for "talent" and assess and evaluate aspiring major leaguers by analyzing relevant statistical reports that depict achievement in hitting, fielding, and base running. Football scouts also evaluate young high school and collegiate athletes by applying traditional criteria that are supposedly predictive of successful achievement in football. Running speed in the 40-yard sprint, amount of weight that can be bench-pressed, body size, and weight are examples of these criteria. In a nutshell, those who evaluate performance must provide evidence of their qualifications for sitting in judgment. The higher the level of performance, the more stringent the criteria for the qualification of the evaluators. The feedback these evaluators provide to performers can be the basis for motivation levels, for training, and for preparation for future performance, as well as for distressful responses that have an impact upon arousal level.

Performances before "juries," or panels of experts (e.g., faculty members, other performers of high reputation), are often reported by music students as well as by those auditioning to be enormously anxiety producing experiences. Musicians claim that they would rather play in front of a sizeable audience of 1,000 to 2,000 people than 4 or 5 jury members. Apparently, the knowledge, ability and experience of jury members, because of their expertise, provokes abundant doses of anxiety. So, in addition to advance notice and behavior of audience members, the reputation and status of evaluators may influence performance quality.

Performers themselves also establish criteria by which their personal successes and failures are determined. Often, a performer is able to identify steps required for high achievement. Making such a plan and carrying it out is an earmark of the accomplished performer.

Without a realistic plan designed to structure and regulate preparation, the performer's training and practice sessions are unfocused, meandering, and unproductive. It is the pursuit of soundly structured "doable" goals that sets the stage for ultimate success.

6.4.1 Goal Setting

T. A. Ryan (1970), an industrial psychologist, was among the first to understand and argue that consciously established goals influence our actions. But what exactly is a *goal*? According to Locke and Latham (2002), who continue to conduct research and write extensively about goals, a goal is the object or aim of an action — for example, to attain a specific standard of proficiency, usually within a specified time limit. Our interest here lies with specific performance goals, rather than with broad intentions such as obtaining a fellowship to graduate school or getting a job after completing a graduate degree. The more specific the goal is, the better the result will be. Therefore, it is best to encourage performers to establish well-defined behavioral targets (rather than simply urging them to do the best they can).

Setting appropriate performance goals is motivational. That is, goal setting accounts for the amount of energy or fuel that underlies our efforts, as well as the direction and intensity of those efforts. The highest or most difficult goals are associated with the highest levels of effort and performance. When our commitment to a highly difficult goal fades or ceases, performance decreases accordingly. Those with high self-efficacy tend to set higher goals than performers with lower self-efficacy. They are also more committed to their goals and are better able to handle negative feedback than are people with low self-efficacy (Seijts & Latham, 2001).

Why does goal setting affect performance so powerfully? The following four mechanisms explain.

1. Goals direct attention toward relevant efforts and away from those that are irrelevant.
2. Goals energize or spark our behavior. High goals tend to do this better than low goals; however, some evidence is available that suggests that with regard to sports performance, moderate goals may be superior (Kyllo & Landers, 1995).
3. High goals prolong effort — that is, they foster persistence. Behavior that is goal driven has a strong "stick-to-itiveness." But goals that are unrealistically high may encourage the performer to take greater strategy risks, and it is conceivable that in the domain of physical performance, injury could be a consequence of unrealistic goals.

4. Goals affect action indirectly by leading to the arousal, discovery, and/or use of task-relevant knowledge and strategies (Wood & Locke, 1990).

Other aspects of appropriate goal setting that encourage commitment (pursuing the identified goal[s] over time) are:

1. Perceived importance of the goal. Goals that are viewed as important are associated with higher levels of effort. When important goals are achieved, high degrees of satisfaction follow.
2. Participating in establishment of the goal, in contrast to accepting goals imposed by others
3. Feedback that provides information about progress toward goal achievement. If a dancer, for example, establishes a goal for leaping higher during performance, or a baseball batter is determined to smooth out his swing, information about goal accomplishment must be forthcoming. When feedback indicates below-goal achievement, performers are likely to try something new or crank up their effort (Matsui, Okada, & Inoshita, 1983). Feedback need not necessarily be derived from external sources. The performer should provide himself with strategies for determining progress toward goals.
4. Task complexity. People are more likely to achieve simple rather than complex goals. Complex goals require more complicated and varied strategies and thereby bring into play more cognitive functioning. Thus, the more complex the goal and associated tasks, the more the performer has to think and make decisions and choices.

Goals may be set for groups as well as for individuals. Goals may be established for subgroups within larger groups. In a symphony, the woodwind section requires goals; the entire symphony orchestra does as well; and each oboe, bassoon, and clarinet player develops and pursues individual goals. The field goal kicker, the quarterback, and the defensive tackle all have individual goals; the offensive team, as a group, also sets appropriate goals; and, of course, all 60 or so members of the football team share large-group goals.

Authenticity and *realism* are two additional characteristics of proper goal setting. Goals should be realizable (realistic). If unattainable, goals will not only fail to influence performance in a positive manner, but may also generate frustration, anger, and diminished motivation for continuation of the behavior. Those who work with young performers in particular should supervise their goal setting, lest pie-in-the-sky, unattainable aspirations be erroneously established.

Proximal and *distal* are terms that also apply to properly established goals. Performers should be encouraged to develop *proximal* (or immediate) as well as *distal* (or far) goals. A shot putter may set a goal for performance at the coming weekend competition but should also create a realistic view of her throwing distance for five months into the future.

As we conclude our discussion of goals, two points deserve emphasis:

1. Goal setting has been shown repeatedly to be highly correlated with achievement (performance).
2. Goals may be either developed by the performer or established and assigned by others such as coaches, counselors, or teachers. When set properly, they exert a strong influence upon motivation.

6.5 SUMMARY

The essential concerns of this chapter were with the processes of performance measurement, assessment, and evaluation. Distinctions are made among these three commonly used procedures for gathering information about performance. Evaluation is considered as a function either of self or of others. By this is meant that performers themselves gather information about the quality of their performances that may or may not be compatible with feedback from mentors, peers, or audience members.

Standards of excellence are usually set according to the perspectives of so-called experts who sit in judgment of performance quality. Evaluation responses provide a variety of emotional reactions from performers who integrate this feedback into their preparation for future performances.

Goals and appropriate goal setting are relevant to performance. In order for goals to exert positive influences on motivation for practice and skill acquisition, certain aspects of proper goal setting must be recognized and incorporated. Among these are (1) goals that are attainable, (2) goals that are identified for individuals as well as for groups, (3) the establishment of near (proximal) and far (distal) goals, and (4) goals that, whenever possible, are set by the performer, although regulation by a mentor may often be necessary.

7

PERFORMANCE AND SELF-PERCEPTIONS

LEARNING OBJECTIVES

After reading this chapter, you should be able to:

- Define *self-concept, body image, self-confidence,* and *self-efficacy*
- List and elaborate upon the five selves that form the self-concept
- Understand the adaptability of body image and self-concept
- Name and describe the four sources of information that can modify self-efficacy
- Discuss the link between biochemistry and emotions as they relate to performance

IMPORTANT TERMS

- Self-concept
- Body image
- Spirituality
- Self-efficacy
- Affect

7.1 INTRODUCTION

In another book, Jerrold Greenberg and I speak of five components of self and their relationship to wellness (Greenberg & Pargman, 1989).

In our interpretation of wellness, we suggest that *physical, mental, intellectual, emotional,* and *spiritual* selves are equally important. The whole is not necessarily always the sum of its parts; but in this case, the well-integrated or total self is the sum of these parts. The overall image you maintain of yourself is beholden to each of its constituent selves. The perceptions we hold about each of these components and our notions about their viability and potency compose the *self-concept.* Some experts argue that self-concept is located at the very heart or core of our psychology.

The person you are or think you are consists of many interrelated selves. Some aspects of self are easy to be in touch with, and others are more difficult to access and evaluate. At times, any one aspect of the self may need more personal attention than others. In our quest for well-being, we seek to strengthen all parts of self and to maintain a balance among them (i.e., one aspect should not overpower others, and none should be underdeveloped). These are the issues dealt with in this chapter. We take a close look at the view of the self in an effort to see how it relates to stress and anxiety.

7.2 THE PHYSICAL SELF

Our basic concern here is with physical performance. In this book, I have used anecdotes, metaphors, and examples taken mostly from the performing arts and sports. However, any observable gross-motor activity executed competitively or during exhibition satisfies our definition of performance. *Body image* is the mental picture one holds of the body, and the relationship between performance and the physical self is clear and strong. It is the physical self, its function (organic, systemic, and mechanical), and one's perceptions about its appearance (observable body parts) that influence the quality of movement. We know and experience our world through our bodies. Physical performance is a medium for developing positive or negative concepts about the body and the entire self.

Wellness and happiness may be achieved in spite of flaws or malfunction of any aspect of the physical self. However, when this is the case, performance is negatively affected in some way(s). Compensatory or "backup" responses may enable performance to proceed, but clearly, the type of performance we speak of here is basically dependent upon an effectively functioning physical self.

When performance is consistent with established goals and aspirations, we acknowledge the efficient functioning of the physical self and we are pleased. Parts of the body that work effectively generally conform to the anatomically desirable model for that part. A leg that is functionally sound is thought to be shaped properly. Its muscles are well developed and well formed. It pleases us to make this observation. We derive pleasure from knowing that our body and its parts are working in accordance with well-established models. We feel good about our bodies when they look good and work well. Performance is a yardstick with which we may assess organic function, which in turn is a basis for formulating a view about our total selves.

Self-concept is very meaningfully influenced by the image we hold of our bodies. If we think poorly of the body, we tend to hold negative attitudes about the overall self. A comforting thought is that unlike personality (behavioral tendencies), which most trait theorists believe in some cases to be resistant to change, body image is modifiable. This suggests that a highly successful performance may alter the body image. In turn, this revised view is expected to influence self-concept. Therefore, if we actually modify physical structure through exercise or weight training (i.e., lose body fat or increase skeletal muscle size), concepts of both physical and total selves may very well undergo positive change. The intriguing thing about this is that your entire outlook on life, the world, and your place in it is colored by perceptions about who you are physically (e.g., "I am strong/weak," "I am a fast runner," "I am graceful"). These perceptions are an outgrowth of physical performance. Performance enables you to know who and what you are physically.

7.3 THE INTELLECTUAL SELF

Although the term *intellectual* suggests mental activity, its use does not imply independence from the physical, emotional, and spiritual aspects of self. Aside from the most basic movements such as reflexive reaction and autonomic functions, physical acts do not proceed without intellectual involvement. The intellectual self is that part of you that is responsible for organizing solutions to problems and converting environmental stimuli into messages that initiate, terminate, or change movement behaviors. There's even an intellectual side to reflexive responses: You attach meaning to your knee jerk when you think about it and make a determination about its frequency, force, or magnitude. In this case, your intellectual involvement is "after the fact," but the point is that there is intellectual involvement.

You also make evaluations about your physical self by employing intellectual abilities. Your conclusion about your performance, whether you executed a required task perfectly or poorly, is a function of reasoning or intellectual activity. As a consequence of your experiences with problem solving (taking a written test) as well as feedback from the environment and people in it (teachers), you make evaluations about your intellectual abilities and your intellectual self. Much of this evaluation is based upon physical experiences or performance that includes a physical or movement component. Not all movement is gross or exhibited. In fact, a good portion of movement is fine and even unobservable to others, but almost all of it somehow relates to knowing yourself and the world in which you live. Knowing involves cognitive processes that in turn suggest intelligence. It is through physical performance that your understanding of total self is enhanced.

7.4 THE EMOTIONAL SELF

Stimuli in our social and physical environments provoke feelings within us. A stranger suddenly lunging at us with a weapon makes us fearful. The tender caress or generous psychological support of a loved one produces a reaction of affection, and the absence or loss of such a person may fill us with longing, desire, or anguish. These kinds of feelings and their various tones are *emotions*. Psychologists also use terms such as *mood* and *affect* to describe such responses. There are, however, distinctions to be made among the meanings of these words. Emotions are less enduring than moods; and *affect* is a generic term, in that it includes mood and emotion.

From a purely scientific perspective, we know more about the negative emotions such as fear, anxiety, rage, and jealousy than we do about love, admiration, pleasure, and the other positive emotions. Poets and lyricists have written about love for thousands of years, but although we are able to define this emotion operationally in terms of our own understandings and purposes, we have difficulty getting a scientific grip on it. Somehow, emotions such as hate, fear, and anger have been easier for us to study. Perhaps they are considered to be more important to study because the behavior they may produce is often problematic.

Apparently, each of us has tendencies to emote in preferred ways at certain times. Therefore, some of us are said to be jealous, nervous, or angry persons. When these emotive tendencies are very pronounced or are no longer within a range considered to be "normal" by trained and experienced observers (clinical psychologists, psychiatrists, etc.), mental illness may prevail. In subsequent chapters, we will review certain of these human emotional responses, notably anxiety, and make an effort to understand ways to manage or control these kinds of reactions, particularly when they relate to performance.

Physical performance can activate emotional responses that may otherwise rarely appear. Through physical performance, an individual may make initial contact with feelings that heretofore remained unstirred. Physical performance, particularly when done in front of an audience, can be a catalyst for the dramatic development of previously dormant feelings. Indeed, for some persons, performance may be the only stimulant for certain feelings. Physical performance may be distinctive in its ability to generate emotional responses in individuals who permit them to occur in performance contexts but tend to stifle their emergence in other settings. Much has been written about the alleged cathartic ("getting it out of your system") effect of exercise relative to emotions, although it has not yet been very well supported by robust, sound, and scientific inquiry. Put simply, the teenager restless with pent-up fury and rage may find opportunities for legitimate release on the playing field, where body contact and physically aggressive behavior is sanctioned. Similarly, some researchers (Berkowitz, 1989; Berkowitz & Hamon-Jones, 2004) have argued that vicariously experienced physical performance (e.g., being a spectator at a football game) may stimulate emotionally based behavior such as screaming, stamping, or throwing objects at others or onto the field.

Physical performance itself and its outcome may stimulate the emergence of strong emotions. Relief, disappointment, or exhilaration related to quality or outcome of performance may be an emotional consequence. If the idea of performance itself has caused anxiety or is associated with stress reactions, then its termination will be a source of pleasure: "Whew, I'm glad it's over with." For many performers, waiting in the wings for an entry cue is much more of an emotional experience than the performance itself. Once the starting gun is fired or the referee's signal to begin is given, many athletes feel relief from emotional constraints.

In the theater and in dance, performers must be able to experience emotional fluctuations and communicate these variations to an audience. Method acting is a technique for training actors and actresses to do precisely this. It encourages retrieval of their own past experiences that had generated the emotion they are presently trying to project. In Chapter 10, we will discuss a technique known as eye movement desensitization restructuring (EMDR), which is designed to assist practitioners in their attempts to selectively disengage from or connect with moods and emotions that inhibit their functions. EMDR originator David Grand has applied this technique successfully with actors, athletes, and other performers.

7.5 THE SPIRITUAL SELF

Belief in a supernatural authority that regulates and influences our lives is a function of the spiritual part of self. The word *God* is commonly applied to this "higher power." Religious persons typically attribute achievements and outcomes of all kinds of experiences to this metaphysical presence. Scholars, theologians, and laypersons alike continue to debate whether God is alive, whether there is but one God or many, and where precisely God is to be found (i.e., is God's presence only located in designated shrines or houses of worship or is God omnipresent?).

The pressures and tensions associated with physical performance are often sufficient to encourage reaching out to this supreme authority. We tend to seek help when we are troubled or burdened, and one source of assistance sought by those with strong and active spiritual selves is God. We try to communicate our need for help or some form of intervention through an experience known as prayer.

Many of us are motivated to "look heavenward" when formidable obstacles to performance appear. Expressions such as "Please God, help me get through this one" or "Give me strength to finish," although not made in a formal prayer setting, may be interpreted as prayerful. Sometimes, such requests for support, strength, or courage are made in the midst of performance. Yet they need not carry a conscious salutation to God or a god. So long as intervention of some supernatural power is implied, prayer is being implemented.

Often, formalized group prayer sessions are constructed for, or by, athletes for such purposes. For years, the Pittsburgh Steelers football team of the National Football League regularly flew a Catholic priest in from Ireland to conduct pregame prayer services. Many major league baseball and professional football teams conduct regular Sunday chapel services for athletes. Such sessions are believed by coaches and management to accentuate the sense of group identity. That is, a team that prays together supposedly plays well together (a very common, but difficult to support, assertion).

It's really difficult to determine to what extent individual performers use prayer. A study conducted many years ago by Marbeto (1967) revealed that 55 percent of coaches and athletes on male baseball, basketball, football, and tennis teams from 23 California colleges and universities indicated that they prayed at least occasionally in connection with athletic contests. Interestingly, most praying was reported as occurring before the contest. Evidently, not very much prayer of the "thank you" kind was offered by athletes in Marbeto's sample. It's probably fair to conclude that individuals who believe in a spiritual power and pray with regularity generalize this practice to all aspects of their lives, including the performance domain. The Fellowship of Christian Athletes is an organization whose members share a belief in the presence and authority of God, whose guidance and benevolence is sought through prayer prior to competition. Thankfulness is also expressed after competition for God's protection and inspiration.

The term *spirituality* need not be applied only when referring to God, prayer, or formal worship. The spiritual part of self and the view we hold of ourselves as spiritual beings also encompasses our appreciation or love of natural resources, environmental beauty, and aesthetic pursuits.

7.6 SELF-CONFIDENCE AND SELF-EFFICACY

Another dimension of the self that relates very meaningfully to performance is the extent to which you believe in your performance abilities, the faith you have that your performance will succeed, and your belief that it will satisfy your expectations and goals.

The strategies used by teachers and coaches to stimulate desired performances in their pupils varies with teaching philosophy, the specific nature of the task (i.e., particular skill requirements), and perhaps characteristics of the social environment (audience) as well. However, one objective invariably pursued by all coaches and teachers is building confidence within performers and, more specifically, confidence in their capacities to fulfill the task requirements.

"You can do it" is shouted from every sideline, pool deck, and dugout. It's whispered gently into the ears of fidgety dancers and virtuoso musicians backstage. If there is but one component of performance success that coaches and teachers universally agree is critical, it is undoubtedly *self-confidence*, which is the degree to which individuals believe in their general capacity to succeed. One of the most important factors contributing to the development of this attitude is a history of personal success and failure.

In contrast, the term *self-efficacy* refers to the degree to which a person possesses confidence in his ability to achieve a specific goal. When a performer contemplates the probability of a successful outcome (victory or positive critical acclaim) as high, he or she is formulating *outcome expectancy*. High self-efficacy and outcome expectancy correlate positively with performance (Bandura, 1997; Gould & Weiss, 1981; Highlen & Bennett, 1979; Mahoney & Avener, 1977; Meyers, Cooke, Cullen, & Liles, 1979). There is, therefore, substance to the cliché "You can do it if you believe you can."

In addition, the activities you select and the environments in which you choose to conduct them are influenced by your efficacy expectations. This suggests that if you believe you are capable of handling a situation, you are inclined to engage in it with assurance.

According to Bandura (1997) — a scholar who has investigated the general area of the relationship between cognition and performance — a person's level of self-efficacy can be modified by four sources of information:

1. *Mastery experiences:* previously successful outcomes from identical or similar situations
2. *Psychological states:* perceptions about level of arousal (e.g., awareness of being frightened)
3. *Verbal persuasion:* encouragement or suggestions (from within or deriving from another) that lead performers into believing that they possess specific capabilities related to task performance
4. *Modeling:* vicarious experience that influences an individual's judgments about the likelihood of performance success (e.g., "If she can do it, so can I")

There are clear implications for improving performance through efficacy training. Teachers, directors, and coaches would do well to invest time and energy in the development of training programs that enhance self-efficacy in performers. Efforts in this direction should incorporate as many of the above four sources of input as possible.

7.7 PERFORMANCE AS AN EMOTIONAL EXPERIENCE

Emotions are *feeling tones*. Rage, grief, fear, and love are examples. It is not yet perfectly clear whether emotions are elicited directly by environmental stimuli that are individually interpreted on the basis of previous experiences (learning) or whether they are consequences of instinctive physiological (sympathetic nervous system) responses to arousing sensations. The psychologist and philosopher William James paraphrased this dilemma in 1890 when he asked, "Are we frightened because we see the charging bear, and then run, or do we see the bear, decide to run, and then experience fear because we find ourselves running?" In the first option, the behavior (running) is caused by the emotion (fear); in the second, the emotion is caused by the behavior itself. James chose to defend the second. He believed that emotions are nothing more than bodily changes (e.g., pounding heart) that in the case of the above example, are caused by running. However, Schachter and Singer (1962) reported findings from their research suggesting that environmental conditions and their interpretations modify emotional responses to bodily changes. So, for example, if your heart is beating wildly and thumping in your chest and you attribute this to the fact that you have just found a sackful of one-hundred-dollar bills while walking along the street, you do not experience the emotion of fear, but rather joy.

Physiological arousal and associated feelings are of special interest to us, particularly as these variables bear upon performance. Let us now examine selected aspects of the relationship between emotions and performance.

7.7.1 Affect

In contrast to the physical and cognitive domains already alluded to, emotions, feelings, mood are brought to mind by the term *affective*. Emotions and moods (longer-lasting than emotions) form one's affect. Sometimes you are in a "funk" — a blue mood that may last all morning. In contrast is the emotion of fear that you experience when your car skids on ice, which lasts for only a minute or two and fades as you regain control of the car. The affective domain contributes meaningfully to the variability of human behavior. Undoubtedly, affective experiences interact with performance to at least the same level of significance as do physical and cognitive factors.

Although at the moment, our concern is basically with emotions and the performer, spectators (e.g., audience members, fans) also respond emotively while, after, or even before they observe a performance. Certainly, you have cried while in the movie theater, leaped wildly to your feet in the stands during a basketball game, or reeled with side-splitting laughter at a nightclub comic's routine. Stringent regulation of emotion is usually not required of spectators, although some sanctions are imposed during certain kinds of events, such as golf and tennis matches, as well as concert performances. At a concert, constraints upon emotive audience responses are loosened when the performance concludes. Then it is appropriate to give vent to stifled feelings. Often, a tumultuous burst of applause and loud shouts of approval fill the hall as soon as the last measure of music ends. Humans are emotional beings, as both spectators and performers alike.

7.7.2 Feeling High or Low, Good or Bad

Some time ago, while pursuing a research interest in motivation for regular exercise, a fairly large number of regular exercisers were interviewed by graduate students and myself (Burgess, 1976; Pargman & Burgess, 1979; Sachs & Pargman, 1979). We questioned and tested them, tape-recorded some of their responses, and occasionally observed their participation in physical activity. We learned many things, and much to our delight, some of our research hypotheses were eventually supported. Among our observations was that the subjects seemed to fall into two groups with reference to the way they felt prior to their scheduled bout of exercise (calisthenics, running, or swimming). One group of participants viewed the regular workout as a mandatory regimen to which they were committed. Health, fitness, physical well-being, and weight control were the goals that members of this group most frequently cited. Prior to their workout, some of these participants felt anxious, irritable, and even slightly depressed. If they failed to show up for exercises or somehow managed to avoid it, they were likely to experience remorse at not having fulfilled their self-imposed contract, and they reported feelings of dishonesty and guilt. Although they were temporarily relieved of the physiological and psychological rigors and stress imposed by the workout, they were displeased with themselves. Discipline and self-control, therefore, became important parts of their psychological reaction to the idea of exercise. They exercised out of an intellectual commitment, and when they didn't exercise, they felt badly.

Subjects in the second group answered differently. Members of this group spoke of the excitement and joy associated with exercise. As the hour of the day in which they were scheduled to swim, run, or do calisthenics approached, they reported an increased excitement. Anticipation of exercise created a positive mood and exuberance. While dressing for the workout, they experienced a thrill and euphoria. We also came across runners who reported this kind of high when participating in prerunning routines; that is, rituals that are second-order, conditioned, or associated reactions, such as lacing up the running shoes or experiencing the smell of the locker room. It is likely that dancers, musicians, actors, and performers of all kinds are also divided into two such groups. Perhaps they can be located on a continuum that accommodates varying degrees of commitment, euphoria, or any of the other motives or feelings we've just mentioned (see Pargman, 1980).

Admittedly, we're concerned here with performance rather than exercise per se. But sometimes it's hard to distinguish between the two. The point, however, is that what my students and I observed while studying samples of regular exercisers is likely to be true of performers in general. For some, performance is a joy, a high, a turn-on, and a veritable fulfillment of drive or drivelike forces — almost a passion. For others, it is a nerve-wracking commitment that they feel obliged to satisfy and an experience that yields release from anguish only when it's over. Along these lines, Solomon and Corbit (1974) developed a very interesting theory that attempts to explain the emergence of positive and gratifying feelings when a difficult commitment is finalized. The theory posits that it is not necessarily the elements of risk or thrill of an activity that yields pleasure and fulfillment, but rather the awareness that the experience is concluded. This, according to Solomon and Corbit, is the source of gratification. They referred to their speculation with the term *opponent-process theory*.

7.8 BIOCHEMICAL ASPECTS

In Chapter 13, we will note that vigorous physical activity promotes change in biochemical status. Now that our concern is with affect (moods, emotions, etc.), we should note that a link between emotions and biochemistry has also been established. The liaison agent is often physical performance. Physical activity in and of itself generates increased amounts of chemical substances such as norepinephrine and dopamine. These chemicals are known as *neurotransmitters* and play vital roles in conveying messages from one nerve cell to another. In other words, they help keep you neurologically sharp. In psychologically depressed individuals (who, by the way, tend to be physically inactive), the blood levels of these chemicals are relatively low. Physical activity elevates these chemicals, which perhaps accounts for the fairly common observation that exercise "makes you feel good." At any rate, when you perform physical acts, you usually *feel* something. You emote, and what you feel may be related to fluctuations in your biochemistry.

Yet another approach to this question was taken by Marvin Zuckerman (1971) of the University of Delaware, who incorporates in his theoretical model elements of Sigmund Freud's *drive reduction* theory. According to Zuckerman, some persons have strong psychological needs for thrills and excitement. Zuckerman considered this to be a personality trait. Physical performance may help satisfy such needs. When this has been accomplished, a good feeling results.

Zuckerman (1990, 1996, 2004) maintains that the need for thrills and excitement is variable and, in part, a function of biological forces within the individual. This suggests that some persons have personality traits that are expressed as needs for high and low stimulation. Clearly, sports provides an environment in which such needs for excitement or stress may be pursued without fear of social reprisal. Indeed, many of the behaviors categorized by Zuckerman as high in risk taking, thrill seeking, and adventure seeking are commonly reinforced in competitive sports. Some sports, such as race car driving, sky diving, gymnastics, and wrestling, provide greater opportunity for physical risk taking than others, such as archery or golf. But for most of us, a need for stimulation may be addressed through almost any kind of performance — not necessarily sports.

Zuckerman, Bone, Neary, Mangelsdorff, and Brustman (1972) described an optimal range of excitement that best suits a particular individual — not unlike that inherent in the inverted-U hypothesis discussed in Chapter 1 (and which we will once again address in Chapter 8). A person, therefore, learns how to maintain optimal arousal as well as to appreciate the types of activities needed. In this fashion, an individual avoids both boredom and overstimulation. Simply put, the need for stimulation influences our behavior (Eysenck, 1998; Pearson, 1970; Petrie, 1967; Ryan, 1969).

The notions, explanations, and models presented by Eysenck, by Pearson, by Petrie, and by E. Ryan (all op. cit.) also describe various aspects of the need for stimulation as a basis for behavior. An athlete's overt behavior may thus be determined by the strength and configuration of his arousal needs.

7.9 SELF-APPRAISAL

We can also feel disappointment, shame, and embarrassment when we are displeased with the quality of our performance. Displeasure of this kind may be a consequence of introspection, self-evaluation, self-analysis, or comparison with other performances of our own or of others. All are cognitive processes that in turn may foster changes in biochemistry and ultimately shifts in arousal. As you recall, if arousal level is moved out of its optimal range for performance of a particular skill, efficiency and accuracy may diminish. On the other hand, an excellent performance engenders positive feelings. Therefore, the perceptions we hold about the quality of our performance influence how and what we feel.

7.10 SUMMARY

Performance vis-à-vis the concepts of self involves physical, intellectual, emotional, spiritual, and social perceptions of oneself. Self-efficacy — a feeling of confidence in one's abilities — is key to successful self-concept as it relates to performance. However, performers also have to contend with emotions and moods (e.g., feeling high or low, good or bad) as significant variables or barriers to self-efficacy.

8

STRESS AS AN INHIBITOR OR
ENHANCER OF PERFORMANCE

LEARNING OBJECTIVES

After reading this chapter, you should be able to:

- Define individual zone of optimal functioning (IZOF) and describe Hanin's method for obtaining it
- Briefly describe various cognitive techniques for managing anxiety, including reframing; eye movement desensitization restructuring, or EMDR; thought stopping; rational approaches; participant modeling; stress inoculation therapy; and imagery
- Identify three areas that are influenced by arousal that may subsequently affect performance
- Define attention and discuss how arousal may modify attentional focus
- Elaborate upon Nideffer's three dimensions of attention
- Recognize that muscular tension and fatigue may impair performance

IMPORTANT TERMS

- IZOF
- Attentional focus

- Muscular tension
- Fatigue

8.1 INTRODUCTION

It was suggested in Chapter 1 that not all stress reactions are associated with negative outcomes. Stress may indeed evoke undesirable consequences, but not on a consistent basis. To make this point, the terms *eustress* and *distress* were introduced. Sexual orgasm, for example, would be an example of eustress, wherein the individual is highly activated, but satisfied. In this condition, homeostasis would assuredly be upset, at least temporarily, and the stress response would prevail.

The point here is that stress-related arousal may actually exert desirable or positive influence on performance. Therefore, we once again bring to mind the notion of an ideal physiological activation range for optimal skill execution. This person-specific range varies according to a host of critical variables. Among these are characteristics of the skill itself (complexity, fine- or gross-motor requirements, etc.), as discussed in Chapter 5; level of competence of the performer (beginner, expert, etc.); and psychological attributes of the performer that bear upon arousal responses (high or low state–trait anxiety, sensation-seeking needs, cognitive style, and information-processing tendencies).

Two performers facing identical tasks are likely to react with different arousal responses. This is especially so if the underlying environmental stimuli require a good deal of interpretation. One may become physiologically activated to a degree that the performance is successful. On the other hand, one's activation level may be above or below that which is optimal, and skill execution may therefore suffer. Each of us has a desirable arousal range for each activity or task. It is desirable in that our performance will be enhanced if we can locate ourselves in this targeted bandwidth. The challenge here is twofold: (1) identifying this optimal location, that is, knowing the target range, and (2) being able to modulate arousal level so that the optimal range of activation is actually attained.

8.2 IDENTIFYING THE OPTIMAL RANGE OF PHYSIOLOGICAL ACTIVATION

One strategy for identifying the preferred or optimal arousal range for a particular task is advocated by Yuri Hanin (2003) and is currently receiving acceptance by many working in the field of performance enhancement. Hanin uses the term *individual zone of optimal functioning* (IZOF) to refer to the desirable range of arousal (in this case, due to anxiety) within which we strive to locate ourselves. While working with various kinds of athletes, Hanin observed that they were able to recall with impressive accuracy the anxiety levels they experienced during various past performances, some of which were good and others poor. Since anxiety (or for that matter, any emotion) is typically accompanied by physiological arousal, a performer who reports a low level of anxiety preceding an exceptional performance may also be describing a low level of arousal (however, it is possible that other emotions may be high, and as a result arousal may be elevated). Hanin therefore recommends that this performer be asked to bring to mind the anxiety/arousal level associated with a past performance similar to the present performance. This recall can be facilitated by use of a paper-and-pencil instrument such as the State–Trait Anxiety Inventory (STAI).

Hanin originally recommended adding and subtracting four points or one-half of a standard deviation from the mean of a number of past anxiety scores, in order to identify the bandwidth zone associated with optimal performance. Thus, each performer strives to locate a personal, preferred range of anxiety/arousal level. Accordingly, the IZOF will vary from performer to performer, and from task to task for each performer. Hanin's IZOF is an expansion of the inverted-U hypothesis; however, it places a premium upon individuality. Some performers do well in arousal bands that are high, and others succeed at moderate or low levels. As we conclude our discussion of Hanin's work, let us be sure to emphasize that although our major interests revolve around stress and anxiety, the IZOF really incorporates all emotions of which athletes and other performers are very much aware. This being the case, instruments other than the STAI may also be employed.

8.2.1 Modulating Arousal Levels

Let's assume that Hanin's IZOF has been utilized to identify the arousal bandwidth appropriate for optimal performance. You now know where you should be in terms of physiological activation, and must figure out how to get there. How may we fine-tune our emotions, particularly anxiety, so that they are at appropriate levels of intensity? Chapters 10 to 13 provide the answers to this question. When we get to these chapters, we will examine a variety of strategies for managing stress and anxiety responses. For the sake of convenience, we will divide these techniques into four categories: *cognitive techniques, muscular relaxation techniques, chemical interventions,* and *exercise.*

8.3 HOW SKILL EXECUTION IS INFLUENCED
BY PHYSIOLOGICAL ACTIVATION

We now turn to the issue of how inappropriate levels of arousal influence the performance of skill. We already understand that over- or underarousal detracts from optimal performance. Why? What are the mechanisms that account for this? Three such factors come to mind: *attentional focus, muscular tension,* and *fatigue.*

8.3.1 Attentional Focus

Attention is a word that pervades our daily discourse, but it is defined and used by scientists in different ways. For our purpose, let's understand attention this way: *It is concentration upon stimuli that are relevant.* By relevancy, I mean that the stimuli have direct bearing upon the particular problem, issue, task, or challenge at hand. At any given moment, we are likely to concentrate on a multitude of environmental cues; however, many of these cues are not germane to our momentary mission. If we are preparing to putt a six-footer on the golf course, then it is not in the best interest of our performance to glance at or think about the unusual hat worn by a spectator. When attempting to shoot from the free-throw line in a basketball game, our concentration must not be directed toward the cheering or pompom-waving fans. When we visually or auditorily gravitate to the signals from both internal (within the body) and external environments that are helpful in task fulfillment, we are *paying attention.* Many tasks confronting dancers, musicians, and athletes require that they maintain the capacity to focus exclusively on stimuli coming from different sources at the same time. This presents a challenge to our information-processing capabilities.

In order for information processing to proceed efficiently, a sharp attentional focus is necessary. In its absence, some of the information moving from the sensory register onward to short- and long-term memory is lost. Think of an insulated cable designed to transmit electricity. If the plastic or rubber covering is torn, despite the fact that the copper wire within is intact, some of the electricity is lost. By way of analogy, failure to attend to appropriate stimuli results in a loss of processing efficiency. In turn, inefficient processing is likely to cause performance decrement, since most physical performance skills have important cognitive components. The bottom line is that arousal is a modifier of attentional processes.

The model by Easterbrook (1959) holds that an increase in arousal (due to emotion) will cause a narrowing of attention. Thus, heightened activation beyond a certain level will restrict integration of task-relevant cues and result in performance decrement. Certain kinds of performances will be impeded when attentional width is narrowed. More recently, other researchers were able to support Easterbrook's assertions when studying rifle shooters (Hatfield, Landers, & Ray, 1984), archers (Salazar, Landers, Petruzello, Crews, & Kubitz, 1990), and golfers (putting) (Boutcher & Zinsser, 1990). The lesson here is that physiological activation associated with stress and anxiety disrupts appropriate attentional focus. When irrelevant and unimportant cues (distracters) become the targets of concentration, appropriate focus is partially or even entirely redirected, and desirable performance is inhibited.

8.3.1.1 Test of Attentional and Interpersonal Style   Perhaps the best-known work in the study of attentional processes relative to performance is that of Robert Nideffer, who in 1974 constructed the Test of Attentional and Interpersonal Style (TAIS). His instrument has been frequently applied to sports. The gist of the many published papers resulting from these applications is that certain sports tasks require performers to focus on many stimuli coming from different sources simultaneously (Nideffer & Sagal, 2001(a), Nideffer & Sagal, 2001(b)). Likewise, musicians must be attentive to a multiplicity of stimuli if they are to succeed as members of an ensemble. Just as the athlete is obliged to be aware of the movements of his teammates and his opponents, so must the musician be alert to cues provided by the conductor or fellow musicians. Performers who are so deeply immersed in the execution of their individual skill to the extent that they are oblivious to a wide range of contextual stimuli will not perform or compete well. This is particularly true of team-sport athletes (in soccer, volleyball, lacrosse, basketball, and football) and musicians accompanying other musicians.

8.3.1.2 Measures of Attention   Changes in physiological parameters may reflect the nature of attentional function. Among the variables that may be monitored to ascertain attention are eye movements, heart rate variability, and electroencephalography (EEG, or brain-wave patterns).

Nideffer (1976) maintains that when we attend, we do so in terms of three dimensions: (1) the width of attention, (2) the direction of attentional focus, and (3) the flexibility to alter attentional width and direction. The width dimension speaks to the number of cues or stimuli that one can accommodate at any one time. Performers with very wide attentional capacities are able to apprehend relatively large numbers of stimuli; those with narrow capacities experience the opposite. Attentional directionality refers to the source of cues to which attention is directed; specifically, whether attention is focused on internal or external locations. An internal stimulus would be a shoulder pain, acute thirst, or a thought about failing, floundering, or falling. In contrast, a stimulus emanating from an external source would be a nod given by the concertmaster in an effort to "tune" the orchestra prior to performance. The referee's whistle or a line given to an actor that prompts him to speak or move are other examples of an external cue.

Nideffer further suggests that all of us have *attentional styles* that dictate how we respond to environmental cues. Our attentional styles refer to our tendencies to focus in certain widths and in certain directions. Most of us are not located at extreme points on the internal/external and broad/narrow continua. As is the case with other psychological attributes, most performers are situated toward the center, however some of us tend to be high in the width dimension, while others tend to be low. Some of us typically and eagerly respond to internal stimuli, whereas others seem to prefer external stimuli. *Attentional flexibility* refers to the way in which we shift along the broad/narrow and internal/external continua.

Since different circumstances require different attentional demands, it may be necessary to shift during performance from broad to narrow or from internal to external. Consider the attentional demands imposed upon the basketball player who must be aware of and react to a multitude of environmental cues. Some cues come from teammates, others from opponents. At one moment, the athlete is on defense—in the next, on offense. She must be alert to gross and subtle body movements of other athletes; she must monitor the ball as it is passed from one athlete to another. In addition, she must anticipate what others might do. Her focus must therefore be broad and external. But when she's fouled, the whistle blows and she's awarded two free throws. As she moves to the free-throw line, her attention must shift to a narrow focus. Now, nothing but the rim and her preshot routine, and perhaps some proprioceptive (internal) cues, are relevant stimuli. She should not attend to what fans are screaming, to the placards they wave, or to the body movements of athletes boxing out in anticipation of rebounding and putting back a missed free throw. The efficiency with which she makes the transition from broad-external to narrow-internal is a reflection of her *attentional flexibility*. By regulating physiological activation, attentional processes essential to performance can be mediated.

8.3.2 Muscular Tension

Skill execution is also related to arousal through another pathway, namely *muscular tension*, or the degree to which muscle fibers are "tight," or taut. Skeletal muscle is always in tonus (state of contraction), but during the physiologically aroused state, the tonus is increased. Anxiety, because it is invariably accompanied by physiological activation, is associated with increased muscular tension. Some muscles are affected in this manner more so than others. Muscles that are excessively taut may not function optimally. The softball pitcher's delivery, the golfer's swing, the billiard player's shot, and the singer's musical pitch may thus be adversely affected by muscular tension. Chapter 12 deals with relaxation techniques designed to reduce muscular tension. The *progressive muscular relaxation* technique developed by Edmund Jacobson, hypnosis, yoga, massage therapy, and biofeedback education are the strategies with which you will become familiar.

8.3.3 Fatigue

Skeletal muscles that sustain high levels of tonus for extended periods of time are vulnerable to fatigue. In other words because they are in a prolonged state of contraction, they tire. Fatigue is a physiological state wherein waste material from each muscle fiber or cell is produced to the extent that it is not dissipated or removed rapidly enough. The by-products of muscle cell metabolism collect in and around the fibers and interfere with their normal functions of contraction and relaxation. As a consequence, availability of fuel necessary for muscular contraction is reduced. Proprioceptor organs (sensors) detect these changes and signal the brain, which processes them. Accordingly, we become conscious of being in a fatigued state. Performance is inhibited. Symptoms of muscular fatigue are limb heaviness, discomfort, and inability to continue with motor performance.

8.4 SUMMARY

Stress can potentially have a positive or a negative impact upon performance. A performer must be within a range of optimal physiological arousal in order to achieve best performance. Stress and anxiety responses, because they are invariably accompanied by activation (arousal), may move an individual in or out of this range. If the response causes movement into this desired range, then we may conclude that the consequence of the stress is positive. If and when the opposite occurs and the preferred range is abandoned because of stress- and anxiety-induced arousal, the undesirable or negative result of stress occurs.

Yuri Hanin conceptualized this dynamic in terms of one's individual zone of optimal function (IZOF). Different IZOFs are indicated for different tasks and different individuals. It is important to modify physiological arousal in order to enter and remain in the IZOF. A few strategies for accomplishing this objective were identified and will be treated more adequately in subsequent chapters.

Three factors were identified in our discussion of how the execution of skill is specifically influenced by physiological arousal: attentional focus, muscular tension, and muscular fatigue. Robert Nideffer's notion of attentional style emphasizes individual attentional tendencies.

Lastly in this chapter, a connection between muscular tension and muscular fatigue and performance was established. Inappropriate tension levels that are sustained typically result in muscular tension and the accumulation of waste products that inhibit performance.

The material presented in this chapter implies that both positive and negative performance outcomes may be associated with stress and anxiety responses.

9

THE ASSESSMENT OF STRESS REACTIONS

LEARNING OBJECTIVES

After reading this chapter, you should be able to:

- Discuss the psychoanalytic approaches to stress and anxiety measurement, including the interview, sleep patterns, dreams, verbal indicators, and hypnosis
- List advantages to utilizing self-rating scales for the measurement of stress and anxiety
- Offer criticism for the use of life-event instruments in assessing stress and anxiety
- Provide two examples of projective instruments used in assessing stress and anxiety
- Elaborate upon characteristics of the Type A personality
- Discuss the importance of assessing social interactions and physiological parameters in understanding stress and anxiety

IMPORTANT TERMS

- Psychoanalytic approach
- Verbal indicators
- Life events
- POMS

- SCAT
- TAT
- Type A behavior

9.1 INTRODUCTION

In Chapter 1, stress and anxiety were examined in a definitional way. Our objective was to understand what stress really is. An operational vocabulary was therefore developed, and distinctions were drawn among stress, fear, and anxiety. Additionally, the concept of activation (or arousal) was discussed. In Chapter 2, the consequences of stress in terms of physiological responses were reviewed.

We discussed four theoretical approaches to understanding the causes of stress in Chapter 3: the psychoanalytic approach, the learning approach, the sociological approach, and the personological approach. By now, you should also understand basic neurological and social-psychological factors that underlie the acquisition of motor skill. You should appreciate that physical performance is dependent upon more than bone and muscle. It involves reasoning, problem solving, and emotional dimensions. Chapters 4 and 5 covered this territory. In Chapter 8, we noted that some kinds of stress might even be beneficial.

Now we proceed to address the question of *measuring the magnitude of stress reactions.* In order to understand how stress interacts with performance, and to ultimately identify ways in which stress and anxiety may be managed, it is important to be able to assess the degree to which they are present in our lives. Therefore, we turn now to an examination of assessment approaches in the *psychiatric, psychological, social,* and *physiological* domains. Each of these areas roughly associates with one of the theoretical perspectives explaining the origins of stress discussed previously. The so-called *learning approach* presents a bit of a problem in that it does not readily affiliate with any particular measurement strategy, or at least it does not do so exclusively. As noted previously, learning is an abstract concept that requires performance in order for its occurrence to be demonstrated (at least according to behaviorists, but not necessarily theorists in other camps). Therefore, observation by others as well as self-reporting techniques are probably the two paramount modes for making stress assessments within a learning framework.

A few qualifying observations are in order before the overview of assessment techniques and instruments is begun. First, many indications of anxiety and stress responses are revealed by a client's attitudes and physical gestures. The observant, experienced, and patient teacher, coach, or co-performer can learn much about the performer's stress and anxiety level by noting nonverbal responses such as posture, depth and rate of breathing, activity of the hands and fingers, skin color, and other aspects of general appearance.

Second, batteries of procedures including techniques for evaluating physiological activity should be used in conjunction with paper-and-pencil instruments. Information derived from these methods would undoubtedly be modified or interpreted in view of the test administrator's intuition and professional orientation. Experienced teachers and coaches who know their performers well can detect deviations from "normal" behavior that are indicative of stress/anxiety reactions.

In addition, the number of published, standardized psychometric instruments for assessing stress and particularly anxiety is formidable. To do justice to all or even most of these would require a small volume entirely dedicated to this end. For this reason, the following overview represents merely a sampling of the many available assessment approaches.

9.2 PSYCHOANALYTIC APPROACHES

A note of caution is appropriate as we begin this section. Let me emphatically establish that probing lower levels of consciousness in order to locate probable causes of stress and anxiety (Freud did not use the term *stress* — only anxiety) requires high levels of training and competence. It is unlikely that the typical reader of this book is adequately prepared to do so. It is important, nonetheless, if you are to assist performers with stress/anxiety issues that you be conversant with the notions and procedures we are about to discuss. Your familiarity should permit you to recommend to performers that they avail themselves of the services of properly trained professionals.

9.2.1 Interview

The psychoanalytic approach to determining the nature and potency of stress reactivity entails exploration of the *conscious* as well as *subconscious* levels of awareness. This typically involves rather detailed and often lengthy interviews. During sessions that traditionally take about 50 minutes each, the analyst probes the client's past experiences in order to determine their bearing upon current stress responses. Conceivably, some of these former experiences are associated with time frames as remote and as early as infancy, and with relationships and happenings that have long been forgotten. Questions are strategically couched within a theoretical framework and evolve from the analyst's speculations about the causes of client stress. Much training and experience are required for the analyst to integrate information provided by the client into a rational explanation for the contemporary stress response. It is often the case that this information is not factual or is not expressed quite objectively. For example, a client may report that she is experiencing no stress at all, when very strong behavioral manifestations of stress are apparent. This may indicate an attempt to deny or camouflage evidence, or may suggest that the client is unable to comprehend the nature of her own reactions. The analyst is obliged to test the validity and reliability of client responses before definitive conclusions and assessments can be reached.

9.2.2 Sleep Patterns and Reported Dreams

In addition to the interview, wherein the client reveals or discusses conscious experiences and insights, other sources of information may be helpful in making assessments about stress reactions. Reported dreams may be revealing, as is client-generated information about the quality and length of sleep. We may cope with our anxieties and stressors more dramatically when awake, but we are still engaged with them during sleep. The depth of sleep and its quality (restfulness) are often related to stress levels, as are the frequency of nightmares and the degree to which certain dreams recur. The analyst must be prepared to probe for this information and place it in an appropriate analytical context. Reported fantasies and aspirations may also indicate high levels of stress.

9.2.3 Verbal Indicators

Donald P. Spence (1982) discusses *verbal leakage*. Spence speculates that length of speech, repetition of words and ideas, tongue slips, hesitations, sentence incompletions, and stuttering may all be forms of catharsis for stress. Apparently, excessive or compulsive talking may be an attempt to discharge underlying anxiety. Frequent use of "ahs" or "ums" may also indicate anxiety. Choice of words may also represent stress leakage. Patterns of speech often reveal important aspects of the speaker's world. Once again, for meaningful interpretation, these clues must fall upon the ears of trained listeners.

9.2.4 Hypnosis

Hypnosis is a much misunderstood procedure. A good deal of what many of us know about hypnosis probably derives from the world of show business. Hypnotic trances are demonstrated dramatically by entertainers who very carefully select subjects highly susceptible to suggestion, because for the most part, suggestion is what hypnosis is all about. Not very much material is available that discusses hypnosis from theoretical perspectives. One very good source is provided by Erickson and Rossi (1979). In this reference, an attempt is made to conceptualize hypnosis in theoretical terms.

In Chapter 11, we will discuss hypnosis as a tool for managing stress. At this point, our aim is to understand the applicability of hypnosis as a helpful procedure in assessing stress. In keeping with this objective, perhaps the most beneficial use of hypnosis is in breaking down unconscious barriers that may prevent a client from revealing the identity of his real stressors. Often, stressors remain consciously unknown to a person. For example, a performer may be aware that in a certain kind of situation his performance is always below par, but he remains puzzled about the reason for this, and conscious exploration of all possibly related factors produces no enlightenment. A skillful hypnotherapist may help the client reveal the nature and strength of psychologically submerged stressors. The hypnotherapist may *suggest* directly or indirectly that the client is able to produce information that will resolve the dilemma, and under the trance condition (see Chapter 12) this may actually occur. Hypnosis can also be helpful in clarifying reasons for physiologically preferred modes of reacting to stressors. For example, some of us are perspirers, others experience upset stomachs, while still others suffer headaches in response to stress, and hypnosis may clarify the reasons behind these manifestations.

9.3 PSYCHOMETRIC APPROACHES

Reactions to environmental stressors are not only personal, but also multidimensional. Many symptoms are produced in response to stress stimuli. A single assessment procedure is therefore usually inadequate to fathom the magnitude and quality of stress. For this reason, a number of procedures are typically used by psychologists. Today, there are probably more than 200 tests available for the assessment of anxiety and/or stress. The selection of any of these should not be arbitrary. The choice should relate to a theoretical framework that the test administrator suspects will clarify the kind of stressors believed to be operational. Let us now turn to a few of these commonly used assessment approaches.

9.3.1 Self-Rating Scales

Self-rating scales are filled out by the clients themselves. Underlying this approach is the assumption that clients' perceptions about their own feelings are correct. As Zung and Cavenar (1980) point out, self-rating scales have the following advantages:

1. They provide information that only the subject can provide.
2. They do not involve the use of trained personnel to administer.
3. They take a short time for the patient to complete.
4. They are easy to score.
5. They provide objective data.
6. They can be used as a separate measurement to document change over time.
7. They can be used in any clinical setting, including through the mail.
8. They are inexpensive.

9.3.2 Assessment of Anxiety

Spielberger, Gorsuch, and Lushene (1970), whose ideas about state versus trait anxiety were discussed in Chapter 6, provided paper-and-pencil instruments for assessing both constructs (the STAI, or State–Trait Anxiety Inventory). Janet Taylor (1953) created the Manifest Anxiety Scale (MAS), which is also a popularly used paper-and-pencil assessment tool.

9.3.3 Life Events

Many of the stress rating scales focus upon crucial *life events,* or significant changes in a person's life. Subjects are asked to check off items from lists of experiences that have occurred to them within specified ranges of time (i.e., six months, one year, or two years). Job loss, marriage, divorce, death, serious illness, and automobile accident are examples of life events. One criticism of such scales is that they emphasize only the consequence of problematic experiences. For instance, subjects may check off "divorce" but have no opportunity to record the length and intensely stressful interpersonal conflicts with a spouse that may have preceded the divorce. Moreover, a person checking off "divorce" need not necessarily have stress as a reference, but to the contrary, a sense of relief.

Similarly, other life events presented are neither categorically negative or positive for all individuals and should not therefore be always assumed to be stress inducing. The birth of a child for many adults may be a positive and rewarding event. On the other hand, it is certainly conceivable that for some persons, such a happening may be entirely undesirable. Pregnancy may not only be unanticipated but unwanted. In any event, some type of adaptation to a life event is usually necessary. Moreover, the adaptation itself may be stress inducing.

Scores on self-reporting, life-event instruments have been linked to illness of various psychiatric and physical kinds. Conditions such as schizophrenia (Jacobs & Meyers, 1976), leukemia (Greene & Miller,

1958), and stroke (Adler, MacRitchie, & Engel, 1971) have been shown to correlate with high scores (a high score indicating many events that are supposedly stressful).

Among fairly well known stress rating scales used for clinical as well as for research purposes are those developed by Holmes and Rahe (1967) and Dowhrend, Krasnoff, and Askenasy (1978). Zung (1971) has constructed the Self-Rating Anxiety scale (SAS), which he describes as being appropriate for psychometric use by clinicians needing a reminder or checklist while interviewing clients. Zuckerman (1960) has produced an instrument for assessing anxiety that employs lists of adjectives that are checked off if they describe the present feelings of subjects.

9.3.4 Affect and Mood Scales

Anxiety and stress reactions influence mood. When the perception of environmental stimuli shifts from stressor to nonstressor, or when coping mechanisms deal effectively with noxious stimulation, mood is expected to change. Therefore, mood assessment is valuable in making determinations about the management of stress reactions.

The Profile of Mood States (POMS) is an adjective checklist that reflects measurement in a number of mood states including tension-anxiety. The subject checks off any of 65 items (adjectives) that represent his/her current mood. The instrument is easy to administer, score, and interpret.

There are also questionnaires that help the psychologist assess the degree to which a client experiences stress when confronted with social interaction of some kind (Wolpe, 1973).

9.3.5 Projective Instruments

Tests that enable subjects to report their perceptions, thoughts, attitudes, or feelings indirectly are known as *projective instruments*. The Thematic Apperception Test (TAT) (Murray, 1943) is an example of a projective test. (The TAT is also used to make assessments about client needs and interests other than those related to stress and anxiety.) Subjects are shown a series of illustrations that they are asked to interpret. The examiner carries the responsibility of analyzing each response in terms of what it suggests about the subject's interaction with stress. This requires considerable skill and experience. Sentence completion tests are also examples of projective instruments. Subjects supposedly reveal much about their anxieties by the way in which they provide endings for incomplete sentences. Again, evaluating or interpreting these responses requires insight derived through professional training.

9.3.6 Sport Competition Anxiety Test

Rainer Martens (1977) has devised the Sport Competition Anxiety Test (SCAT) to assess anxiety in sports situations. The test comprises 15 questions that deal specifically with competitive sports performance. It is a useful tool for coaches and researchers interested in studying anxiety in athletes. Both child and adult forms of the SCAT are available.

9.3.7 Type A Behavior

Cardiologists Meyer Friedman and Ray Rosenman (1970) observed that persons with certain *behavioral* inclinations tend to succumb to premature heart disease. This tendency toward cardiovascular illness, they concluded, has little to do with genetic or dietary (e.g., high fat content) factors, but with behavioral style. They label this profile the *Type A personality.* These individuals demonstrate the following attributes:

1. An intense sense of time urgency; a tendency to race against the clock; the need to do more and obtain more in the shortest possible time
2. An aggressive personality that at times evolves into hostility (this person is highly motivated, yet may lose his/her temper very easily); a high sense of competitiveness, often with the desire to make a contest out of everything; the inability to play for fun
3. An intense achievement motive, yet too often this "go for it" attitude lacks properly defined goals
4. Polyphasic behavior, that is, the involvement in multiple and diverse tasks at the same time

Apparently, these characteristics contribute to a generalized stress response and thereby predispose the cardiovascular system to considerable overload and consequent deterioration. The heart and blood vessels are obliged to cope for long periods of time with a litany of stress reactions, including elevated levels of physiological activation because of behavioral style.

Ironically, Type A persons consider their behavioral tendencies to be admirable. They may feel this way because their style enables them to accomplish a good deal. Their competitive, aggressive, time-oriented manner produces achievement and "success," both of which are highly valued in our society. They therefore receive substantial social and vocational reinforcement that encourages their way of functioning.

Friedman and Rosenman (1970) suggest that Type A behavior is learned. If this is indeed the case, then it can also be *unlearned.* This means that one is not permanently locked in to Type A behavior.

9.3.8 Attentional Style

Attention refers to the ways in which individuals respond to environmental cues.

Robert Nideffer (1976) whose work we discussed in Chapter 8, has suggested that there are several aspects of attention that are important correlates of performance. Accordingly, the width and direction of attention are attributes that critically influence performing behavior. Since different tasks impose differential attentional demands, performers with particular attentional strengths or vulnerabilities are inclined toward relative success or failure. Further, according to Nideffer, the ability to shift from one kind of attentional focus to another is associated with arousal. If changing attentional mode is problematic for the performer, then performance control may be lost and a stress reaction may be the consequence.

Some performance tasks involve very narrow attentional demands, such as in the case of sighting the target in archery. In this example, the amount of information to be processed (the number of cues) is relatively small. An unnecessarily wide attentional focus would permit the accommodation of many extraneous stimuli and probably result in an undesirable performance; that is, the arrow would be considerably off the mark.

On the other hand, some performances are actually benefited by broad attentional focus. Many relevant environmental cues must be amalgamated and processed in order for certain performance tasks to be executed desirably. If the football quarterback is too narrowly focused, he is likely to ignore open receivers, blitzing defenders out for his hide, or blockers behind whom he can safely run. Some kinds of performances require rapid shifting from narrow to wide and/or from wide to narrow attentional focus. Baseball is a good example. The attentional demands for a player are not the same in batting as in playing the field. A broad attentional focus is also likely to benefit orchestra conductors who must be aware of sounds emanating from different musicians and directions.

Nideffer also refers to the performer's internal or external *attentional direction*. For example, is the performer concentrating on personal feelings or thoughts (internal direction) or is his attentional focus directed to the surrounding environment (external direction)?

Nideffer (1976) believes that attentional style is modifiable by training. First, an assessment procedure is appropriate to determine the tendency of the performer toward external/internal and narrow/broad attentional focus. To this end, he offers his Test of Attentional and Interpersonal Style (TAIS). It comprises 144 items (as a self-report, paper-and-pencil inventory) that are typically completed in approximately 25 minutes. Scores on the test supposedly provide insight into a performer's ability to "control mental and physical processes, especially under pressure" (Nideffer, 1981, p.225). What Nideffer refers to as pressure is undoubtedly the very same experience we have been referring to with the word *stress*.

9.4 SOCIAL INTERACTIONS

The importance of social relations as a source of stress was emphasized in Chapter 3, where we considered various theoretical perspectives on stress causality, and Chapter 6, where we discussed the impact of others on performance. We noted that orientations emphasizing sociological factors coexist with psychoanalytic, learning, and personological considerations as important breeding grounds for stressors.

Insofar as interpersonal relations can and do produce social disharmonies, the observation of such interactions and the expressed feelings associated with them yield information about the magnitude and scope of the stress experience. Therefore, as we consider various ways of assessing stress reactions, we are obliged to acknowledge problematic or dysfunctional social interaction as a source of information. Tendencies toward argumentativeness, inability to establish or sustain relationships or friendships, and perhaps shyness and withdrawal from social interactions may all be part of the stress response. These inclinations may be tested for with certain paper-and-pencil inventories (Willoughby, 1973); through direct observation of an individual; or through oral self-reporting, whereby the recent social history of a client/subject is revealed.

When coping with stressful situations, some individuals resort to patterns of behavior that temporarily make them unattractive social interacters. They are not fun to be with, may become wrapped up in their own problems, and abandon their typical concern for others. Final-exam week is stressful for many college students, and parents learn to understand the irritable behavior of their children during this period. On the other hand, parents may be understandably more easily annoyed and more sensitive to loud music, laughter, or noise in the house while working on their income tax forms.

9.5 PHYSIOLOGICAL MEASUREMENT

Another approach by which the magnitude of stress reactions may be assessed utilizes physiological measurement. In Chapter 2, we reviewed a number of organic responses to stressors. These typically involve numerous shifts in internal biochemical balances that result in readily observable changes in the way you feel. They may also result in illness (Zegans, 1982). For example, heart and respiratory rates tend to increase in many persons coping with significant stressors; so may blood pressure and body temperature. The cellular chemistry is often altered, and complex chains of hormonal and enzymatic reactions are consequently precipitated. Stress is physiologically unsettling, and by comparing how subjects experience certain variables in situations that are assumed to be stress free with the same variables during bouts of stress, the extent of the stress reaction may be better understood.

Many of the physical effects of stress are gross and detectable by its victim. However, very precise degrees of change in physiology may not be easily discerned. Special equipment or procedures are therefore often necessary to measure subtle changes in such parameters as respiration, blood pressure, perspiration, muscle tension, and blood chemistry. Other reactions such as general fatigue, cold extremities, constipation, frequent urination urgency, diarrhea, nausea, salivary secretion, mouth dryness, sleep deprivation, and abuse of alcohol and chemical agents are more readily noticeable and may be assessed informally by most alert individuals.

A *sphygmomanometer* measures blood pressure. Palmer perspiration associated with stress may be measured by electrodermal (EDR) or *galvanic skin response* (GSR) apparatus containing a Whetstone bridge, which measures electrical conductance. Muscle tension may be measured with *electromyographical* (EMG) equipment, and various blood analyses are conducted with eletrophotometers and spectrophotometric devices.

9.6 SUMMARY

In order to control stress and anxiety responses, the degree to which they are manifest must be determined. Certain levels of stress-related arousal may even benefit performance.

Various approaches measure categories of stress and anxiety causal factors. The psychoanalytic approach considers conscious and subconscious revelations derived from personal interviews, interpretation of dreams, history of sleep patterns, and hypnotic trance.

Psychometric techniques include projective instruments such as the Thematic Apperception Test. Life-event scales and tests specifically designed to measure anxiety include Martens' SCAT, Taylor's MAS, and Spielberger's STAI.

Another approach to measuring stress and arousal examines dysfunctional social interactions as revealed through self-reporting instruments. Problematic personal relationships may reveal the nature and magnitude of psychological and physiological stress. Lastly, this chapter briefly reviewed various procedures for measuring physiological responses to stress. More detailed accounts of these kinds of reactions are included elsewhere in this book.

10

COGNITION AND COGNITIVE STYLE

LEARNING OBJECTIVES

After reading this chapter, you should be able to:

- Understand what is meant by the term *cognitive style*
- Describe ways in which cognitive styles interact with performance
- Differentiate among field dependence, field independence, association, dissociation, and attentional flexibility

IMPORTANT TERMS

- Cognitive style
- Field dependence/independence
- Association/dissociation
- Attentional width
- Internal/external attentional focus
- Attentional flexibility

10.1 INTRODUCTION

Cognition is a process that includes such mental experiences as making comparisons, judgments, and decisions, and in general, thinking. To be sure, all performers are obliged to "think" and "remember." In fact, one way to look at performance itself is as a problem in need of a solution. We bring to this problem-solving process personal dispositions and ways of doing things and thereby possess and display individual cognitive styles. Our responses to environmental stressors rely heavily upon interpretive and experiential factors and are individual and idiosyncratic. We think "our way." Individuals differ in how they prefer to approach problems.

With this in mind, it is obvious that for some of us, certain cognitive coping strategies are more suitable than they are for others. Some of us do well with particular strategies and others do not. This may be accounted for by individual *coping styles*. In Chapter 4, I discussed information processing, and it would be a good idea to review this content before reading further. First, a brief word about cognitive style. In the next chapter (11), specific cognitive techniques for managing performance-related stress will be reviewed. In this chapter, we establish a foundation for the review by focusing upon the process of cognition itself.

10.2 COGNITIVE STYLE

The word *style* refers to a patterned way of doing something, and here explicit reference is made to thinking and problem-solving tendencies, although emotional and physiological factors are also style components. Some persons process information quickly, think well on their feet, and produce decisions in the blink of an eye. Others are relatively more contemplative. They integrate incoming stimuli with great patience and deliberation and proceed slowly and reflectively through the process of *perception* (attachment of meaning to environmental stimuli). Some of us are deep processors; others find meaning in environmental stimuli after only brief and comparatively shallow processing. Experienced elementary school teachers often encounter children whose hands shoot into the air before a particular question is even finished. Such children are quick responders, whereas others in the classroom require lengthy time periods before being able to react. This variation in processing tendencies accounts in part for heterogeneity in learning efficiency and makes teaching a formidable challenge.

Let us now consider some of the stylistic ways in which performers may approach performance-related cognitive tasks. Implicit in this treatment is the notion that selection of an appropriate strategy for managing performance-related stress and anxiety should be related to the cognitive style of the performer.

10.3 FIELD DEPENDENCE/FIELD INDEPENDENCE

For some of us, decision making is contingent upon information from the environment, or so-called field. That is, before selecting clothing to wear for a party, information is required about what the other attendees might wear. Herman Witkin (1964) hypothesized two perceptual-cognitive tendencies: *field independence* and *field dependence*. According to Witkin, the need to extract information from both internal and external environments in order to deliberate, decide, and behave is related to these two perceptual-cognitive tendencies. Field dependence/independence is among the most widely referred to of all cognitive styles. Those who deliberate and arrive at decisions and execute a variety of behaviors with little information from the environment are said to be field independent. Those who must integrate a good deal of environmental input to resolve cognitive challenges are strong in field dependence. Both tendencies were referred to by Witkin (1964) as measures of *psychological differentiation*.

Witkin's original research utilized specially developed apparatus such as the tilt-a-chair and tilt-a-room devices. In the former, the subject sat in a chair mounted on a mechanism that enabled movement in various directions so that a distorted awareness of the upright position was attained. The subject was assigned the task of maneuvering a lever that would realign the chair so that it attained a perfectly upright location in space. The tilt-a-room task required that the subject in a small, roomlike structure realign it to the relatively correct position. Later, Witkin devised the much more simple Rod-and-Frame Test (RFT), which involved manipulation of a dial in order to relocate a displaced fluorescent illuminated line on a frame into the vertical. Witkin identified subjects who had difficulty in locating the upright position as high in field dependence. Those who were able to solve the problem easily were considered to be high in field independence. Still later, a paper-and-pencil procedure for assessing this cognitive style was developed by Witkin, Oltman, Rasking, and Karp (1971), known as the Hidden Figures Test and later as the Embedded Figures Test (EFT). Subjects who can easily locate embedded geometric figures in a field are said to be highly field independent, while those who are unable to do so, or who have difficulty in doing so, are considered field dependent (Figure 10.1).

Witkin insisted that individuals are not entirely field dependent or field independent but are located on a continuum (this observation was also made when Robert Nideffer's attentional style was discussed in Chapter 8). It is therefore best to speak of *degrees of strength* of this cognitive style. Being located toward one end of the continuum or the other is not necessarily better, but as you shall see later in this chapter, certain performance domains or specific tasks within them seem to accommodate individuals with either field dependent or field independent strengths.

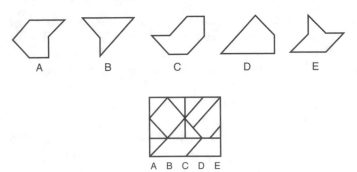

Figure 10.1 Embedded figures test. A sample item representative of the problem in the Hidden Figures Test. The task is to determine which one of the five simpler figures is hidden in the more complex figure. The correct answer for this problem is "A".

Field independence is associated with cognitive restructuring tasks, and persons who are strong in field independence tend to structure circumstances on their own and are more autonomous (make decisions easily and confidently) with reference to the social environment. This cognitive style may have implications for performance-related stress. Performers placed in situations requiring cognitions and behaviors with which they are not stylistically compatible may respond stressfully or anxiously.

Cognitive style, although enduring and stable, interacts with context. Those who think and address cognitive challenges from a strong field-dependent perspective tend to use and rely upon existing information provided by the environment as they predict and extrapolate. On the other hand, field-independent people use absolute information almost exclusively, that is, information the way it is, in its natural state.

Recently, findings from some studies suggest that field dependence/independence as originally conceptualized by Witkin may reflect cognitive ability (Miyake, Witzki, & Emerson, 2001). In other words, the tendency of some of us to be highly analytical and, relatively speaking, able to separate components from the whole configuration in which they are located may be part of a person's spatial ability or even an indication of fluid intelligence. However, the idea of field dependence being a "style" rather than an ability is still prevalent in cognitive psychology circles.

Where does cognitive style come from? Definitive answers to this question are not yet available. However, some interesting speculations are. Some authorities believe that field dependence/independence probably reflects operations of the visual-spatial component of short-term memory (Miyake et al., 2001). Apparently, this form of cognitive style develops progressively from field dependence to independence until about age 17 (Witkin, Dyke, Faterson, Goodenough, & Karp, 1962). Goodenough (1986) raises the possibility that cognitive style may be a function of cortical control — more specifically, of the left and right hemispheres. This control may have hereditary bases. Goodenough suggests that cultural forces may operate in determining cognitive style, and Witkin (1977) has hypothesized that field dependence is a dimension of personality, but he is definitive in his assertion that it is not a component of or related to intelligence (others have recently disputed this; e.g., Miyake et al., 2001).

Can field dependence be manipulated or trained? Probably not, but it is to a performer's advantage to know approximately where on the continuum he lies, so that he can invest effort in strengthening skills that might compensate for his strong field-dependent or field-independent tendencies. Coaches and others who direct practice and performance sessions should also factor-in the field-dependent or -independent idiosyncrasies of subordinates when making arrangements or selecting personnel for certain performance situations.

For instance, in their discussion of field dependence as a perceptual cognitive variable that may distinguish athletes in different sports, Pargman, Schreiber, and Stein (1974) reported higher levels of field dependence in team-sport athletes compared with those in individual sports. However, they caution that most of the team-sport athletes in this study were football players and that if these athletes were removed from the analysis, no differences would have been observed. Likewise, others have reported that athletes in sports dominated by closed skills (see Chapter 4) were significantly more field independent than those in sports dominated by open skills (Liu, 2003). Golf is an example of a closed-skill sport, since the ball is stationary when addressed and moves only when struck. Thus, the golfer is not faced with the challenge of processing a large amount of environmental stimuli in order to perform. Wrestling, on the other hand, is predominantly an open-skill sport, since the competition is obliged to receive, interpret, and act upon a continuous flow of environmental variables (stimuli that are variable in their intensity and presence or absence). If the sports are categorized according to the openness or closedness of the frequently employed skills, then differences in cognitive style become identifiable. For example, swimming and gymnastics (closed-skilled) have higher frequencies of field-independent athletes than do basketball, volleyball, and soccer (mostly open-skilled).

A performer's visual disembedding might correlate not only with performance (Riding & al-Salih, 2000), but also with performance-related choices such as whether or not to be part of an ensemble, choice of instrument (Pargman, Bender, & Deshaies, 1975; Pargman & Ward, 1976), and levels or intensities of effort for various kinds of performances (Mangum, Hall, Pargman, & Sylva, 1986) or activities (Pargman et al., 1974). It is conceivable that actors might reject certain roles, or at least not pursue them, because of unsuitability of what they perceive to be their cognitive style. Some evidence exists that field dependence/independence may also be associated with incidence of sports injury (Pargman, Sachs, & Deshaies, 1976; Pargman, 1976). Musical pitch and memory have also been related to visual disembedding ability in autistic children (Heaton, 2003).

Solo musicians, whose cognitive style is oriented toward field independence, may be more facile in hearing various individual parts of an accompanying orchestra's sound than may highly field dependent soloists whose tendency would be to hear the "whole" sound. It would therefore seem that orchestra conductors would benefit from being located in the center of the field dependent/independent continuum, since it is vital that they respond to the pattern, or whole, as well as to the selection's separate parts. Performers who are obliged to coact or interact in some way with others (actors, dancers, and musicians) would be benefited by higher degrees of field dependence. There is also evidence that persons matched with regard to psychological differentiation (degree of field dependence or independence) are likely to develop greater interpersonal attraction than are mismatched persons (Oltman, Goodenough, Witkin, Freedman, & Friedman, 1975). This suggests that group performances contingent upon member cooperation and interaction (musical ensembles, actors in a play, team sports) would benefit from homogeneity of member cognitive style.

The term *cognitive style*, which many educators refer to as "learning style," is not by any means limited to disembedding tendencies. Other styles include association/dissociation, deep/shallow processing, and imaging ability.

10.4 ASSOCIATION/DISSOCIATION

As noted previously, the term *attention* refers to the act of concentrating upon environmental stimuli that are relevant to the task at hand. Our innate sensory mechanisms are responsive to both internal and external environmental sensations. These responses are ongoing in all of us; however, our interpretation of such sensory input is idiosyncratic. We attach meaning to certain stimuli in ways that differ from those of others sharing the same environment and degree of exposure to it. Athletes who are elite tend to gravitate to important stimuli. They do this selectively. They know what environmental stimuli are essential and contribute to desirable outcomes, whereas novices tend not to. Experienced athletes seem to be aware of what to focus on and which stimuli may be ignored without sacrificing performance quality.

Association means conscious direction of attentional focus to stimuli affiliated with performance. *Dissociation* means the opposite; that is, attentional focus is intentionally directed away from performance stimuli. The runner who counts passing convertible automobiles during his morning jog is thus attempting to "get his mind off" the discomfort of the run. Conversely, the competitive marathoner competes effectively by incorporating information about her body's physiological responses during the race ("I'm exhausted and therefore must slow down," or "I'd better drink water when it's next offered and not try to pass anyone on that big hill that's coming up soon"). The same is undoubtedly true for those who sing on the operatic stage. Being in touch with personal energy resources and monitoring other information about readiness to tackle particularly challenging aspects of a role is essential. Performers should therefore learn to listen to their body messages and utilize information provided by specialized sensory mechanisms.

In addition, performers should be familiar with their tolerance levels for sensations such as pain, which can be unsettling during performance. Knowing that an ache or discomfort perceived while on stage is "nothing to worry about" or something "that will soon pass" enables continuation of the activity. But concluding that "I'm injured" or "something is very wrong with me" could also lead to a wise decision about continuing or discontinuing. Distance athletes such as swimmers, cyclists, and runners may be affected with sharp pains (stitches) that experience suggests will soon pass if the performer can hang in and dissociate. Sometimes, it's advantageous to get one's mind off certain sensations and sometimes it is best to tune in.

Although association and dissociation have circumstantial aspects, it appears that certain individuals tend to be more or less inclined to concentrate associatively or dissociatively. Some evidence suggests that athletes may actually shift in their association/dissociation during the course of competition. Needless to say, it becomes increasingly difficult to dissociate in the face of fatigue and discomfort (Tenenbaum, 2004). Signals from tiring muscles and severely taxed circulatory and respiratory systems are difficult to ignore. Attentional focus, therefore, tends to gravitate to such stimuli when a certain intensity of effort (about 70 percent of maximum) is reached (ibid.).

Which is better: an internal or external focus? The available research findings suggest that external focus may be more beneficial during competition or performance (Fillingham & Fine, 1986; Pennebaker & Lightner, 1980; Wrisberg & Pein, 1990).

Which is better: an associative or dissociative strategy? Conventional wisdom favors associative (Okwumabua, Meyers, Schlesser, & Cooke, 1983; Saintsing, Richman, & Bergey, 1988; Schomer, 1987). However, performers working in dissociative conditions report comparatively lower perceptions of physical effort (Russell & Weeks, 1994). One explanation for this may be that less attentional space is available for cues about physical exertion, thereby permitting a more comfortable feeling (Rejeski, 1985).

10.5 ATTENTIONAL FOCUS

Robert Nideffer (1976) postulates a two-dimensional structure for attention: broad versus narrow, and internal versus external. The former relates to the number of stimuli that can be accommodated at one time; and the latter to the source of the stimuli (the self or the external environment) that receive a disproportionate amount of our attention. Nideffer had constructed a paper-and-pencil assessment instrument, the Test of Attentional and Interpersonal Style (TAIS). By placing the two dimensions on respective continua and aligning them perpendicularly, an individual's attentional style may be depicted. Figure 10.2 presents the two continua, which provide for a four-quadrant matrix. Thus a person who scores high in the "broad" component and low in internality would be positioned in the lower right quadrant. On the other hand, someone whose attentional style is narrow and external would be located in the lower left quadrant.

In keeping with Nideffer's popular model, it may be concluded that those with different attentional styles would perform optimally in certain tasks or playing certain sports positions, since their style would be

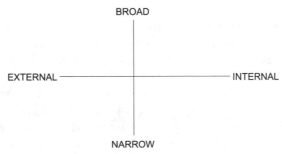

Figure 10.2 Nideffer's four different types of attention.

compatible with the attentional demands of the situation. A baseball or softball catcher with a markedly broad component should therefore be advantaged because he or she would be able to integrate numerous important stimuli emanating from the field and base paths. The attentional scope would be wide and helpful. The swimmer with tendencies to attend to stimuli deriving from the body (internal) would therefore be able to gauge her preparedness to make an all-out effort in the last 50 meters of a 1,500-meter race. Attention to her internal physiological processes and their by-products would permit evaluation of her reserve capacities and readiness to sprint. Her tendency to focus upon body signals enables her to make an educated decision about what she "has left."

A narrow-external style is likely to be helpful in activities that involve striking a stationary or moving target (golf or baseball/softball batting). Here, the "feel" of the swing and awareness of the position of hip, head, and shoulders, all kinesthetically derived, should inform biomechanical function. The tendency toward attentional narrowness would serve to restrict the performer's focus to a relatively small (and preferably relevant) number of cues. Distracting, unimportant, or inappropriate environmental stimuli would thus not be integrated into the information processing, much to the performer's advantage.

According to Nideffer, individuals must also be able to move volitionally along the two aforementioned continua. At times during competition an athlete may be obligated to shift from one mode of attentional focus to another. A case in point is the basketball player who must make the transition from offense to defense, where different attentional demands prevail. Obviously a need for change in attentional focus occurs where the same athlete is positioned on the free-throw line. There, focus should narrow so that extraneous stimuli such as those emanating from the crowd are not processed. Nideffer therefore uses the term *flexibility* to refer to this ability to alter attentional focus when necessary. This so-called attentional flexibility may not be at a premium in all kinds of performances, as it is in the sports domain. The musician is typically not called upon to shift focus dramatically from narrow to broad or vice versa. A focus that is relatively stable is probably preferred. However, in theater the actor may frequently be obligated to project variations in feelings. It may therefore be necessary to shift from an external to an internal focus and then, once again, redirect attention externally. Acting utilizes the performer's very own emotions associated with past personal experiences.

One final comment before moving on to the next topic: *Physiological arousal narrows attentional width, and stress and anxiety responses invariably involve physiological arousal.* Since a stressed or anxious performer is invariably highly aroused (physiologically activated), his or her attentional capacities may very well fluctuate accordingly. In some instances, attentional narrowing may be beneficial — in others, it may be anathema. I hasten to add that attentional focus is not the exclusive determinant of performance success. By this I suggest that when attempting, for example, to thread a needle, an aroused person might benefit from a narrowed focus; however, his activation may also result in heightened muscle tremors in the hand and an increased volume of palmer perspiration — both of which would undermine the attempt to efficiently carry out the task. A narrowing of attentional focus due to stress and anxiety may also be observed in a group context. For instance, a change in team or musical-ensemble perspective or attentional focus, so vital to its performance, might accompany heightened anxiety-related arousal (Driskell, Salas, & Johnston, 2000).

10.6 SUMMARY

The focus of this chapter is upon stylistic variations in the way individuals think, make judgments, and address problems. The chapter begins with a brief discussion of the process known as cognition and moves on to identify and describe particular styles such as field dependence-field independence, association/dissociation, attentional focus, and flexibility.

Those individuals with tendencies to integrate a substantial amount of information from both internal and external environments in order to address problems, make choices, and then behave accordingly, are said to be high in field dependence (FD). On the other hand, those who proceed cognitively, in large measure, with relatively minimal information from the field are said to be high in field-independence (F-I). Both F-D and F-I probably are influenced in childhood by cultural as well as hereditary forces, and it is likely that by age 17 a definitive field-dependent/independent style has developed. The term disembedding is often used in discussions of F-D/F-I and makes reference to a person's ability to extract stimuli that are embedded in the field. F-I people are strong in this capacity.

The next cognitive style discussed in the chapter is association/dissociation, which refers to the degree which a person can concentrate upon environmental stimuli that are relevant to the present task. Pain, for instance, is an internal stimulus from which some people are better able to disconnect than others. When one's perceptual-cognitive style leans more toward association, then it is harder to be distracted from pain.

Lastly, the chapter deals with attentional style and the hypothesized framework for its description provided by Robert Nideffer. Those with an internal attentional focus tend to respond to messages from the body – those with an external orientation tend to gravitate attentionally towards stimuli emanating from the external environment. A broad style enables those with this disposition to integrate a relatively large number of external and internal environmental stimuli at one time, in contrast to those with the antithetical narrow style.

The chapter includes discussion of advantages and disadvantages of these cognitive styles for performers. Of course, performers are advantaged when their dominant style is compatible with the performance requirements.

11

COGNITIVE STRESS MANAGEMENT TECHNIQUES: PLANNING AND UNDERSTANDING COGNITIVE STRATEGIES

LEARNING OBJECTIVES

After reading this chapter, you should be able to:

- Describe the process of *coping* and distinguish it from adaptation
- Discuss a variety of stress and anxiety coping techniques, such as reframing, eye movement desensitization and reprocessing (EMDR), thought stopping, rational thinking, participant modeling, systematic desensitization, and imagery
- Understand how each may be used to regulate stress and anxiety responses

IMPORTANT TERMS

- Coping
- Reframing
- EMDR
- Thought stopping
- Participant modeling
- Stress inoculation therapy
- Mental imagery
- Systematic desensitization

11.1 INTRODUCTION

In this chapter, my aim is to present stress management strategies that depend upon mental activities. Such interventions involve conscious efforts to cope with undesirable stressors by "using the mind" or by thinking. Drugs (Chapter 13), such as beta-blockers, and muscle relaxation procedures, such as the Jacobson method (Chapter 12), do not therefore fall in this category. Our primary interest in this chapter is in coping mechanisms that emphasize mental processes.

Since performance-affiliated stress and anxiety are major concerns in this book, we shall in this chapter describe cognitive interventions that are appropriate. Background material indicating the basis for the development of these techniques and examples of how they may be implemented are provided.

11.2 COPING

Willful attempts at controlling or managing stress responses are popularly referred to as *coping*. To cope with stress means that you voluntarily apply techniques that modify the somatic and psychological consequences of stress. And this is done in ways suitable to your personal and momentary arousal needs.

Coping is not the same as adaptation. The former suggests strategically instigated approaches that have been learned; and the latter, the development of tolerance for the negative consequences that are physiological outcomes of repeated encounters with stress (Selye's general adaptation syndrome). Coping suggests taking action about something that is considered to be disturbing. In a sense, therefore, cognitive assessment of a stimulus as being harmful precedes coping.

Coping strategies continue to attract a good deal of popular attention in both professional journals and lay periodicals. One need only type in "stress management" or "stress coping" in a favorite search engine to find a trove of commentary, advice, references, and caveats — all related to stress and anxiety.

Cognitive techniques are varied, creative, and usually affiliated with any number of theoretical perspectives that supposedly explain the origins of stress. For instance, clinicians who emphasize chronological factors as being stressors may encourage the use of time-management techniques that facilitate a client's daily planning. "To do" lists may also be constructed based upon goals for the day. Similarly, "not to do" lists are used to assist the stressed client in avoiding time-consuming behaviors that are unproductive. Such techniques may also prove helpful to the performer having difficulty finding time for practice. Biofeedback training that is concerned with the body's physiological responses to stress is another popular approach. This method will be addressed in Chapter 13.

Assertiveness and attributional training are often utilized when a performer's stress reactions are believed to be due to feelings of low self-esteem, low self-confidence, and other weak concepts of self. Along these lines, improved social relations may be the therapeutic goal.

Cognitive coping mechanisms are optimally effective when the performance task or tasks are high in thinking or reasoning components, that is, when the performer's success is contingent upon "figuring things out" or "outfoxing" an opponent. Playing chess would exemplify this; swimming a 1,500-meter freestyle event would not. Physical performance activities that contain many mental aspects are particularly amenable to cognitive interventions (Ryan & Simons, 1983). If cognitive activity prior to or during performance is believed to induce anxiety or stress reactivity and thus disrupt it, then coping strategies that include cognitive emphasis would be the techniques of choice.

The interventions introduced in this chapter should be considered skills, and as such, they require practice to ensure their effectiveness. They should prove helpful in managing many of the performance-related stress and anxiety disorders discussed earlier and may also be useful in preventing stressful events from occurring in the first place. Further, they have the potential for exerting remediative influence in relatively short periods of time (i.e., a few months). Some of the assessment tools previously described may be used to determine changes in coping style and are typically incorporated in research designs.

All stress coping strategies are not necessarily healthful and positive. For instance, some individuals are known to deal with stressors by intentionally elevating their blood pressure. This response results in a sedative effect which provides temporary relief from other physiological consequences of stress (Miller, 1980). However, the obviously negative consequences of such a strategy over extended periods of time hardly enable us to consider it as a recommended approach to stress management. Similarly, for obvious reasons, alcohol/drug abuse fails to qualify as a positive coping strategy, and has no cognitive basis. But then the term *cognitive,* which is being applied here, is essentially suggestive of *thinking processes* that stressed individuals employ.

Two more points are noteworthy before I get to the specific cognitive-behavioral techniques:

1. Folkman and Lazarus (1980) observed some 25 years ago that stress coping is multidimensional. That is, a person attempts to deal with stress responses by simultaneously invoking a number of problem-centered approaches. With this in mind, the performer would do well to cultivate a repertoire of techniques to be available for coping opportunities.

2. Not only must appropriate techniques be accessible in the repertoire, but the performer must be able to summon them on propitious occasions. Coping really doesn't happen until a technique is actually applied.

The second point is emphasized by Cameron and Meichenbaum (1982), who offer a caveat to this end. They suggest that in a stressful situation, it simply may not occur to a person to employ potentially effective responses (production deficiency). I am reminded of one of my university's varsity tennis players whom I had been assisting in regard to stress coping techniques. During one such session, she confessed that sometimes she is so nervous and upset precompetitively that she simply forgets to effectuate any stress management approach. Sometimes, available coping responses are not activated even though an appropriate mediating cue is present.

11.3 COPING STRATEGIES

Some stress and anxiety management strategies are more heavily contingent upon cognitive processes than others. They place a premium upon thinking — in contrast to behavioral interventions that merely provide contingencies or reinforcing agents designed to increase the likelihood of a future desired response to a stimulus. Among the better-known cognitive stress/anxiety management techniques are:

- Reframing
- Eye movement desensitization and reprocessing (EMDR)
- Thought stopping
- Rational thinking
- Participant modeling
- Stress inoculation therapy
- Systematic desensitization
- Imagery

Each of these will now be presented with the hope that you will understand how they may be used to regulate stress/anxiety responses, how they came to be developed, and how to go about implementing them.

It is assuredly not the aim of this section to prepare the reader for a psychotherapy career or even to suggest that upon completing its reading you would be ready to apply all of the described strategies and procedures. What is expected is that insights gained will improve your understanding of performance stress. In addition, you may be motivated to pursue training and further study in some of the techniques presented here.

11.4 REFRAMING

Reframing is a mental process wherein perceptions about a situation or person are strategically altered. When reframing, people tend to change the value or meaning of something they have experienced or are experiencing, so that these things become supportive of their existence, their efforts, and realities. Reframing may be viewed as an *editing of situations* so that they become pleasant, or at least less unpleasant than they were previously. Undesirable aspects of a situation are thus displaced by something that may be viewed as correct, pleasing, or valuable. These strategies are elaborated by Bandler and Grinder (1982). They make a plausible case for reframing being an effective agent of change and development of solutions to problems.

In the field of business, reframing is successfully used to alter perceptions of prospective customers. Successful salespersons convince potential purchasers of their products to reconfigure the perception of need for what they are selling. David Posen (2004) calls this "the act of reframing." The successful salesperson is able to convince the buyer to possess the item in such a way that the spotlight shifts from the product's qualities themselves to other possible outcomes of the purchase — for instance, "It will make me look good in the eyes of my girlfriend."

Posen, a former physician, relates the story of a young student who contracted infectious mononucleosis. When Posner told the boy's mother of his diagnosis, she expressed despair; but her son revealed a broad smile. Upon Posner's inquiry, the boy confessed a measure of relief upon learning of his illness, since it would enable him to miss two exams in the following week for which he was woefully unprepared. He was, so to speak, "off the hook." The boy had reframed a bad situation and found a silver lining. *Interpretation* is the thing — and by reframing, we can reduce stress and anxiety. A clarinetist is unsuccessful in an audition for an available orchestral position. She is one of three finalists but doesn't prevail. She therefore uses the following frame to modify the unpleasantness of not getting the job: "I now have more time to prepare for another audition that's bound to come up soon. I have a chance to practice and improve more."

In January 2005, the Super Bowl was played between the Philadelphia Eagles and the New England Patriots. The Patriots won, 24–21, and their fans reveled in their team's success. Conversely, according to an account in the Philadelphia *Daily News* (Knipe, 2005):

> The growling city [Philadelphia] screeched to a sullen silence yesterday as weary Eagles fans moped around town like little lost children. A normally bustling suburban station was oddly quiet, restaurants were closed or empty, offices were sparsely staffed. Many people took the day off—call it Eagles Flu.

Philadelphians were depressed, disillusioned, and disappointed. However, those who were able to reframe the situation may have avoided the "flu" by saying, "After all, we did make it to the Super Bowl" or "We have a young team — most of the guys will be back next year and we'll win," thus permitting themselves to feel better and avoid negative moods.

A note of caution is appropriate here. Construction of a new frame that will enable a change of perception of an event must be realistic and not be little more than a self-deceiving palliative. Mind you, reframing does not alter outcomes — the young boy in Posner's scenario still had to deal with mononucleosis, the clarinetist did not win the audition, and the Eagles did lose the Super Bowl. But the cognitive technique permitted the reframers in these examples to think and feel differently. Unrealistic reframing may succeed in protecting the ego (Freud's defense mechanism) but may not be helpful in stress management in the long run.

11.5 EYE MOVEMENT DESENSITIZATION AND REPROCESSING

EMDR dates from the early 1990s and is a psychotherapeutic intervention that is contemporary, complicated, and controversial. Its advocacy, although widespread and considerable, stems mostly from anecdotal sources, and this is an issue upon which many of its critics dwell.

The controversy involved in EMDR lies not with what it is or what it does, or for that matter with procedures necessary to achieve its professed results — according to its critics, what is conspicuously lacking is a clear idea of how and why it might indeed be effective. EMDR has been administered to many persons throughout the world who have claimed reprieve from stress reactions and various kinds of trauma.

The originator of EMDR, Francine Shapiro (2001), refers to it as an *integrative* approach because it attempts to bring together major psychotherapeutic orientations, namely psychodynamic, behavioral, and cognitive theoretical frameworks. I include it in this chapter because EMDR incorporates its clients' negative and positive belief systems as well as the insights and *changes in cognition* they undergo — although admittedly other kinds of changes are also pursued (e.g., affective, physical). It is an approach that can be effective in managing performance stress and anxiety.

11.5.1 How Does EMDR Work?

EMDR uses an eight-phase approach that is very much client oriented. This suggests that the therapist doesn't interact with the client in a highly structured format, but "the clinicians are taught to follow the lead of the client rather than to be dictating or molding the different treatment aspects" (Shapiro, 2001).

Much speculation prevails as to how EMDR procedures actually work. There are those who believe that it unblocks the information processing system due to rapid eye movement. However, others believe that the alternating left-right brain activity initiated by the eye movements or by other forms of rhythmical stimulation restructure or dump old memory. Negative, stress-causing recollections that have been triggered repeatedly are trashed, while others replace them. One premise inherent in this explanation is that the human information processing mechanisms are geared toward protecting and healing the organism and that the tendency to achieve health and wholeness is within all of us. EMDR permits this quest to be fulfilled by enabling the client to disconnect from stored painful networks that resurface to cause stress and anxiety. EMDR provides for new, comfortable, and protective cognitions, since old and troublesome thoughts are unlocked and reprocessed.

EMDR's eight-phase approach engages clients according to their needs and abilities. Therefore, not all clients are involved in the eight phases in an identical manner. These phases or stages are:

1. *Client history and treatment planning.* The client's susceptibility for EMDR is assessed and his or her treatment goals are established.
2. *Preparation for EMDR.* The client is educated about the process and its methods.
3. *Assessment of the target.* Specific memories are identified, as are visual images associated with them. Also, current negative thoughts connected to the target memory held by the client are elicited. The client further is asked to bring forth a positive cognition to place

alongside the negative one. The client then uses a scale (from 1 to 10) to rate the validity of the positive image and the intensity of feelings associated with the negative belief.

4. *Desensitization and reprogramming.* While the client is receiving bilateral sensory stimulation, the therapist moves fingers or a lighted rod from side to side in front of the client's eyes. The therapist may rhythmically tap on the client's hand or present pulsating auditory stimuli while the client's focus is directed toward the visual image, associated emotions, and bodily sensations. All of these are focused upon while the client visually tracks the therapist's moving fingers for 15 to 30 seconds. The client then discusses the material that surfaced during the completed stimulation set. This material becomes the focus for the next series of bilateral stimulating sets. The therapist observes changes in client affect, cognitive insights, and physiological state.

5. *Cognitive installation of the positive self-statement.* In this phase, the client is asked to link the previously identified positive self-statement with the original trauma as another set of bilateral stimuli is introduced.

6. *Body scan.* Since stress and anxiety responses are usually manifest through physiological status, the client is asked to monitor bodily sensations while experiencing the image and positive cognition. Sensations that are identified become the focus of additional bilateral stimulation until they are no longer perceived.

7. *Closure.* When cognitions, affect, and physiological indications are brought to a desirable status, therapist and client attend to closure and anticipate future sessions.

8. *Reevaluation.* In this final phase, assessment is conducted by the therapist as to maintenance of the treatment gains.

EMDR may be applied to the performance domain in an effort to assist stressed or anxious competitors' or performers' fear of humiliation, loss, or even nothing more than being evaluated by others, which may be so unsettling to the performer as to create significant impediment to motor and cognitive function. When applied to performers, EMDR would be designed to assist in the disconnection from previously processed experiences, related cognitions, and bodily sensations that interfere with competition and performance.

One treatment goal might be to simply enable the performer to be comfortable while performing and to enjoy the experience. During the assessment phase, the client would provide information about circumstances under which basic fears were initially acquired. For example, in the case of a dancer, when and where did the earliest dance lessons take place? And were parents or siblings present? Did they provide feedback about the lessons during travel home? What kind of person was the teacher? When and where did the first recital take place? Who comprised the audience and what were their reactions? What were the dancer's feelings about the performance, as well as the feedback it engendered from others? The therapist would thus explore the performer's *schemas* (networks, images, knowledge, attitudes, recollections, etc., derived from past experiences and stored in long-term memory) relating to skill acquisition, early performance, and associated feelings. A therapeutic attempt would then be made to expunge or trash negative cognitions and associated images and feelings while replacing them with helpful, supportive, positive self-statements.

11.6 THOUGHT STOPPING

Undesirable, negative thoughts that pervade consciousness are a bane to performance. Unwanted thoughts crop up and interact with our attempts to deal with important environmental stimuli. They undermine our efforts to concentrate. They are disturbing and disruptive and inhibit attainment of optimal performance. These negative ideations may be prophetic of failure, as in: "I'm going to mess up this passage" (music), "If I blow this free throw, we'll lose the game" (sports), "Don't drop her, if you do, it'll be a disaster" (dance), and "I'm afraid I'll forget my lines and I'll get lost" (theater). Negative thoughts invariably reflect fear or anticipation of catastrope and can cause problems in a variety of ways which may dominate thinking to the extent that they filter out helpful or supportive thoughts — the result being a focus only on doom or failure.

Negative thoughts reduce thinking and problem solving to an either-or level ("I'll drop her/I won't drop her," "I'll make the free throw/I won't make the free throw"), whereby creative or alternative thoughts cannot surface. Another pitfall of negative thinking is that it may cause fear or anxiety to be generalized to other, similar situations or to dire consequences ("If I blow this free throw, the coach will put me on the bench for the rest of the season"). And lastly, negative thinking tends to go hand-in-hand with *should*ing ("I should have done this or that. Why didn't I?"). Shoulding is, to say the least, not helpful in managing stress and anxiety. Since negative ideations are indeed thoughts, cognitive techniques may be employed to purge them.

Intrusive thoughts that carry *failure messages* are performance impediments. They deprive the performer of confidence and interfere with development of positive convictions about success. They are undesirable, unnecessary, and unprovoked. In arguing for an approach that places a premium on using a variety of cognitive-behavioral stress management techniques, Short and Curran (2004) raise an appropriate question: "Could it be that the problem is the way they [those under the influence of negative thinking] are responding to their thoughts and not necessarily the thoughts themselves?" (p.107). By so positing, Short and Curran suggest that rather than suppressing thoughts about not succeeding or performing optimally, which are common among competitors prior to "going on," a better approach would be to distract the performer or assist him in interpreting such stimuli in alternative ways. They refer to evidence that the attempt to suppress naturally occurring, unhelpful, and unwanted thoughts may, ironically, increase their production. For instance, what comes to mind when someone says, "Don't think of a zebra"? (McNally & Ricciardi, 1996; Rassin, Diepstraten, Merchelbach, & Muris, 2001; Rutledge, 1998).

Thought stopping is a technique that may be employed to empty your mind of negative representations — the advantageous result being that you will no longer have to ruminate about troublesome thoughts, images, or memories that may be unhealthy, harmful, or counterproductive to performance.

11.6.1 Thought Stopping Techniques

The strategy in all thought stopping techniques is to simply put an immediate end to improper notions that interact in some undesirable way with the execution of appropriate task-specific behaviors. Disengagement from negative thoughts may be accomplished in a number of ways:

1. Firmly articulating the word "Stop" either to oneself (in the *mind's ear*) or out loud in real speech.
2. Snapping a rubber band worn on the wrist, which interrupts negative thinking (or for that matter, any kind of thinking) due to the stinging effect. Snapping fingers or clapping hands is likely to accomplish the same effect. I introduced the rubber band technique to a collegiate place kicker, who reported considerable success in expunging thoughts about "kicking wide" or "not getting the ball high enough." Truth be told, he snapped his wrist red and raw after each practice during the week and during the weekend games. But the thought stopping technique worked well for him.
3. Bringing to the mind's eye a traffic stop sign, that is, the universally identifiable, octagonally shaped red symbol that signifies an

immediate halt. Capitalized, boldface block letters — STOP — may be envisioned.

11.6.2 Practicing Thought Stopping

Whether thought stopping is pursued with the rubber band, finger snapping, or auditory or visual imagery (stop sign), two important items must be attended to:

1. Not only must the negative thought(s) or images (falling, fumbling, failing, etc.) be terminated, but *replacement* thoughts or images must be installed. A single word or phrase such as "accurate," "calm," "strong," or "I'm okay," may also work for some performers. Positive imaginal representations of behavior may be brought to mind. The figure skater mentally visualizes his successful execution of a difficult portion of his routine. The musician uses auditory imagery to "hear" the challenging passage played flawlessly. Or a comforting thought may be invoked, such as "You're okay, the audience is friendly, and it consists of many of your relatives and supporters." The idea is to get rid of nonsupportive thoughts that impede optimal performance and to install helpful, positive ideas or images into the cognitive processes.
2. Thought stopping is a cognitive skill that must be practiced in order to be well learned and ultimately utilized effectively. (I discussed skill acquisition in Chapter 5.)

Here are some guidelines for practicing thought stopping, as provided by James J. and Constance M. Messina (personal communication, 2005):

1. Use relaxation training and breathing exercises to get yourself relaxed. It is important that you be at ease to stop a recurring thought.
2. Record the word **stop** in alternating 1-, 2-, and 3-minute intervals on a 30-minute tape. Using the **stop** tape in a relaxed state, think your unwanted thought, and every time you hear **stop**, discontinue the thought. Go back to the thought again and cease the thought only when you hear **stop**. Do this for 30 minutes every night for two weeks or until you can consistently discontinue the thought when you hear **stop**.
3. After you are trained to arrest your thought using the **stop** tape, you are ready to try arresting your thought by yelling **stop** out loud. Think of your unwanted thought for 30 minutes and yell

stop to discontinue the thought. Once you arrest the thought, go back to thinking about it for awhile, then yell **stop** again. Do this for 30 minutes each night for two weeks or until you are able to consistently discontinue the thought by yelling **stop**.

4. After you have trained yourself to stop thoughts by yelling **stop**, you are ready to train your thoughts to end by whispering **stop**. For 30 minutes, repeat the process of dwelling on your unwanted thoughts, but this time whisper **stop** to halt them. Do this for 30 minutes nightly for two weeks or until you are able to consistently discontinue the thought by whispering **stop**.

5. After you have trained yourself to discontinue unwanted thoughts by whispering **stop**, you are ready to train your thoughts to discontinue by thinking the word **stop**. Repeat the process of dwelling on your unwanted thoughts for 30 minutes, but this time simply think **stop** to discontinue them. Do this for 30 minutes nightly for two weeks or until you are able to consistently discontinue unwanted thoughts by thinking the word **stop**.

6. The technique of either taping, yelling, whispering, or thinking **stop** can be effective in discontinuing unwanted thoughts. Ideally you could get to the point where simply thinking **stop** would work; however, use whichever mode works best for you and keep practicing. Remember to start the process in a relaxed state.

11.7 RATIONAL THINKING

Negative thoughts may be challenged by a lucid, honest cognitive counterattack. Thought stopping, if done effectively, results in the cessation of cognitions that undermine performance. EMDR allegedly provides the opportunity for the reorganization and modification of previously processed traumatic experiences that are stubbornly lodged in long-term memory, then enter high levels of awareness and cause trouble. Sometimes, the performer can challenge (not delete or reprocess) negative thoughts by arguing rationally against their validity. In this strategy, an objective view is adopted whereby the performer, in effect, employs available empirical evidence that actually countermands the negative thinking. Logical questions are raised by the performer about her readiness to perform, about the quality of her preparation, and about the nature of feedback provided by colleagues, teammates, coaches, teachers, and mentors. Self-regulation is a linchpin of this *educational approach*. The performer, knowing and expressing much about himself and the nature and complexity of the forthcoming performance, employs rational thinking to dispel insecurity, doubt, and threats to self-efficacy.

However, as Dugdale and Eklund (2002) indicate, the performer may actually lose this debate. Ironically, such attempts at self-regulation may induce errorful performance. Wenzlaff and Wegner (2000) therefore apply the term *ironic processing* to refer to stress and anxiety control gone awry. The performer may unfortunately be rendered weaker in his efforts because negative thoughts have not been suppressed but linger and intrude upon information processing and skill execution. Negative thinking may take the form of well-intentioned cautions provided by teachers, coaches, or mentors, but phrased negatively, as in: "Don't do this or that, or you'll fall." Ergo, the performer indeed does "this or that," and consequently, falls.

Another technique designed to address undesirable or negative thoughts is *cognitive diffusion*. Here, the context of such cognitions are altered, instead of their frequency or form being manipulated (Masuda, Hayes, Sackett, & Twohig, 2004). The believability of the thoughts are challenged. In other words, recognition is made that the surfacing of certain thoughts is inevitable. But the individual changes them so as to reduce their potency. He permits their emergence but has changed their framework. This strategy is similar to reframing.

11.8 PARTICIPANT MODELING

A very fruitful area of psychological inquiry during the past 40 years has been *social learning theory*. This theoretical approach to learning postulates that we learn from each other or by copying the behavior of others. It also suggests that others learn from us. This copying, or *modeling*, has been one of the major research interests of Albert Bandura (1965), a proponent of what he calls *observational learning*. Bandura and his disciples argue that without actually physically experiencing a particular behavior, an observational learner may observe the actions of others, take note of their behavior's consequences (e.g., being punished or rewarded for it), and thereby acquire it *vicariously*. In addition, the observational learner is involved in thinking about the behavior, making assessments about its relevance, and rendering judgments about his ability to accomplish it. He must also apprehend or see or hear the model and process an image of it — all of these things involve cognition.

Bandura insisted that we all learn from models; however, we discriminate and do not personally acquire everything we see others do. We don't merely copy everything. We have the capacity to self-regulate what we learn. We plan to learn and we determine what we want to learn. Moreover, the attributes of the model influence the extent to which we emulate his or her behavior. We are inclined to learn and copy behaviors of others who we consider peers, or people like us ("I can do it if *she* can. I'm as smart, or strong, or fast as she is"). If we vicariously experience someone similar to us being reprimanded or punished for acting in a certain way, we are likely to avoid acting that way ourselves. We learn much from models — sometimes wrong or inappropriate behaviors, as well as highly correct ones. This accounts for the scrutiny of parents regarding inappropriate models for their children ("I don't want you hanging out with those kids").

Our capacity for vicarious learning is by no means restricted to peers. We also learn from what is provided on television, in movies, and by teachers, teammates, and admired elite performers. And what we acquire through modeling is not restricted to overt behavior. Attitudes about studying, fair play, hard work, sexism, ageism, and racism may also be learned through modeling. According to Bandura (2001), social cognitive learning theory accounts for a large measure of what children and adults learn. Among skills that may be acquired through modeling are those that may be applied to stress and anxiety management.

11.8.1 Modeling and Stress Management

We are often not alone when performing, since many coactors operate within our social environment. In individual sports, others simultaneously perform, although actual physical interaction may not occur. The swimmer or track athlete competes in her lane and dares not cross its boundaries lest she be disqualified. She does not speak to or touch other competitors after the starting signal is given, but she is usually aware of the presence of others. Members of musical, dance, and theatrical ensembles may perform solo, but they must also *interact* (perform with others) as well as *coact* (perform individually but at the same time as others). Performers interact socially with group and team members, in locker rooms, dressing rooms, and other off-the-field or backstage venues. They witness the stress and anxiety responses of other performers, who may inadvertently serve as models.

Performers are exposed to a potpourri of demeanors — loss of temper, emotional and physical outbursts, as well as very admirable coping strategies. Veteran performers who may experience powerful preperformance stressors but who manage to control them may serve as resource persons or models for rookie athletes or young neophytes. Directors, conductors, team captains, and coaches who throw and kick inanimate objects in response to stress and anxiety may be modeling behavior that subordinates accept and emulate. Thus, they may demonstrate to impressionable beginners inappropriate ways of dealing with stress. Such loss of control may result not only in an official's whistle and a costly penalty, but injury as well. A hostile outburst in sports may include biomechanical error. And, of course, the individual to whom the behavior is directed may unfortunately and understandably be injured.

Loss of temper is believed to be a consequence of exposure to aversive stimuli. Performers should know what environmental stimuli irritate them, and avoid or find ways to curtail them. Stimuli in the locker room, dressing room, or backstage that may generate frustration and loss of temper include tobacco smoke, noise that interferes with mental preparation, excessively high or low room temperatures, and unpleasant odors. The aforementioned are common; however, others cause stress in idiosyncratic ways, calling for like responses. Some athletes who are comforted by exposure to certain kinds of music (country-western, rap, heavy metal) prior to performing may wear headphones so as not to annoy or offend others with their choice of stress-reducing sound. The ways in which performers respond to aversive stimuli may be modeled by members of their team or group.

A variety of theories are available that attempt to clarify aggressive behavior (e.g., loss of temper). Some indict biological (endocrinological, hormonal) factors; others emphasize psychodynamic causes, whereby aggressive behavior is viewed as having subconscious roots. Other theoretical approaches take a learning, or more particularly, a social learning perspective. This theoretical approach is consistent with what we have been discussing in the above paragraphs — that is, people *learn* to behave with anger and to respond to stressful stimuli accordingly (Berkowitz, 1989). In some instances, the feeling of anger may be sought because of its potential for augmenting performance. Undoubtedly, many noteworthy performance outcomes have stemmed from anger. Actors are obliged to call up this emotion in order to interpret a scene with purpose and validity, and without doubt many a victory or spectacular play on the football field or wrestling mat (i.e., combative sports) has been predicated upon anger, or other emotions as well (Jones, 2003). My point here is that much more than motor or cognitive skill can be acquired through participant modeling. Management of stress and anxiety responses and of aggressivity are examples.

11.9 STRESS INOCULATION THERAPY

This cognitive stress and anxiety management approach places a premium on *imaginal confrontation* with anxiety-causing circumstances.

The performer first learns to recognize stress and anxiety reactions and to understand the scope of his or her physiological correlates. Then, some stress management skills such as deep muscle relaxation (see also Chapter 12) are taught to the performer. Because it results in a condition of reduced muscular tension, a relaxed state is incompatible with the physiological reactions to stress. Other skills may also be introduced, such as role playing and modeling. Following this, the performer is required to imagine anxiety-provoking stimulations and thereby initiate a veritable "flood" of anxiety responses. The relaxation method is then applied to the imagined stressful situation. In this way the connection between the stress or anxiety stimulus and the learned or conditioned stress or anxiety response is extinguished.

The risk taken by performer and psychologist alike is that if the imagined stressor and stress reaction are strong and realistic, and the relaxation or management technique is ineffective, future real-world stress/anxiety reactions will be stronger than ever. When considering use of this strategy, a performer should seek assurance that the person administering it is well trained and professionally qualified. My purpose in introducing it here is to familiarize you with its various aspects so that you may reach prudent decisions about its potential value and perhaps recommend it or discourage others in its use.

Psychologist Donald Meichenbaum (1996) was among the first to explore the stress coping possibilities of this approach, which he labeled *stress inoculation* (SI). SI therapy typically consists of 13 to 15 sessions conducted over a period of three months to a year. In a physical performance context, it may be exemplified by the following case.

> Sheila has prepared her recital program diligently. She can play all its pieces flawlessly for her teacher. Unfortunately, she has great anxiety about performing in a dimly lighted full auditorium. She believes it will be extremely difficult for her to walk on stage the evening of her recital. She is fearful she will be a nervous wreck. In order to deal with this problem, she embarks upon a program of SI.

First she learns how to enter a state of deep muscle relaxation, wherein her breathing is slow and full; her body heavy, her attitude calm and relaxed. With this accomplished, Sheila then imagines herself walking confidently onstage toward the piano. In her mind's eye, she takes note of the full audience. Imaginally, she senses its presence in the darkened concert hall. She remains calm. She begins to play. Her performance is perfect. Amidst warm applause she bows, smiles appreciatively to the audience, and walks offstage. Stress inoculation has enabled Sheila to cope with stress reactivity imaginally, while experiencing a state of voluntarily induced relaxation. She continues to do this over a period of a few days, until onstage performance becomes associated with the pleasantness of the deeply relaxed state. Visual, auditory, and tactile responses are incorporated into her imagined performance.

The concept employed in SI is fundamentally the same as that used in medical immunization procedures, wherein a measured and carefully determined dose of microbial stressor (antigen) is introduced in order to eventually strengthen the body's biological ability to cope with its negative impact. SI would be ideally constructed in a customized manner to accommodate each performer who likely presents different variations of the performance stress problem.

11.10 SYSTEMATIC DESENSITIZATION

Systematic desensitization is an extremely popular stress management tool among behavior therapists today. It involves the gradual association of steps or antecedent behaviors that lead to the stress experience with a state of calmness and relaxation. Anxiety and stress responses once linked to a stressful stimulation are approached through imagery in a step-by-step fashion.

A baseball pitcher having anxiety about facing a particular batter with a notorious slugging reputation would imagine his infamous opponent emerging from the dugout. Then the relaxed condition would be evoked through the Jacobson technique or autogenic training. Relaxed and calm, the pitcher would mentally see the batter leave the dugout and approach the on-deck circle again and again until this image produced no aversive reaction. This might take a few minutes, hours, or days of training. After a while, the image of the slugger would be changed so that he was seen digging into the batter's box. Again, this would be done in association with the relaxed state until this image was no longer linked to a stress/anxiety reaction. In this fashion, all previous cues conditioned to anxiety about facing and pitching to the slugger would be counterconditioned or neutralized. Subsequent separate steps requiring counterconditioning would be the batter knocking dirt from his spikes with the bat, digging into the batter's box, and checking the third-base coach's hand signals. All of these steps leading to the ultimate windup and pitch to the batter in his stance would be systematically connected with a new response — relaxation.

The psychiatrist Joseph Wolpe (1958) developed this cognitive-behavioral approach based upon classical conditioning. Although he originally envisioned its application in the treatment of phobias, systematic desensitization is also used as a stress coping technique. Essentially, it utilizes a series of increasingly anxiety-generating scenes that are alleviated individually in progressive order.

Numerous other cognitive-oriented stress and anxiety managing techniques are also in the marketplace. Some seek to overload the thought processes with heavy doses of precisely the type of thought that causes anxiety. In this way, the performer is compelled to confront the full force of the stressor and hopefully realize that the alleged source of fear or harm is realistically far less potent than previously believed. Clearly, some of these strategies carry risk in that they may cause undesirable consequences if applied inauspiciously. Most have common core elements and are concerned with overt manifestations as well as thoughts that are a result of, or associated with, performance-related stress or anxiety. This is why these techniques are referred to as *cognitive-behavioral*. In one fashion or another, most attempt to alter the ways in which performers think about their performance. Many of these strategies enable the performer to disengage from unrealistic concerns (another way of referring to anxieties) and accompanying emotions. All of the techniques require practice, since they comprise cognitive skills that must be learned.

11.11 IMAGERY

Imagery is a popular cognitive technique for coping with performance-related stress and anxiety. These images are formed in the mind as a result of input from our organs of sensation (eye, ear, nose, etc.). With practice and attention to precise details, images may be made very realistic — and the more kinds of sensations employed, the more effective is the technique. The idea is to include in an imagined performance scenario varied sensations that typically characterize real-world activity. If this is done well, the performer is benefited by having already "been there" at the time of actual function. She's seen it, smelled it, heard it, and felt it. Such prior experience may contribute beneficially to stress and anxiety management.

Ironically, negative prior experience may sometimes provide an undesirable set of memories that result in real-world performance decrement. To avoid this, it is wise to incorporate as many positive sensory experiences as reasonable during imagery training. None the less, the keynote is realism. The imagined event should be highly consonant with what is to occur onstage or on the field/arena of play. In this manner, imagery can be used to rehearse or practice performance skills so that greater levels of comfort (less fear/anxiety) may occur during the actual event. When imagery (referred to as *visualization* when the visual sensation is exclusively emphasized) is employed to improve skill execution, be sure to attend to and achieve the following three elements: (1) accuracy of movement, (2) a relaxed state, and (3) feelings of confidence.

Sometimes the source of a performer's trepidation is centered on forgetting, falling, or making an error. A word of caution is appropriate here: Imagery and mental practice are not the same. Imagery may be employed to "calm" your physiology — to relax you without necessarily addressing skill acquisition or improvement. Mental practice, however, suggests trial-by-trial repetition of an act in order to optimize skill attainment. You practice mentally or physically (or perhaps both) to enhance skilled performance; however, you do not necessarily image relaxing scenes or circumstances, as would be the case if your aim were to subdue your body's biochemical turbulence.

If a reasonable probability of failing or making an error in actual performance or competition exists, efficient recovery may be an important goal to imagine and practice. For example, the gymnast or skater who often falls during a performance faces the challenge of getting up and carrying on. The musician or actor who "loses his way" while performing must learn to regroup and catch up. These performance failings and recoveries from them may also be imagined and practiced in training. If the notion of falling or losing one's place is anxiety producing, then imaginally rehearsed error followed by recaptures of position and poise may be of considerable benefit in stress/anxiety management.

Imagery techniques should be practiced until various shapes, colors, and sizes of objects can be quickly brought to mind. Then, your own body may be installed in the image. Imagery is often initiated spontaneously, without forethought or design. However, when imagery is used as a coping strategy, the term *mental training* is applicable. The mind appears, on occasion, to want or need to imagine, since it often moves into such a mode voluntarily, that is, without forethought.

Performers may apply *imagery* (the broad term that encompasses mental practice or training) to manage stress response or to improve or change their behavior in competition or exhibition. When this can be done fairly well, then your imagined body or that of another may be assigned motor tasks. In this fashion, various problems, including emotional responses to stressors, may be played out and their negative consequences marginalized.

Thoughts are capable of stimulating various aspects of the nervous system in ways that are very similar to actual events. You have the capability to organize, install, and respond to your very own images. And you may do so in a manner of your own choosing. Therefore, it's important to construct and utilize images that represent what you want. In so doing, incorporate as many of the senses as possible in order to provide image strength. And while engaged in this cognitive strategy, use your mind's ear to listen to affirmative responses from group/team members and audience members.

For best results, images should be expressed in terms of the first person. That is, you yourself are imagined to actually be experiencing the event, rather than observing yourself engaged in an activity. For instance, if you were imagining a soccer event, instead of watching yourself in third person (as if in a movie), you would imagine the situation as if you were playing — seeing the field in front of you, perhaps seeing your feet come into and out of your vision as you run down the field, seeing your opponents in your peripheral vision. Some research findings point to no meaningful difference in first- or third-person applications of imagery. However, it is my impression that more research findings favor first- than third-person techniques.

11.12 SUMMARY

Thoughts are cornerstones of anxiety responses and therefore essential components of strategies designed to manage them. Implicit in the clarification of these different cognitive styles is the idea that performers with certain stylistic proclivities might benefit from adapting particular cognitive strategies, or that the strategy selected should advantageously incorporate certain elements or directions in recognition of an emphatic style. Not all techniques work equally well with all performers. Care must be taken to select the appropriate coping strategy for each performer in each situation.

All of the cognitive techniques discussed in this chapter require practice if they are to be employed effectively. Typically, one or two sessions a day over a period of a few weeks should suffice for most performers. Although individual practice is essential to the development of these stress management techniques, the participation of a trained and experienced leader/helper in the beginning stages of their acquisition cannot be overemphasized. Many of these techniques require guidance from well-prepared and experienced others if they are to be learned and eventually applied successfully.

The foremost stress and anxiety management strategies are: *reframing*, whereby interpretation and meaning associated with an event or other persons are manipulated, so that unpleasant or aversive situations are "edited" and rendered acceptable or pleasant; *eye movement desensitization and reprocessing (EMDR)*, whereby bilateral (and other) movements of the eyes create an optimal opportunity for the mind to "trash" old and troublesome thoughts that create anxiety, which are replaced by more wholesome and protective cognitions; and *thought stopping*, whereby negative thoughts (e.g., failure) are nipped in the bud when the performer signals himself to abruptly stop thinking negatively—snapping a rubber band on the wrist or bringing to mind the universally recognizable octagonal STOP sign immediately causes cessation of negative thinking, and the cognitive void is filled with affirmative ideation ("I can do it," "I'm strong" etc.).

Other cognitive stress management techniques are participant modeling, stress inoculation therapy, rational thinking, systematic desensitization, and imagery.

12

RELAXATION TECHNIQUES

LEARNING OBJECTIVES

After reading this chapter, you should be able to:

- Understand the value in managing stress and anxiety responses by use of progressive relaxation and autogenic training
- Describe the steps necessary to implement progressive muscle relaxation
- Appreciate the differences between progressive relaxation and autogenic training
- Discuss the goals of hypnosis interventions and their relevance to management of stress and anxiety responses

IMPORTANT TERMS

- Progressive muscle relaxation
- Autogenic training
- Hypnosis
- Age regression
- Autohypnosis
- Mindfulness
- Hatha yoga
- Pain
- Melatonin

- Prefrontal cortex
- Cortisol

12.1 INTRODUCTION

In the coping techniques described in the previous chapter, as well as in the following pages, frequent reference is made to two common elements, *relaxation* and *imagery*. In this chapter we will become familiar with management strategies that rely substantially upon these skills.

12.2 PROGRESSIVE MUSCLE RELAXATION

Cognitive techniques are more effective in management of stress reactivity when they are applied during the relaxed state. By relaxation I mean the presence of a minimal amount of muscular tension and reduced metabolic, respiratory, and heart rates. A frequently utilized relaxation procedure was developed by Edmund Jacobson in 1938. The original version has undergone abbreviation (Benson, 1975; Bernstein, Borkovec & Hazlett-Stevens, 2000), and both revised and original versions remain popular and effective self-regulatory stress management procedures.

As a result of observations made with rudimentary electromyography equipment (analysis of various brain waves), Jacobson was able to conclude that states of heightened anxiety as well as many forms of psychological stress are incompatible with deep muscle relaxation. As the body prepares to deal with a stressful stimulation, the skeletal muscles become tense. Jacobson also observed that many of his patients or subjects had very vague understandings about what a relaxed muscle group really feels like. They typically sustained fairly high degrees of muscular tension in areas such as the neck and shoulder while expressing confidence that they were relaxed ("Who, me? I'm fine!"). Therefore, in the procedure that Jacobson eventually developed, the initial aim was education as to the difference between tense and relaxed muscle. His method continues to be advantageously taught to persons afflicted by migraine and tension headaches, essential hypertension, chronic neck tension, cancer-chemotherapy and osteoporosis pain, and breathing problems (Baird & Sands, 2004; Carlson & Hoyle, 1993; McComb, Tacon, Randolph, & Caldera, 2004).

The leader or instructor of a Jacobson progressive relaxation session begins by requesting participants to be comfortably seated. Articles of clothing such as neckties or tight-fitting jewelry (bracelets, necklaces, etc.) are loosened or removed. Subjects are instructed to close their eyes gently and focus upon their breathing. In and of itself, deep, rhythmical breathing is relaxing and it appears to have a neutralizing effect on autonomic nervous system response to stressors. It is handy and effective in modifying many physiological manifestations of stress response.

Beginning with the hands, the body's large muscle groups (nearly 30, as originally proposed by Jacobson) are *intentionally tensed*. Participants are instructed to:

> Clench the hand — hold it — feel the tension — feel the tightness. And relax. Let the muscular tension escape. Now let the hand relax. Notice the difference in how your hand feels now and how it felt a moment ago when it was firmly clenched.

Major muscle groups are alternately tensed and relaxed in this fashion. The neck, facial, shoulder, abdominal, leg, and foot muscles are all first tensed and then relaxed. Each episode is accompanied by encouragement to observe the difference between tension and relaxation. After a number of practice sessions, the tensing part of the procedure is abandoned and subjects are instructed to directly "relax" a particular muscle group. With additional practice sessions subjects are expected to be able to relax all major muscle groups simultaneously in a matter of seconds.

A number of streamlined procedures (Bernstein, Borkovec, & Hazlett-Stevens, 2000; Carlson & Hoyle, 1993) have been developed that shorten Jacobson's original agenda, which required as many as 40 sessions in order to acquire proficiency. However, evidence exists of the superiority of the original, albeit longer, technique (Lehrer, 1982). Furthermore, individual instructors compose their own "scripts," which they use to train clients. Some use images or words that are typically associated with relaxation, such as "the cloudless, blue sky" or "the gentle summer breeze softly stirring the green grass." And some purveyors of progressive relaxation tape-record their instructions, suggestions, and cues and encourage users to "follow along." My experience is that the Jacobson technique works best when administered on an individual (one-on-one) basis. When spot tension can be reduced at will, a performer is able to find relief from pre-, mid-, or postperformance stress-related tension.

12.2.1 Psyching Up

More often than not, stress and anxiety are viewed as undesirable reactions. To most persons the word *stress* immediately brings to mind negative consequences. The inclination of most performers would therefore be to minimize the potency of these reactions. But sometimes a performer's arousal level is too low to satisfy task demands. This situation may occur in the case of gross-motor skills, wherein muscular strength and endurance are essential performance elements. This was noted previously on a few occasions when we discussed optimal level of arousal.

Coaches and theater directors sometimes attribute poor play or performance in athletes and actors to "not being up" for the game or show. In this way some of the aforementioned coping techniques may be applied to raise arousal by increasing stress or anxiety reactivity. Often the term *psyching up* is used to refer to this strategy. However an accurate insight on behalf of teacher, coach, or helper into the performer's appropriate arousal range for a given activity is necessary before such interventions should be attempted. Miscalculations resulting in overreduction of stress levels do not carry the same degree of potentially harmful consequences that overstressing may cause. That is, performance is less likely to be inhibited by too much psyching down than by too much psyching up. Moreover, as I have already indicated, sustained interaction with stress-inducing stimuli may take a serious physiological toll.

12.3 AUTOGENIC TRAINING

Similar to the Jacobson technique, autogenic training, originally described by Schultz and Luthe (1969), emphasizes feelings of body heaviness and warmth, particularly in the arms and legs, in connection with suggestive cues such as "comfortable," "still," and "serene." Autonomic nervous system responses are brought to the performer's attention passively. Unlike progressive relaxation, where the large muscle groups are strenuously contracted in order to create high levels of tension, muscular tightness is avoided. So-called passive concentration is encouraged, as is self-regulation (which is what autogenic means). As is the case with Jacobson's protocol, or for that matter, any of its shortened versions, autogenic training should be practiced daily until it can be invoked volitionally. I suggest to performers with whom I work that they practice twice a day.

Here are some self-administered cues to incorporate in your practice:

- My right arm (left arm, right/left leg, right hand, left hand, etc.) is warm and heavy.
- My breathing is smooth and rhythmic.
- My heartbeat is regular and strong.

Two additional items to remember about autogenic training are: (1) It may be practiced and employed any time and anywhere, and (2) it is self-induced (unlike progressive relaxation). One particular application of this technique is with insomnia (sleep disturbance), a common preperformance problem.

In essence, both progressive relaxation and autogenic training attempt to counteract the flight-or-fight response discussed earlier, while directing our physiological processes into the balanced, or *homeostatic,* condition (Selye, 1982). Autogenic training may be considered a form of self-hypnosis.

12.4 HYPNOSIS

Franz Anton Mesmer was no charlatan. An Austrian physician, educated at the University of Vienna, he was able to successfully treat some of his patients' illnesses by inducing a condition known as *hypnotic trance,* a state wherein the subject is accepting of suggestion. Ultimately, a French governmental commission appointed to investigate Mesmer's techniques and claims produced an unfavorable report. As a result, he fell into disrepute and lost a considerable amount of his previously held prestige and popularity. But he was no fraud. He was able to understand the curative potentialities of temporarily changing a subject's perceptions, mental sets, and beliefs in order to pursue therapeutic objectives. And this is basically the goal of hypnosis.

Further, hypnosis may accurately be viewed as a cognitive-behavioral strategy (hence its legitimate place in this chapter). Hypnosis aims at retrieval of information and catharsis of experiences embedded in various layers of memory. These intellectual/emotional past experiences may play important roles in the development of current stress reactivity associated with performance. Additionally, hypnotherapy may provide information not previously accessible to conscious reasoning. Such information liberated by hypnosis may be integrated into ongoing cognitive processes and ultimately influence motivation for current behavior.

For a period of time, hypnosis flourished mostly as an entertainment medium. Vaudevillians and nightclub entertainers used hypnotic trances to reveal their mystical and magical powers. Demonstrations were often couched in secret and arcane settings. Volunteer subjects from the audience would be carefully chosen. In fact, selection of the appropriate subject — an individual suspected of being especially susceptible to suggestion — has always been the most critical task of the entertainer-hypnotist, whose objective is obviously to amuse those observing the demonstration. This is clearly *not* the aim of hypnosis as it is presented here. There is a world of important differences between hypnosis as entertainment and *hypnotherapy,* which is our professed interest. Hypnotherapy uses hypnosis in order to bring about change or resolution of a problem.

We shall consider hypnotherapy as an approach to the control of stress and anxiety. When used advisedly, it may be helpful in enabling a performer to restrict his/her responses to a narrowed range of environmental stimuli. In terms of performance, this translates into *concentration*.

12.4.1 An Objective View of Hypnotherapy

Perhaps the one person who has been most influential in elevating the reputation of hypnosis to its current status of a legitimate psychotherapeutic method is Erik Erikson. For more than 40 years Erikson explored, extolled, and experimented with the use of hypnosis in treating an amazingly broad sweep of physical as well as mental disorders. He has written prolifically about his successes and failures in casework format and has established a theoretical framework upon which his models and specific practices rest.

According to Erikson, hypnotherapy evokes subjects' very own previous life experiences in order to effect beneficial or therapeutic change. This is accomplished through indirect suggestion. Individuals undergoing hypnosis must desire to be hypnotized and not resist carefully considered suggestion from the therapist. Suggestions are presented by the therapist in accordance with his/her perceptions of the subject's stress-related problems. It is unlikely that a performer who does not wish to enter hypnotic trance will be hypnotized.

Hypnotic responses may take many dramatic forms. Anesthesia, amnesia, age regression, and hallucination are examples. But these manifestations of trance are subordinated in importance to the therapist's decisions about what to do with the subject in the trance state. And of equal importance is the reason for this decision.

Trance induction is not a standardized procedure for all subjects or even the same for a particular individual on different occasions. As long as attention may be fixed (on the therapist's eyes, a bright light, or a spot on the wall), a subject *who wishes to enter trance* may usually be hypnotized. Some authorities consider hypnotic trance to be exactly that — a state of focused attention distinguished by a lack of initiative or willful movement (Dietrich, 2003). This acute attentional focus may be associated with a change in prefrontal circuitry in the brain's cortex resulting in a change in information processing. We'll have more to say about this speculation shortly in this chapter when yogic meditation is explained.

The progressive relaxation technique described earlier is, for all intents and purposes, the same as (or at least extremely close to) the fixation stage of trance. And this suggests that the fixation of attention need not be accomplished relative to an external object, but an internal focus may serve to attract attention as well (e.g., the subject's rhythmic breathing).

The hypnotized subject remains essentially the same person. Hypnosis will not provide any additional skills. The dancer will not be able to perform new movements. Nothing that the subject doesn't wish to do, or doesn't have the skill to do, will be accomplished. However, some behavior may be altered by trance if inhibitions and psychological impediments to improved performance are removed by hypnotherapy. Stimuli that heretofore were interpreted as stressors may in trance be reorganized in the perceptual field as nonthreatening. And if the original stressful perception of a stimulation is removed, performance may thereby be enhanced.

In trance, a subject may reexamine personal psychological experiences and perhaps acquire the freedom to express them. Put simply — many memories, fears, and anxiety-provoking stimuli act and interact at various levels of consciousness. Under the influence of hypnotic trance, contact with these troublesome stimuli may be made and resolution sought. During the trance a probe of the unconscious mind for embedded information, feelings, and experiences may be initiated by suggestion, and the causes of some anxiety and stress responses may be clarified.

Hypnosis may be introduced to enable a client/performer to recall an exemplary performance that may be used as a model for future performances. Another beneficial outcome may be that the affective state (feelings) of the performer during a noteworthy past exhibition or competition may be caused to surface into awareness. Feelings of confidence and calmness may be recalled so that an affective goal may be established and pursued for future performances. Fear-laden, confused images related to certain events may be brought to higher levels of consciousness, where they may be addressed and clarified. The hypnotherapist avoids suggestion relating specifically to victory (e.g., "You will win," "You will receive a standing ovation") — the therapist as well as hypnosis itself may be discredited in the performer's view if these outcomes are not realized. A more appropriate suggestion would be, "You will feel strong and confident," "You will be eager to succeed," or "You will be free to give an outstanding performance." Eriksonian hypnosis advocates the avoidance of direct commands being given to a subject and thus uses an *indirect* approach. Nondirective hypnosis is permissive in that subjects remain in control of their own trance state. There is no immobilization, and participants may even be mobile and take themselves out of trance at will.

Morgan (1993, 2002) has reviewed the relationship between sport behavior and hypnosis and describes a variety of applications. Others have demonstrated the effectiveness of hypnosis in reducing performance anxiety in musicians (Scholz, 2001; Stanton, 1994). But here we are chiefly concerned with anxiety and stress control rather than quality of skilled performance per se.

12.4.2 Three Stages of Hypnotherapy

In the above paragraphs, some of the more prominent potentialities and realities of hypnotherapy were identified. Perhaps most important of all is the preparedness, rapport, trust, and insight of the therapist. Hypnotherapy may be a remarkably effective approach to managing stress and anxiety in motor performance; however, only trained, professional clinicians should attempt to administer it.

The approach usually taken by experienced professionals involves a three-stage process, as described by Erikson and Rossi (1979, pp.1–11):

1. *Preparation,* in which the therapist, establishing rapport, explores the subject's past experiences and needs and then determines therapeutic goals
2. *Trance,* in which the subject's usual perceptual framework is altered in order to facilitate problem solving
3. *Evaluation* and discussion of therapeutic change

According to Erikson and Rossi, anyone who wishes to enter trance, can. Only the desire and ability to disengage the conscious mind and the ability to achieve a state of deep relaxation are necessary. Meditation is not the same as hypnosis. The latter attempts to relax the participant and utilizes a goal orientation, whereas the former strives to eliminate thoughts, aims, and objectives. Meditation purports to eradicate stimuli — to empty the mind. Hypnosis, most assuredly, does not.

12.4.3 Autohypnosis

A performer who has been hypnotized by a therapist may be given the suggestion that he or she may induce trance volitionally. Trance is by no means a rare experience. We have all entered it frequently. Anytime your attention is so intently riveted on one thought or object as to leave you oblivious to other stimuli, you may be in a trance experience. This has happened to me often while driving on a very boring stretch of interstate highway when other cars are not present. When some environmental change suddenly prods me out of my altered state (e.g., observation of a dog roving on the roadside), I am surprised at how long I remained unaware of my "real world" — of how many miles and minutes had gone by.

This condition may be self-induced either due to previous suggestion (e.g., "You can hypnotize yourself whenever you wish") or through practice. In the domain of performance, the wherewithal to autohypnotize is bound to be helpful. Upon observation that one's arousal level is inappropriate, autohypnosis may be employed as a coping strategy.

12.5 YOGA

All well-contrived research articles include operational definitions. Important terms and words quintessential to reading and understanding the report are defined so that the reader comprehends precisely how the author is interpreting and using them. A word such as *elderly*, for example, would be in need of an operational definition so that the reader is clear about the age range meant in a particular article. For the purposes of this section, an operational definition is in order for *yoga*, a widely known term and the subject of numerous journal articles.

The word *yoga* has its origins in the ancient Indian language Sanskrit and is evocative of a system of exercising the mind and modifying consciousness in an expansive manner. It does this through practicing and sustaining various physical positions, breath control, relaxation, concentration, and contemplation. All of these methods are pursued simultaneously. Some yoga training techniques accentuate concentration and others are more emphatic about relaxation. Some schools of yoga training utilize the word *meditation* exclusively and others are content with the term *yoga*. Yoga is an unconventional combination of physical exercises and meditation that involves intensely focused awareness, so much so that in its advanced format, altered consciousness and a changed sense of time and space occur. Some books and articles use the two terms *yoga* and *meditation* synonymously; however, I understand yoga to be a form of meditation. Although yoga is now practiced throughout the world and is enjoying unprecedented popularity, it was for many years associated with Eastern philosophy and religion. Hinduism and Buddhism are examples. *But in itself, yoga is not a religion,* and a practitioner may retain his or her own religious beliefs.

The purposes of yoga are to keep the body toned and flexible and to center and balance the mind. The second of these two purposes is a bit more vague than the first and suggests a calm state of mind and an objective and highly rational mode of thinking and processing of sensations. In addition, I interpret the *centered mind* to mean a focus upon helpful, relevant, and satisfying environmental stimuli.

Supposedly, yoga facilitates one's power of self-awareness, thereby enabling incisive communication between body and mind — a relationship that ancient pundits and many contemporary scientists alike have recognized and extolled. The term *centered state* also suggests a connection between, and interpretation of, one's internal and external events — that is, events occurring in the world at large in juxtaposition to what one feels.

Yoga practitioners also claim an attending spiritual process and outcome. Yoga is alleged to provide for a religious reckoning, a contact with a metaphysical authority or universal source of strength and power (God?). Nonetheless, as mentioned earlier, yoga is not claimed to be a religion, and practitioners of many different spiritual persuasions feel comfortable in their adherence. Supposedly yoga encourages an inner harmony and self-awareness. Note my use of the words alleged and supposedly, by which I express recognition of some prevailing skepticism in the scientific community about some claims made on yoga's behalf. Yet, a link between the practice of yoga and stress and anxiety management is sustainable.

Yoga's promise of inner peace, harmonious connectiveness of mind and body, and sharpened powers of concentration notwithstanding, yoga is a physical experience as well as an exercise form. And as you'll see in Chapter 13, exercise continues to be revealed in study after study to exert a meaningful and mostly beneficial influence upon mood and psychological state. All of the salubrious exercise outcomes may therefore also be anticipated from yoga participation — notably strength, flexibility, and respiratory improvements. And through inference, might we not also anticipate improved resistance to physical injury?

A number of different kinds of yoga are practiced. Each is designed to accommodate persons of different interests and inclinations. The one with which most Westerners are familiar is *hatha yoga*, and it is this form that will represent our treatment of yoga here. Males and females who practice yoga are referred to as *yogis* and *yoginis,* respectively. Hatha yoga is sometimes referred to as *physical yoga,* since it emphasizes *asanas*, which are physical poses named after their (mostly) Indian inventors.

Asanas are not akin to exercises that are typically done in the traditional gymnasium setting, such as push-ups, sit-ups, or other such calisthenics. Perhaps the fundamental aim of these asanas is to calm and relax (lower the activation level) of the yogi or clear the mind, so to speak, in order to enable meditation. To this end, emotions are dramatically reduced in intensity or temporarily eliminated from awareness. Asanas are taught by trained teachers and learned through practice.

Inward focus, or *mindfulness,* is foundational to yoga. It is achieved through a coordinated breathing rhythm of which the yogini is aware, with movement of the body (the asanas) involving twisting and turning as well as postures that are static. One critical element of the asanas is *relaxation.* Another action present in many asanas is stretching, which in and of itself provides a host of benefits to the musculoskeletal system (Ghoncheh & Smith, 2004; Raub, 2002).

A sizable number of published materials appear in lay periodicals that have not received the scrutiny typical of the peer review process. Moreover, charges of faulty data collection, inappropriate methods of testing, and vulnerabilities in statistical analysis have even been levied at articles published in most scientific journals (Bunce & Stephenson, 2000). To be sure, all scientific disciplines, subdisciplines, specialty areas, and "-ologies" are, on occasion, criticized on the basis of methodological flaws in research. Yoga and similar meditation systems are certainly no exception (Bishop, 2002). Nonetheless, an impressive body of material does testify to the efficacy of hatha yoga and other forms of mindfulness as legitimate and effective stress and anxiety management strategies (e.g., Kabat-Zinn, 2003).

Let us overview a sample of what is available by dividing the literature into two broad categories: (1) *psychological changes* in stress and anxiety parameters resulting from yogic or mindful intervention, and (2) *physiological and biological changes* associated with such interventions. Let us see what has been generated by researchers who have studied yoga in relation to stress and anxiety. What do they tell us and in what helpful ways might we apply this information to performance anxiety and stress?

12.5.1 Psychological Changes Due to Yogic Interventions

Yoga and other forms of meditation have been shown to be associated with positive psychological effects in dance students (Elkins, 2003; West, Otte, Geher, Johnson, & Mohe, 2004). Medical school students, who typically function under high levels of performance-related stress, though not always of the physical kind, have also been shown to decrease overall psychological distress during their difficult exam period when practicing mindfulness-based relaxation protocols (techniques akin to yoga) (Shapiro, Schwartz, & Bonner, 1998). A meta-analysis conducted by Eppley, Abrams, and Shear (1989) on the effect of different relaxation techniques indicated that meditation was as efficacious in reducing anxiety as were any others incorporated into the study. (A *meta-analysis* is a statistical technique popularly employed today that permits pooling of data from studies that address similar hypotheses and employs similar kinds of subjects and interventions to test hypotheses or uncover new conclusions derived from data across numerous investigations.)

12.5.1.1 Pain   Various relaxation and meditation strategies have been recommended for the management of pain (Morley, Eccleston, & Williams, 1999). Among the most well known of contemporary pain researchers is the psychiatrist Jon Kabat-Zinn. With his colleagues, he has studied a variety of issues and strategies aimed at clarifying and ameliorating this perceptual-cognitive experience, often associated with performance of various kinds. Kabat-Zinn has consistently reported experimental as well as qualitative research (single-subject interviews, surveys, etc.) that revealed positive effects of meditation-based stress management programs (Kabat-Zinn et al., 1992; Kabat-Zinn, Lipworth, & Burney, 1985; Kabat-Zinn, Lipworth, Burney, & Sellers, 1987).

Back pain, a frequent malady encountered by athletes, dancers, and many other types of performers, and undeniably an impediment to optimal performance, has also been shown to be responsive to yoga (Graves, Krepcho, Mayo, & Hill, 2004). I'll offer additional comments about pain later in this chapter when I discuss massage therapy. At that point I'll describe Melzack and Hall's gate theory as a model for understanding pain perception.

The human nervous system is multidimensional in that it consists of numerous subsystems. We therefore speak of such neural entities as the *peripheral nervous system,* the *central nervous system,* the *autonomic nervous system,* etc. That portion of the nervous system that responds automatically to internal and external stimulation is known as the *autonomic nervous system.* In this network of neural connections, cognitive processes are minimally involved and mechanisms that do operate are said to respond *autonomically* (see Chapter 5). Mindfulness such as that present in yoga and other meditation experiences influences the function of this subsystem, as reflected in electroencephalographic (EEG) activity. In the mindful condition, brain-wave characteristics undergo change, thereby supporting the claim for a relaxed state (Takahashi et al., 2005).

Yoga asanas have also been shown to improve affect and decrease self-reported symptoms of depression, anxiety, fatigue, and other negative moods when administered during a five-week intervention period (Woolery, Myers, Sternlieb, & Zeltzer, 2004). These changes are attributed to higher *cortisol* levels observed in those participating in yoga. Cortisol is a neurotransmitter (a chemical messenger found in the bloodstream) associated with feeling good. Coincidentally, and very much in keeping with one of our primary interests in this book, rigorous physical activity (exercise) is also associated with elevated cortisol levels. *Melatonin,* another chemical factor found in the blood and related to positive mood change when elevated, has also been shown to increase as a result of a yoga intervention (Harinath et al., 2004). Perhaps both the cortisol and melanin increases noted during yoga participation account for or at least contribute to the observed improved sense of well-being. Generally speaking, individuals with relatively higher trait anxiety scores are associated with deeper relaxation while meditating (Murata et al., 2004).

12.5.1.2 Attention The ability to concentrate on stimuli that are relevant to a particular task (attention) was observed to improve significantly in boys diagnosed with attention deficit hyperactivity disorder (ADHD) after 20 sessions of yoga training (Jensen & Kenny, 2004). Appropriate attention focus is critical to performance success (this point received elaboration in Chapter 8). If yoga could be of help to those with marked attention deficiencies, might it not contribute to both the long- and short-term preparations of many different kinds of performers who, although not faced with ADHD, might nonetheless be challenged by formidable attention demands inherent in their performance areas? Sports behaviors that typically contain a multiplicity of constantly varying and interacting stimuli would exemplify this point.

12.5.1.3 Reaction Time Whether our interest is momentarily centered on dance, sports, musical or theatrical performance, one human function in particular is quintessential to all; namely *reaction time* (RT). RT indicates the way in which our central nervous system processes information and provides a convenient means of determining sensory-motor function. Both visual and auditory RTs have been shown to improve (decrease) as a consequence of yogic training, which indicates improved sensory-motor performance and enhanced processing ability of the central nervous system. This improvement may be related to a faster rate of information processing and improved attention focus (Bhavanani, Madanmohan, & Udupa, 2003). Implications for sports performance in particular are obvious.

Although an overview of the literature can at times be somewhat dry and difficult to present in a reader-friendly fashion, it is at the same time a helpful and necessary component of a text. The discussion and interpretation of reported research findings by others goes a long way toward convincing readers of the appropriateness and validity of one's premises and advocacies. A credible foundation must be established in order to permit conclusions, applications, and recommendations. Those considering helping others manage performance-related stress and anxiety or are interested primarily in controlling their own require such information. What may we glean from the findings we've so far reviewed?

1. There exists a sizable body of research literature, much of it well conceived and judiciously discussed, that portrays yogic interventions as having a positive and helpful impact upon various psychological measures.
2. Yoga appears to have implications for stress and anxiety management that in turn may be extrapolated as beneficial to performance.
3. This positive influence of yoga is likely to be of benefit to those preparing to perform as well as to performance itself.

12.5.2 Yoga Efficacy

Are there also benefits of a physiological and biomechanical nature that accrue to practitioners of mindfulness? Now that we've concluded a discussion of various perceptual-motor, mood, and attention capacities (psychological factors) and the manner in which they are enhanced by yoga, let's look at the connection between biological status and yoga.

A literature overview by James Raub (2002) summarizes a good deal of medically substantiated information about the physical health benefits of yoga. This overview, which contains 75 references, enables us to draw inferences for performance-related stress and anxiety management. Raub generally concludes that hatha yoga in particular can improve muscular strength and flexibility and may also be influential in regulating physiological variables such as blood pressure and heart and metabolic rates. All of these are contributors to overall exercise capacity. These findings are for healthy people as well as for those with compromised musculoskeletal and cardiopulmonary systems. Physically active persons with physical disabilities, such as Special Olympics participants, or performers who are physically challenged in sundry ways would also benefit from yoga and other mindfulness training regimens.

Among the many citations offered in Raub's review is the work by Manchanda and colleagues (2000), who reported improved exercise capacity and decreases in body weight, serum total cholesterol, low-density cholesterol, and triglyceride levels — all in comparison with control subjects deprived of the yoga experience. Another research finding included in the review, also pertinent to our concern, addresses recovery time from rigorous exercise as being shorter under the yoga condition in comparison with a nonyoga rest (Bera, Gore, & Oak, 1998). Boyle, Savers, Jensen, Headly, and Manos (2004) reported similar findings.

Systolic, diastolic, and mean blood pressure were significantly reduced in middle aged men with hypertension (high blood pressure) who participated in four weeks of daily yoga training (Vijayalakshmi, Madanmohan, Bhavanani, Patil, & Babu, 2004). However, of additional relevance to our interests here was the observed improvement among yoga participants in sympathetic nervous system response to a stressful stimulus and restoration of the autonomic regulatory reflex mechanism (in lay terms, improved reflexes). To brush up on the meaning of these terms, have a look at the discussion in Chapter 5.

Melatonin production has been shown to increase as a result of yogic training (Harinath et al., 2004). This chemical produced by the body is believed to be linked with the sense of well-being and sleep function, which is implicitly related to stress management because disordered sleep is a frequently reported preperformance (and sometimes, postperformance) anxiety-related problem.

One other study generated findings that are also germane to our interest here. Subjects who participated in yoga training demonstrated significantly improved work output (on a treadmill) while consuming a reduced level of oxygen per unit of work, without demonstrating any significant increase in heart rate. This suggests a stronger, more efficient heart function that generalizes from yoga, not from treadmill training (Raju, Prasad, Venkata, Murthy, & Reddy, 1997).

Yoga has also been shown to assist in the modification of cardiovascular risk factors and in the rehabilitation of postmyocardial infarction. A rather convincing review of the scientific literature that supports this assertion is provided by Jayasinghe (2004). We have already discussed linkages between accumulated stress and cardiovascular disease in Chapter 2. Yet another researcher, Parshad (2004), offers a terse summary of observed effects of yoga participation as they relate to health: "Physiological benefits which follow, help yoga practitioners become more resilient to stressful conditions and reduce a variety of important risk factors for various diseases, especially cardio-respiratory diseases" (p. 191).

Finally, two questions seem appropriate: What is really happening organically during yogic activity, or for that matter, during any state of altered consciousness, such as the "runner's high," hypnosis, and even daydreaming; and where in the human nervous system is this happening? The seat of control is the central nervous system. Consciousness, mindfulness, and individual changes in these capacities are under the aegis of brain activity. Some sort of neuroanatomical experience kicks in and takes control. Do we know the exact location within the brain that is responsible for yoga's effects in mood alteration, sensation change, physiologic function, and various fitness parameters (all performance related, with implications for stress and anxiety management)? No, not for sure. However, scholarly speculation places this control center in the *prefrontal cortex*, a part of the cerebral cortex.

Such is the hypothesis of Arne Dietrich (2003). Dietrich explains that an anatomical hierarchy describes the juxtaposition of all parts of the cortex; the higher cognitive functions being located at the top. Attention, perception, and some arousal functions are all lined up here, with consciousness located on top of the ladder. Its function is therefore said to be executive. Perhaps a better way to express this is to say that the prefrontal lobes do not, in and of themselves, regulate consciousness, but integrate or facilitate it. In this way, according to Dietrich, altered states of consciousness are a result of changes in prefrontal regulation and deregulation. But one additional factor contributes importantly — physical activity.

The kind of physical performance we refer to in this book is largely of a gross-motor nature (running, jumping, dramatically moving the body in space, etc.). For the most part this type of performance takes place in sports, exercise, and dance. Of course, rigorous gross-motor activity may be involved in theatrical performance, but to lesser degrees — the behavior of the symphonic conductor in concert and the members of a chorus line in musical theater being notable exceptions. In particular, physical activity of the endurance kind is associated with decreased prefrontal activity; that is, a decrease in brain activation (Dietrich, op cit.). Other forms of exercise requiring high levels of cognitive involvement (football, basketball) may not be accompanied by a decrease of prefrontal activity at all.

During yoga, or any other form of meditation, sensory input of a continuous nature is drastically reduced — and so is prefrontal activity, where high-order cognitive function occurs (see Chapter 5). It may be that during meditation the quietude and intense concentration upon the mantra, breathing rhythm, or other internal events serve to cut off or at least minimize a sizable number of stimuli typically requiring processing.

Prefrontal mechanisms undergo change that result in consciousness alteration. Shifts in wave patterns determined through EEG assessment during meditation provide evidence of this change in the prefrontal cortex. Perhaps this also clarifies the *anxiolitic* (anxiety-reducing) effect of both meditation and vigorous, rhythmic aerobic exercise. This speculation may also be helpful in explaining what happens during hypnotic induction. Hypnosis may not be a true state of altered consciousness as much as it is a state of intense attention focus.

Under the rubric of *relaxation*, ample evidence from the medical and psychological research literature supports a case for the efficacy of progressive muscle relaxation (the Jacobson method), hypnosis, and yoga in stress/anxiety management.

12.6 MASSAGE

In research methodology a *dependent variable* is a factor that is under observation in order to see if it changes when exposed to an experimental intervention, which is the *independent variable*. Say, for instance, that I hypothesized that a certain drug would alleviate pain better than another. I would introduce both pharmaceutical agents (*interventions* or *treatments*) to a *sample* of participants (*subjects*) under identical conditions (time of day, location, environmental temperature, etc.) for the same length of time. Then I would somehow assess pain perception in my subjects and compare the findings resulting from the two conditions. Pain would be the dependent variable in my study, and each of the pharmaceutical treatments would constitute an independent variable.

Massage, administered as a therapeutic intervention to ameliorate performance-related stress and anxiety, has been but sparsely incorporated in well-designed studies. A considerable amount of anecdotal material is available that portrays massage as being very helpful; however, hard, cold *empirical* (observed from experimental research) data are few and far between. This is not necessarily the case with regard to a litany of other dependent measures. According to published research results, massage therapy has been used in attempts to alleviate anorexia nervosa and bulimia (two eating disorders, the former often associated with female athletes participating in sports such as figure skating and gymnastics), ADHD, back pain, various communication disorders, autism, fibromyalgia (a neurological condition), academic stress, cystic fibrosis (a respiratory disease), tobacco craving, clinical depression, sleep disturbance, chronic fatigue syndrome, rheumatoid arthritis, multiple sclerosis (a disease of the protective sheath covering nerve axons), and tension headaches (Field, 1998; Martin, Lane, Dowen, Homer, & Milton, 2004).

Of the studies that have been presented in professional journals (about 200 articles, according to Field [1998]), many are methodologically vulnerable. Among the criticisms leveled at this body of work are that sample sizes are too small and the studies fail to include control groups (groups not exposed to the experimental condition(s) but used for comparative purposes). The multiplicity of massage techniques incorporated in the studies also contributes to mixed and/or conflicting results. An additional criticism is that a good deal of what is available in the research literature is restricted to athletic populations and is focused upon reduction of muscle soreness after performance. These shortcomings have resulted in equivocal findings that have raised doubts and generated cynicism from the scientific (medical) community.

Two questions surface at this point: Could not similar criticisms be levied against other techniques, strategies, and interventions described in this and the previous chapters; and if indeed massage therapy has not been subjected to rigorous and methodologically correct research procedures and reported findings are suspect, why consider massage as a legitimate strategy in stress and anxiety management in the first place? My answer to the first question is *yes*. I say this because I am aware that methodological and procedural flaws are unfortunately to be found in just about all areas of research. However, the enlightened reader has the prerogative of culling those that are weak and vulnerable from a large number available and focusing on the remaining ones that are well conceived and that satisfy high standards. This can be done when a body of professional literature comprises thousands of published papers. Only two meta-analyses are provided in the literature with a focus on massage therapy (Field, 1998).

My response to the second question is this: Massage or *touch therapy* (a broader term under which massage is subsumed) is currently receiving a good deal of attention in the "alternative medicine" movement. Many performers with whom I interact professionally praise its effectiveness and encourage me not to ignore it in my writing, teaching, and lecturing.

Models that may clarify the effects of massage and touch therapy originate from two questions: What physiological mechanisms may account for the effectiveness of massage therapy; and why is touch a potential mediator of performance stress and anxiety? A number of possibilities exist.

12.6.1 Alleviation of Pain

One may pursue an entire professional career as a musician and not suffer performance-related injury, although injury to fingers, hands, shoulders, and neck would certainly not be uncommon. Those who participate in sports and dance or who are inveterate exercisers may anticipate eventual injury. It is likely to occur sooner or later. Injury is a bane (Pargman, 2005) to all athletes, dancers, and others who make their living or immerse themselves for pleasure in gross-motor activities. Injuries hamper, severely restrict, or entirely prevent participation. Invariably, *pain accompanies injury.* Pain is an unpleasant and often odious perceptual-cognitive experience whose intensity is largely dependent upon the personal meaning attached to it. Prior experiences with similar injury and pain, in combination with insight into the injury's prognosis, interact with sensitivity and tolerance levels (and other psychological variables as well, such as cognitive style and attention style) to determine the degree of perceived discomfort. Massage and touch therapy are often used to alleviate pain.

The process of *nociception* underlies pain (*noci-* = pain). This involves transmission of stimuli that signal tissue damage or potential tissue damage if maintained. Removal of the source of damage or potential damage is sought by the traumatized individual. The same is true of rest, for purposes of healing.

Among the more venerable models attempting to clarify pain perception is *gate theory* (Melzack & Wall, 1965). This theory hypothesizes the existence of gates along the spinal cord through which pain stimuli must ascend en route to the brain, where they undergo nociception. Pressure sensations such as those created by massage, exerted on appropriate sites in the stimulus pathway, travel more rapidly than pain messages, since they proceed along byways that are shorter. They therefore supersede the pain message, and the result is that the brain issues a command to close the gate(s). The sensation of pain is thus thwarted and not felt.

One additional explanation of the positive effect of massage on pain relates to the increase of *serotonin* levels usually observed after massage therapy (Field, 2004; Hernandez-Reif, Field, Krasnegor, & Theakston, 2001; Ironson et al., 1996). Serotonin's effect is to modify mood, emotion, sleep, and appetite. It is believed to play an important role in anxiety. A decrease in the stress hormone cortisol has also been reported following massage therapy (Field, 2004; Ironson et al., 1996). Cortisol levels typically rise during states of agitation, or stress (Greenspan & Stewler, 1997).

Quiet and restorative sleep is associated not only with relaxation and healing of injury, but also with pain relief. This is believed to be due to a substance known as *somatostatin* that is released during deep sleep. An absence of this substance increases the perception of pain. Massage therapy has been shown to be soporific (sleep inducing). Deprivation of deep sleep results in reduced levels of somatostatin and consequently increased sensitivity to pain (Sunshine, et al., 1996). The studies I have cited include data supporting decreases in anxiety levels in subjects pre- and postmassage intervention (Hernandez-Reif et al., 2001; Ironson et al., 1996; Martin et al., 2004; Sunshine et al., 1996).

Respiratory rate has also been reported to drop significantly after massage, which explains the concomitant decrease in anxiety and perceived stress (Zeitlin, Keller, Shiflett, Schleifer, & Bartlett, 2000). A positive correlation between these two dependent variables would be expected. Both are apparently correlated with breathing rate, which is responsive to massage therapy.

12.7 SUMMARY

The term *relaxation* suggests a change in the status of muscular contraction, as well as a general reduction in metabolic activity. Therefore, the procedures described in this chapter — Jacobson's progressive relaxation, hypnosis and autohypnosis, yoga, and massage therapy — differ from those introduced in Chapter 11, which dealt with thought and ideation.

Both the Jacobson and autogenic techniques involve administration of a relaxation protocol, the difference being that the latter is self-administered, while the former requires initial administrative leadership from another.

For the purposes of stress/anxiety management, hypnosis enables a performer to enter a state of trance, which simply means that his/her responses are restricted to a narrow range of environmental stimuli, so that the performer can concentrate on execution. Autohypnotic (self-administered) techniques are also available.

Yoga is presented not as a religious experience, but rather as a meditative technique that employs physical exercises known as asanas. Mindfulness is emphasized in yoga. Meta-analyses have shown the efficacy of yogic practice in recovery from pain experiences and exercise exertion, in cardiovascular health, and in reducing depression and negative affect.

Massage, or touch, therapy also (like yoga) contributes to muscular relaxation. In particular, massage therapy is related to alleviation of the perceptual-cognitive experience known as pain. The point is made that pain is something that accompanies injury, which is a concomitant of overuse or damage to various of the body's systems during or as a consequence of many types of performance.

13

BIOFEEDBACK TRAINING, CHEMICAL INTERVENTIONS, AND NUTRITIONAL CONSIDERATIONS

LEARNING OBJECTIVES

After reading this chapter, you should be able to:

- Describe a biofeedback system
- Explain how biofeedback training may be used as a stress and anxiety reduction intervention
- Identify four biofeedback measurements
- Describe the effect of beta-blockers upon anxiety response
- Discuss the relationship between at least three hormones and stress and anxiety response
- Discuss the connection between stress and nutrition

IMPORTANT TERMS

- Biofeedback system
- EMG
- EEG
- GSR
- Beta-blocker
- Adrenaline

- ACTH
- Epinephrine
- Testosterone

13.1 INTRODUCTION

Biofeedback interventions are effective stress management tools. They permit awareness of the physiological status and fluctuations of selected systems and organs of the body. Once apprised of the intensity and frequency of their systemic response to stressors, performers consciously strive to regulate them through cognitive processes (thinking). The simplest way to explain or define *biofeedback* is to suggest that it is a means to make its user more aware of what is happening in the body. It is a process that allows access to biological information not usually available to your consciousness.

Once you develop an awareness, for example, of how fast your heart or lungs are functioning per minute, you may then learn to voluntarily control the rate at which these organs perform. In other words, when stressors initiate the physiological reactions we examined in Chapter 2, the stressed individual is able to consciously countermand them. Blood flow to various body parts can be regulated, as can the amount of perspiration and heart and breathing rates. In the first section of this chapter, we will discuss biofeedback management.

The key concept underlying this approach to stress is learning. Feedback is an essential element of all learning. Biofeedback training is essentially a method of teaching subjects to self-regulate their organic and systemic responses. The learner becomes aware of bodily activities that are measured and amplified by biofeedback machines, which translate personal physiological data into interpretable information through use of various kinds of visual, auditory, or sensation feedback modalities. Typically, this feedback corresponds to functions such as heartbeat, muscle tension, brain wave activity, blood pressure, and peripheral skin temperature. Devices are also available that will provide feedback for such functions as penile erection and the production of hydrochloric acid in the digestive system.

With feedback training, the stressors themselves are not removed, lessened, or affected, but your response to these stressors is modified. Control of physiological arousal is a critical step in stress management. Imagine how much less troublesome stress would be if the physiological changes associated with it were drastically reduced; biofeedback training often accomplishes precisely this. It has been applied effectively in performance enhancement as well as anxiety, pain, and fatigue reduction.

Let us briefly review some of the stress-related physiological responses discussed in Chapter 2. Some of these are intricate in that they involve chains of reactions, where each reaction is instigated by an antecedent response. The following idealized scenario illustrates a series of such events that would be perceived as undesirable:

> Suddenly, an enzymatic increase occurs due to activation of a particular brain part that interprets an environmental event as harmful. Consequently, electrical-chemical impulses are transmitted along neural pathways to certain glands, whose hormonal productivity is increased. As a result, the blood's concentration of these hormones is elevated. The circulatory system carries these hormonal messages to especially sensitive tissue in the body, as well as to the central nervous system itself. In turn, the sympathetic nervous system is activated. Organic response quickly occurs as the body becomes aroused in its reaction to the stressor. Emotions change and the perceptual field narrows. Heartbeat quickens, breathing becomes rapid, and muscles tense.

However, if the stimulus precipitating these responses is, in reality, nonthreatening (as is often the case in anxiety or apprehension), then the entire physiological preparatory episode may be unnecessary, biologically costly, and in and of itself debilitating. Conscious control of these arousing processes may therefore be extremely desirable. Biofeedback training can provide for this.

Biofeedback permits selected information about biological functions to directly reach the client's perceptual awareness. Thus, the trial-by-error training emphasis is diverted from the therapist toward the subject. Moreover, with the use of the simple (but sometimes expensive) machinery typically used in this type of stress management program, the information provided is easily interpreted. It is simply a matter of understanding that as the visual or auditory frequency increases, there is a corresponding increase in the activity or intensity of the associated organ (e.g., the heart). Essentially, biofeedback enables a communication between subtle but meaningful "internal" bodily activity and conscious awareness. Without the benefit of this type of training, most of us would maintain awareness of only those functions that are reasonably dramatic and have external manifestations. We might very well be aware of elevated body temperatures when our forehead burns and headache strikes, but we would be unlikely to recognize the very slight changes in skin temperature of the finger due to constricted blood flow. We are certainly unlikely to know when alpha brain waves begin to predominate in relation to other waves.

Biofeedback converts internal physiological experiences into recognizable, measurable, and usable information. This feature distinguishes it from some of the other stress management approaches we have so far discussed. In Chapter 12 we dealt with autogenic and progressive muscle relaxation training. But for now, take note of the following criticism of these two approaches by Budzynski and Peffer (1980). A number of important implications favorable to biofeedback are identified:

> Although progressive relaxation and autogenic training are effective, the training can be lengthy, and success depends on the trainee's ability to discriminate extremely subtle proprioceptive, kinesthetic, and interoceptive sensations. Discriminations of this sort appear to be particularly difficult for those who most need the training; that is, individuals who have a chronically heightened arousal level. Because various components of their arousal patterns are frequently high, these individuals tend to become adapted to, and are therefore lacking in awareness of, these sensations. Consequently, training might be improved by the addition of a technique that would aid in the development of these fine discriminations (p. 419).

In addition, feedback can relieve the client from the responsibility of recording and storing the wealth of observations about physiological change. Data can be easily stored by recording devices incorporated into the feedback equipment, or recorded by the therapist.

13.2 BIOFEEDBACK MEASUREMENTS

Let us now describe in a little more detail some of the specific assessment procedures and their necessary equipment. Irrespective of the body functions to be measured and displayed, some procedures and pieces of equipment are common in virtually all forms of biofeedback training. Figure 13.1 illustrates the basic system.

The client is connected to electrodes that are attached to the skin (in standardized locations) above the organ or tissue about whose function information is sought. In some applications of feedback, such as muscle rehabilitation, where the detection of single motor neuron activity is significant, needle electrodes may be used. Basically, an electrode conducts or picks up electrical current or body heat. When muscle tissue contracts, electrical charges are emitted. Since the heart is a muscle,

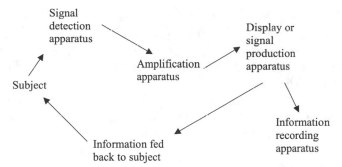

Figure 13.1   The basic biofeedback system.

each of its beats produces an electrical current. The conduction of the electrical impulse is usually facilitated by an electrolytic cream or solution and/or a sensor that is applied to the skin, on which an adhesive tab connected to the electrode is placed. The electrode is connected to an apparatus that adds up the signals within an appropriate time frame and converts the electrical charge to an observable stimulus such as a bleep on a screen, a light, or an auditory signal such as a buzz. The trainee is thus made aware of the magnitude or frequency of a particular organic function. She is then able to use cognitive strategies, such as imagery, in an effort to reduce or increase the signal.

It might be helpful to note that the performer does not wear electrodes or carry paraphernalia such as a signal amplification apparatus while competing or exhibiting his or her performance skills. Biofeedback training occurs during regular therapeutic sessions, wherein manipulation of physiological function is learned under the guidance of a professionally prepared therapist. This applies not only to cardiovascular feedback, but to all forms of biofeedback discussed in this chapter.

Biofeedback training is often only one of several techniques used by mental health professionals for purposes of stress and anxiety control. Stress management techniques are often combined with psychotherapy for purposes of relieving stress disorders, which are rarely isolated events and are often the symptoms of broader-based problems.

Many biological processes that were heretofore assumed not to be under conscious control have been shown to be manageable through biofeedback training. A number of biofeedback training modalities are in use, and as long as the basic training model presented in Figure 13.1 is implemented, any and all of them should be effective. These include electromyography (EMG) (muscle data), electroencephalography (EEG) (brain wave data), electrocardiogram (EKG) (heart data), galvanic skin response (GSR), and gastrointestinal (digestive) functions.

13.2.1 EMG Biofeedback

The electromyogram, or electromyograph, is a graphical record of muscle activity produced through application of the above model. EMG enables even very minute muscle activity to be perceived through auditory or visual senses.

EMG biofeedback can be useful in managing performance-related stress that is manifest through muscle tension. Excessive tension can play havoc with motor control and reduce the accuracy and efficiency of fine-motor acts. Undoubtedly, it would benefit the performer to be able to manipulate the degree of tension in selected muscle groups, particularly when they carry basic responsibility during certain skill executions. The billiard player, the archer, and the marksman are all eager to reduce tension in a wide array of muscle groups immediately prior to shooting. On the other hand, the discus thrower and weight lifter are likely to benefit from an increase in tension. The guitarist and flutist would probably strive for tension reduction, particularly in their hands and jaw muscles, respectively. An actor's performance would probably be best served by tension-level flexibility or adaptability. With the ability to willfully vary tension in a wide range of muscle groups, including those that regulate voice and speech during performance, the actor would satisfy the fluctuating demands of each scene, as well as the role itself.

Muscle relaxation may also help relieve emotional problems. Barbara Brown (1977, p.53) has written:

> Schultze and Luthe, from clinical work with autogenic training, suggested that primary muscle relaxation relieves emotional problems by decreasing muscle tension impulses to the cortex, in turn decreasing the cortical influence on lower muscle control centers keeping muscle tense in the defense posture. Many emotional problems, however, are complex, and in such cases the objective of EMG biofeedback as used to decrease muscle tension is to afford enough physical relaxation to allow for decreased mental tension impulses going to the central nervous system. This in turn appears to allow the patient's attention to shift to more productive memories, insights, and control which he and the therapist can use for the resolution of the emotional problem.

Brown suggests that EMG biofeedback be combined with other clinical methods in order to maximize success in emotional or psychosomatic illness. Boris Blumenstein (2002), who has applied biofeedback training to various issues in sports performance recommends use of EMG training together with relaxation and imagery.

The frontalis muscle of the forehead is the target muscle that many clinicians use in treating subjects with tension-related headaches. However, researchers who have attempted to establish the effectiveness of EMG biofeedback training in relieving tension headaches by coupling the frontalis with visual feedback have had difficulty in producing consistent findings. Auditory, rather than visual, feedback is more effective for tension-reduction programs based on the forehead muscles; with visual feedback, the placement of electrodes on the frontalis with eyes open permits artifact due to ocular movements.

13.2.2 EEG Biofeedback

Man is distinguishable from lower-order animals in many obvious ways. Perhaps the most dramatic and telling difference between humans and infrahumans is in brain development. The capacities of man's brain are vastly great (or so man continues to assume) when compared with those of any other species. At the expense of incurring the pitfalls of self-delusion, we believe that such capacities as abstract reasoning and high-level problem solving distinguish us from lower-order animals. The human brain, therefore, with its intricate and virtually incredible capabilities, is perhaps man's most distinctive possession, for it permits us to claim cognitive and intellective successes perhaps unknown to most other living creatures.

EEG is a biofeedback modality that provides an awareness of electrical activity in the brain. By measuring emitted brain waves, each of which roughly correlates with some form of brain state (such as sleeping, reading, or solving mathematical problems), the feedback trainee may learn to maintain desired wave patterns. For example, alpha waves are associated with wakeful relaxation and peacefulness. Being able to volitionally trigger this wave into predominance immediately prior to a performance that requires neuromuscular relaxation may be an extremely useful and profitable technique. Conversely, it would be to the performer's benefit to strategically "turn off" alpha before a performance requiring heightened arousal.

Volitional control over brain wave predominance results only from *learning*. This learning is accomplished through the use of feedback, which provides awareness of currently prevailing wave patterns. In addition to alpha, the activity of other waves are also identified through EEG feedback (for instance, delta, beta, and theta waves). Each wave is characterized by a range of frequencies per second. The hertz (Hz) is the unit of measurement that expresses this. The alpha wave has a frequency between 9 and 12 Hz. Beta wave voltage is approximately 13 to 28 Hz. Delta waves that occur during deep sleep have a frequency range of about 0.5 to 3 Hz. Electrodes attached to the scalp in accordance with the schema illustrated in Figure 13.1 measure these frequencies. Apparently, not only the predominant frequencies are relevant; the relative synchrony (in-phase properties) are also important.

Brain wave manipulations may also offer postperformance benefit. Such interventions may induce relaxation, even restful sleep, in an individual who would otherwise carry the heightened arousal that had benefited him during pre- or midperformance for hours after the performance was completed. However, in the case of relaxation as an objective, an important observation to note is that brain wave manipulation has not yet been conclusively shown to generalize its effects to other bodily functions such as that of muscle tissue. That is, if your desire is to reduce tension in the calf muscles, a conscious switch to alpha brain state may not produce the desired effect. It would be necessary to induce overall relaxation by using both EMG and EEG manipulations (Daniels & Hatfield, 1981).

13.2.3 EKG Biofeedback

In the Dutch language, the word corresponding to the English term *cardiac* begins with the letter *K*. Some of the original work done in this area was by Dutch physiologists, who published their observations in their native language. Thus, an EKG is a picture of the electrical currents emitted by the heart (or ECG, in English).

When we bear in mind the critical responses of the heart and vascular system in the body's reaction to stress, it is not difficult to understand how conscious control of the cardiovascular system would be extremely helpful in the performer's pursuit of optimal activation levels. The sympathetic nervous response to stress is complicated and biologically dramatic. Hormonal transport is conducted through the vascular network and results in marked physiological changes as you prepare biochemically to encounter your stressors. In fact, it may very well be that chronic sympathetic arousal for any reason or reasons may result in stress disorder. The rate of heartbeat and the pressure exerted upon the blood by the constricting and dilating muscular walls of the blood vessels are examples of controllable cardiovascular functions.

By attaching electrodes and thermisters (which measure temperature) to various parts of the body, many of these cardiovascular functions may be monitored in the general manner described in the opening paragraphs of this chapter. Accordingly, a performer may be trained to develop an awareness of "what's going on" cardiovascularly. The ability to control these functions at appropriate times may be subsequently acquired.

13.2.4 GSR Biofeedback

Reaction to psychological stress very often includes an increase in palmar perspiration. The sweat glands in the palms of the hands do not respond to heat and friction as do those located, for example, in the armpits and scalp. The palmar sweat glands are activated mostly by stress. Feedback machinery containing a device that measures small electrical currents conducted by the water in sweat provides an awareness of heightened arousal due to stress. This response is known as the GSR. Some researchers and clinicians also refer to it as the electrodermal response, or EDR.

In musical instrumental performance, gloves or hand coverings are usually not worn, because of delicate fingering requirements that would be undermined by the bulkiness of fabric, and stress-related palmar sweating can be a formidable problem in such instances. Today, many golf, tennis, and baseball players and weight lifters who must handle implements apply resin or other sticky substances in order to prevent their hands from slipping, and many of these athletes wear gloves. Because hand covering may not be compatible with scene motif, theatrical performers and dancers are not likely to include them in their costumes, and for them, sweaty palms are likely to be a terrible nuisance. Many a stage prop or dance partner has undoubtedly been dropped, erroneously placed, or moved due to stress-induced palmar perspiration.

13.2.4.1 Peripheral Skin Temperature Biofeedback Cool peripheral skin temperature (below 90° F) is often associated with heightened arousal due to stress (Budzynski & Peffer, 1980). With thermister electrode attachments to the skin, particularly the little finger or toe, a feedback system may be employed to train a subject to overcome the typical cause of this response, which is the vasoconstriction of small blood vessels servicing the area. Cold hands due to stress or any other reason can be detrimental to fine-motor performance that depends upon kinesthetic awareness. Thermal feedback training can be very useful in such cases. Often, voluntary manipulation or peripheral skin temperature correlates well with skeletal-muscle tonus control. Therefore, clients who learn to regulate skin temperatures (either upward or downward) usually have also acquired manipulative muscle tone capability. According to Brown (1977), an impressive variety of medical problems have been improved or solved entirely by use of temperature biofeedback training (including menstrual distress, essential hypertension, and migraine headaches).

13.2.5 Gastrointestinal Biofeedback

One of the most common, noticeable, and disturbing manifestations of preperformance anxiety is the unsettled stomach. The digestive tract is apparently a very vulnerable target for the stress offensive. Stressors seem to ravage the gastrointestinal area with greater fervor than any other organ or system. Preperformance "butterflies" (Taylor, 1983) or general stomach nervousness including cramps, spasms, diarrhea, and rumbling are frequently reported inconveniences related to stress.

Performers employ numerous creative, time-honored remedies and preventative measures to counteract nervous stomachs. Professor Jean Williams, presently a faculty member at the University of Arizona, Tucson, and a former graduate student in my program at Florida State University, remarked in a presentation to a meeting of the Sport Psychology Academy of the American Alliance for Health, Physical Education, Recreation, and Dance (Anaheim, California, April 1984) that we may not be able to entirely eradicate the butterflies in our bellies, "but we can sure make them fly in formation." Every performer has a stomach story. In fact, Taylor (1983) concludes by confessing that for him, "[f]inding ways to overcome 'nerves' for performance is part of the challenge and excitement of dance." One popular approach to managing such conditions is the use of *beta-blockers*, which will be discussed below.

Biofeedback training can also be helpful in combating gastrointestinal difficulty. Its implementation enables the performer to avoid the sometimes troublesome stigma of drug use concomitant with use of agents such as the beta-blockers. Unfortunately, gastrointestinal biofeedback involves techniques that are also troublesome and uncomfortable. Some sort of sensing device must be placed within the digestive tract. This may be accomplished by swallowing the device or inserting it anally. Impressive successes using very creative approaches have been reported in the research literature (Blumenstein, 2002).

Despite many inconveniences, the potential of gastrointestinal feedback training for resolving the debilitating effects of preperformance anxiety makes an attractive option. Clearly, it is an approach that requires a competent, well-trained, and experienced biofeedback therapist to establish and monitor the learning of the self-regulation techniques described in this section.

It is worth noting here that gastrointestinal disorder is highly correlated with inappropriate GSR responses. A person reacting unusually on GSR measures often identifies stomach problems as a most disturbing stress symptom. Therefore, GSR training may be used to alleviate or prevent gastrointestinal disturbances such as ulcer.

13.3 BIOFEEDBACK PROCEDURES

A number of biofeedback approaches and their anticipated beneficial applications have already been reviewed in this chapter. What needs to be emphasized at this point is that considerable care must be taken in the selection of appropriate feedback strategies for specific stress- and anxiety-related problems in individual performers. The same procedures may not be appropriate for all individuals, despite similar stress symptoms. Biofeedback diagnostic procedures may be used to determine an individual's unique way of responding to stress.

Essentially, feedback training is a learning experience. The effectiveness of any learning program varies with a long list of factors. These include degree of motivation for learning, previous experiences, sensitivity toward information being fed back, and the form in which feedback is made available. The therapist should therefore conduct both informal and formal inquiry into the client's overall physical and psychological health, as well as the above-mentioned parameters. Clients should be asked to respond to questions (administered in written or oral form) that probe important factors relating to readiness for self-regulation training. Clients seeking this service should anticipate such inquiry. The initial concern of both clinician and client is therefore two-pronged: (1) Am I (the client) ready for this type of learning/training? and (2) Which kind of feedback modality is indicated for my (the client's) stress-related problem?

There are, however, a number of steps that should be taken irrespective of modality choice. One such general approach is outlined by Zaichkowsky (1982), one of the first to apply biofeedback to motor performance. Zaichkowsky describes the procedures he uses when working with athletes troubled by competitive stress. Following is a summary of these procedures slightly modified by my own recommendations.

In the initial interview with the athlete, his or her athletic history is discussed. During the interview, an attempt is made to determine whether the stress-related problem involves hyper- or hypoarousal. Short- and long-term goals are also discussed. Some standardized tests are administered (such as the State–Trait Anxiety Inventory and the Test of Attentional and Interpersonal Style). The strategy for the training program is established with information derived from the interview.

In the typical second session, as described by Zaichowsky, baseline data are collected on selected feedback measures. Information about the program's goals, characteristics, and potentialities are provided.

Next, the athlete is encouraged to use feedback in order to change EMG, EKG, GSR, etc., values. The athlete is encouraged to somehow experiment with cognitive intervention (such as thoughts, imagery, etc.) in order to alter the feedback displays.

Relaxation techniques are taught to the athlete, and cognitive strategies are refined. These become tools to be used in self-regulation training, and consequently tools for moderating reactions to stress.

Home practice is assigned to the athletes. Biofeedback training as a learning experience involving skill acquisition (i.e., conscious control of physiological responses) requires practice. An individual's progress is therefore a result of motivation to practice.

Analogous general steps are also identified by Brown (1977) and Budzynski and Peffer (1980), although nuances of procedural differences are present in their respective approaches.

13.4 BETA-BLOCKERS

One learns through the grapevine that many desperate performing artists take beta-adrenergic blocking agents, or *beta-blockers,* in pill form. Although reported use of beta-blockers among athletes is uncommon, large numbers of musicians use such interventions in order to control performance anxiety. A survey by the International Conference of Symphony Orchestra Musicians, which represents the 51 largest orchestras in the United States, indicated that well over 25 percent of musicians queried had at one time or another used beta-blockers. This survey was conducted in 1987, and it is likely that the number of users today is considerably higher.

Consider the following testimony provided by a flutist who was for years afflicted by severe performance jitters (Tindall, 2004):

"My hands were so cold and wet. I thought I'd drop my flute," Ms. McClain said recently, remembering a performance at the National Flute Convention in the late 1980's. Her heart thumped loudly in her chest, she added; her mind would not focus, and her head felt as if it were on fire. She tried to hide her nervousness, but her quivering lips kept her from performing with sensitivity and nuance.

However much she tried to relax before a concert, the nerves always stayed with her. But in 1995, her doctor provided a cure, a prescription medication called propranolol. "After the first time I tried it," she said, "I never looked back. It's fabulous to feel normal for a performance."

Ms. McClain, a grandmother who was then teaching flute at Rhodes College in Memphis, started recommending beta blocking drugs like propranolol to adult students affected with performance anxiety. And last year she lost her job for doing so.

Do beta-blocking drugs work? How do they work? Are they safe? What exactly are they? First, let's address the question, What exactly are beta-blockers?

Many of our body's major organs contain beta-receptors, which receive fight-or-flight messages, as touched upon in previous chapters (1, 6). The hormone *adrenaline*, or epinephrine, stimulates responses from the sympathetic nervous system and provides such messages. Reception of these kinds of stimuli in turn initiates chains of physiological reactions that prepare the body for action and may be indicted as one causative factor in tummy turmoil. Here's where the beta-blocking drugs come in. Their effect is to arrest or interfere with the production of adrenaline. They prevent these stimulating signals from reaching the receptors in the heart, lungs, and numerous other organs.

Fear of performing inadequately during audition and not winning the available position, anxiety about being evaluated negatively by others, and losing one's place in a piece are frightening possibilities of which musicians are often aware. Referred to collectively as *stage fright*, these thoughts are not alleviated by blockading beta-receptors, but the consequences associated with the physiological activation caused by them often are. At least they may be made more bearable. To this end, we may conclude that beta-blockers do work (Lehrer, Rosen, Kostis, & Greenfield, 1987; Neftel et al., 1982).

My strong conviction is that there are many other effective ways of dealing with performance anxiety that are preferable to beta-blockers. But they require skill development and practice. Considerable treatment of these preferred strategies has been included in the two preceding chapters. But because beta-blockers have become so inculcated in the classical-music performance culture, I feel obliged to include a discussion of their use here.

It is my belief that an essential part of preparing for a career or high status in sports, dance, theater, or musical performance is anxiety management. Use of chemical agents (assuming their effectiveness) deprives the performer of the opportunity to develop coping skills; and although believed not to be physiologically addictive, chemical blocking agents may well produce a psychological dependence from which it may eventually be difficult to disengage. The cognitive strategies and techniques presented in Chapters 10 and 11 provide long-lasting and perfectly safe ways of addressing performance anxiety. Beta-blockers, at best, are quick fixes. Some authorities, such as Nagel (1993), argue that stage fright among musicians is causally related to an individual's life history, and its symptoms are manifestations of complex unconscious processes. If this speculation is correct, then chemical solutions are not likely to be the most effective or sensible way of addressing the problem.

Are beta-blockers safe? Many would argue that they are, but bear in mind that one may obtain beta-blockers only with a physician's prescription. Originally developed as medication for heart problems and not intended for anxiety control, beta-blockers were first prescribed for abnormal heart rhythms and disorders such as angina (heart pain). Blockers may cause serious medical problems in consistent users, especially those who are afflicted by slow heart rate, bronchial asthma, low blood pressure, and diabetes.

Responses to beta-blocking drugs vary from person to person and may be dose specific as well. A performer would be ill advised to use a blocker for the first time prior to a major performance. Under a physician's direction it would be advisable to search for the appropriate performance dose during a few experimental trials. This is also preferable in order to be sure that no adverse reactions are related to its use. Certain of the beta-blockers have been linked to hallucinations, nightmares, and depression. Those blockers that cross the blood–brain barrier more easily may generate such negative side effects. A dose of 5 to 20 milligrams is considered moderate and, if taken only on occasion, is not likely to result in the aforementioned symptoms in healthy persons.

Not all beta-blockers are the same, or act on the receptors in identical ways. Some are unable to enter the brain easily and are therefore not as likely to produce the above effects. Those that are directed to beta-receptors outside of the brain seem to have a greater impact upon anxiety. Most beta-blockers exert their maximal impact at about an hour to an hour and a half after ingestion. They are therefore not effective when taken during performance.

Perhaps the most commonly used beta-blocker of the many available today is Inderal (propranolol hydrochloride). Varying degrees of its success in performance-anxiety management continue to be reported anecdotally, with some musicians insisting that without its use they would never have achieved the level of accomplishment they now claim. Conversely, others maintain that performances supported by chemical agents such as beta-blockers, although executed with decreased levels of anxiety, are lackluster and without the element of intensity so necessary for superlative execution (Green, 1980).

For some reason, athletes do not report use of beta-blockers to nearly the same extent as musicians. Why? I'm not sure. However, I am aware that in some Olympic sports, such as riflery and bobsledding, beta-blockers are banned. Games administrators and authorities believe that the playing field becomes uneven when their use is permitted. In shooting sports, beta-blockage has the potential to steady the hand so that tremor, for example, would not interfere with a timely squeezing of the trigger. Perhaps for this reason, those who use blockers may be at an advantage. Why shouldn't we also be concerned with the uneven playing field on which musicians must compete and entertain when experiencing the enormously anxiety producing and feared audition? Perhaps regulation of foreign substances should be introduced into this domain as it is in sports. Would musicians who use beta-blockers have an edge over those who don't? (An interesting question.) One thing is clear, however. Beta-blockers will not enhance skilled behavior but may reduce anxiety that inhibits optimal performance.

13.5 BIOCHEMICAL CHANGES AND CHEMICAL INTERVENTIONS

In Chapter 2, attention was directed to our body's organic responses to various environmental stressors, such as stimuli interpreted as harmful, risky, or potentially troublesome, and the behavioral and somatic reactions they tend to elicit. We therefore spoke of changes in blood pressure and other cardiovascular and respiratory functions, as well as increases in sweat volume and muscle tension. It was noted that individuals respond to stressors and anxiety-provoking stimuli in person-specific fashion. Some people are "sweaters," while others are more inclined to react with dry mouth or tremors. The term *homeostasis* was introduced and defined as a condition in which biochemical equilibrium was achieved, with the bodily fluids containing just the right amount of the many constituents necessary for optimal psychological health. But our main concerns were with reactions that were more or less readily detectable because of their surface manifestations. That is, they were seen or sensed in some dramatic way.

In this section, our focus is directed at acute changes in biochemistry as associated with anxiety and stress, but at the *hormonal* level. We'll deal briefly with what's going on inside your body about which you are likely to have absolutely no clue. We speak now of products of the endocrine glands that are shunted into the bloodstream for rapid distribution. Known as *hormones*, these substances exert a wide range of powerful influences on the functions of all major organs and systems. For our purpose, I focus on adrenocorticotropic hormone (ACTH), aldosterone and the catecholamines, and testosterone.

13.5.1 Adrenocorticotropic Hormone

ACTH is produced in the brain — more specifically, in the anterior portion of the *pituitary gland*. The pituitary is stimulated to this end by signals from another brain center, the *hypothalamus*. In chain-like fashion, ACTH next stimulates the outer portion of the adrenal gland (*cortex*) to secrete the hormone *cortisol*. During stress responses, ACTH production is increased, and thus cortisol is as well. Cortisol then triggers activity in the sympathetic nervous system such as those delineated in Chapter 5. When we are in the throes of a stress or anxiety response, ACTH levels rise, adrenal function increases, and the fight-or-flight reaction kicks in. For this reason ACTH is referred to as a *stress hormone*. But bear in mind that an overabundance of these hormones may be metabolically disruptive in that it may generate feelings of fatigue and insomnia. Also, aging is associated with increasing levels of cortisol, with higher levels present in the elderly.

13.5.2 Aldosterone and the Catecholamines

Aldosterone is also secreted by the cortex of the adrenal glands (one atop each kidney) and is very much involved in stress response. The innermost part of each gland, the adrenal *medulla,* produces the catecholamines *epinephrine* and *norepinephrine,* which in turn stimulate general physiological excitation in preparation for fight or flight. High levels of catecholamines are typically reduced when environmental stressors are removed or when effective intervention strategies are introduced (West, Otte, Gehr, Johnson, & Mohr, 2004). These hormones are detectable in body fluids such as blood plasma and saliva, and their concentrations are indicators of degree of stress or anxiety experienced by an individual. Catecholamines are therefore often used as measures of dependent variables in research projects. They are used as indicators of stress reactions.

13.5.3 Testosterone

Low concentrations of this hormone in certain body fluids may be indicative of stress response. The more stress, the lower the testosterone level. Its particular molecular structure enables it to be classified as a *steroid,* as also is cortisol. When stress is reduced, testosterone levels in saliva and plasma rise (Cruess et al., 2000; Bahrke, Yesalis, & Wright, 1990). In males, low levels of this hormone are also associated with depression, reduced sexual drive, and erectile disturbance. And although typically appearing in males in higher concentrations, testosterone is also to be found in females. Testosterone levels in males are highest in the mornings and progressively decrease during the day. Research that studies stress response by assessing levels of this hormone should therefore take cognizance of its diurnal variations in the investigation's design.

Interestingly, testosterone levels have been shown to increase before a sporting event for both participants and spectators, and to decrease in both groups upon loss of the contest (Bernhardt, Dabbs, Fielden, & Lutter, 1998; Booth, Shelley, Mazur, Tharp, & Kittok, 1989). Evidently, loss of competition is stressful for both participants and those who are vicariously involved in the activity, namely, the fans. In a nutshell, feelings of success are associated with increase in testosterone levels, while failure is associated with a decrease.

Too much exercise (overdoing it) as well as lack of exercise will also reduce testosterone levels in males. For instance, prolonged endurance training is likely to cause a decrease in levels, since testosterone is also needed to maintain muscle health, and the "supply" may be temporarily reduced or depleted. In Chapter 14 you will see that when done excessively, or improperly, exercise becomes a stressor.

Where does testosterone come from? It is converted from a substance known as DHEA (dehydroepiandrosterone) that is produced in the adrenal glands. The adrenal glands thus play a major role in stress response.

13.6 NUTRITIONAL CONSIDERATIONS

You are what you eat. You ask, "So, what else is new?" since you've come across this platitude before, and you consider it to be trite. But might there not be substance to this platitude? Might there not be a real link between what you eat or drink and the degree of anxiety and stress that you experience? And for that matter, might there not be a connection between what you eat and the way in which you cope with anxiety and stress? Knowledgeable scientists say yes (Cartwright et al., 2003; Lieberman, 2003). Of equal interest is yet another, but related question: In addition to what is eaten, under what conditions is the eating taking place? Or, phrased as a statement, the patterns of your food intake — or how you eat — may be as important as what you eat (Hill, 1991).

There appear to be connections between stress and nutrition, and nutrition and performance. It is these associations that interest us most. Two perspectives surface with regard to the alleged linkage between stress and nutrition: (1) how nutritional factors may be causally related to stress and anxiety response, and (2) how nutritional interventions may mitigate stress and anxiety response.

13.6.1 Nutritional Factors as Causes of Stress Reactivity

In a fascinating and compelling argument, Lonsdale (1986) reasons that in each and every case of disease, there is a fundamental interplay among three variables: *genetics, stress,* and *nutrition*. He observes that only nutrition may be manipulated, since barring application of sophisticated technological intervention, genetic influence cannot be curtailed volitionally. In other words, the influence of one's genetic composition is stable and internal. Stress variables, on the other hand, typically, or at least most often, derive from external sources that are not likely to be under our immediate control. As was indicated in previous chapters, these variables differ in intensity, frequency, and origin.

We may be able to regulate the ways in which we respond to stress stimuli, but we have little direct control over the multitude of sources that generate them. Unfortunately, they assault us regularly. But fortunately, nutritional factors are mostly within our control. True, even today, people in various countries are nutritionally deprived and challenged, but in advanced Western societies nutritional problems revolve around choice of food (diet) rather than nutritional availability. People often eat poorly not because of dire need, but because their choices are ill conceived. These poor choices are manifestations of three factors: ignorance about the essentials of what is referred to as a balanced diet; insufficient discipline to avoid unhealthy foods; and failure (laziness) to secure and prepare nutritious foodstuffs.

In teenagers, greater amounts of stress have been found to be associated with high intake of fatty foods, low levels of fruit and vegetable intake, high levels of snacking, and reduced likelihood of daily breakfast consumption (Cartwright et al., 2003). These findings, based upon a survey of more than 4,000 American teenage subjects, suggest that stress response may contribute to vulnerability to disease by encouraging poor dietary choices. And not incidentally, these findings cut across gender, body type, socioeconomic status, and ethnicity. They suggest that when we grapple with environmental stressors, the tendency to make improper decisions about what, when, how, and even where we eat increases (e.g., eating on the run).

As noted previously, participation in sports carries a high probability of physical injury. I include dance performance in the category of sports, since it is characterized by rigorous, gross-motor activity done within a competitive framework. Athletes, and dancers in particular, are continuously beset by physical stressors that require execution of explosive movements, rapid changes in direction while moving, and the generation of large quantities of muscular force.

Hence, they are frequently injured. And injury itself is a significant stress stimulus. Furthermore, because injury increases the body's energy requirements (needed for repair), appropriate dietary measures are indicated.

Anabolic (tissue-building) metabolism requires minimal amounts of dietary factors such as glycogen (sugar), protein, and fat. Protein is a critical component of the diet of injured persons. Energy requirements (derived from food) increase according to injury type and nature of the stress and the stress response. For example, rehabilitation from a burn injury requires considerable amounts of dietary protein (Gillespie & Devine, 1982). Failure to provide adequate amounts of dietary factors during the body's search for homeostasis following injury may in and of itself be stressful.

Evidence is also available that supports a connection between nutrition and cognitive function (Blundell, Gumaste, Handley, & Dye, 2003; Kaplan, Greenwood, Winocur, & Wolever, 2000). A drink enriched with glucose was shown to improve cognitive function in subjects with poor glucose regulation and low levels of cognitive ability. Similar findings were also reported with subjects who had no glucose regulatory or cognition problems. In both subject sets, improvement in cognitive function was observed.

In another study (Kaplan, Greenwood, Winocur, & Thomas, 2001), a carbohydrate supplement was associated with improved memory performance. Mood and vigilance were also observed to improve as a result of dietary carbohydrate supplementation. *Vigilance* involves detecting and responding to stimuli over long periods of time, especially against a background of distracting stimuli. In many sports performances, vigilance is critical to success, and carbohydrate deficiency in the diet may therefore place an athlete at a significant disadvantage. Perhaps neurotransmission efficiency was improved by carbohydrate supplementation in the aforementioned study. The neurotransmitter *serotonin*, known to be associated with alertness, may be implicated. It is manufactured in the brain from *tryptophan,* which has been observed to increase in the body in response to a carbohydrate-rich snack (Lieberman, Falco, & Slade, 2002). Vigor, one of six subscales of the Profile of Mood States (POMS), was also shown to increase in the same study, as a consequence of supplemental carbohydrate.

Caffeine also has undeniable beneficial effects on vigilance, particularly among sleep-deprived individuals. It tends to stimulate adrenal gland function and consequently stimulate the nervous system (Lieberman, 2003).

The research literature is clear in suggesting that optimal mental as well as physical performance is contingent upon proper nutrition. Children in particular perform relatively poorly in school when they have had no breakfast (Bellisle, 2004). It appears that optimal brain function is dependent upon an adequate glucose (sugar) supply. This reservoir is decreased overnight, and an appropriate breakfast meal tends to replenish it. A key word here is *adequate*, which does not for a moment suggest that children should overload their various physiological systems with sugary foods.

13.6.2 Vitamins and Minerals

Cognitive function is also highly contingent upon vitamins and minerals in the diet. Vitamins C, E, and the B complex (vitamins B_1 to B_{12}) play important roles in thinking and memory (Craig, 1986). In times of stress, hormonal function (discussed previously) may result in the body's excretion of minerals such as chromium, copper, magnesium, iron, and zinc. If losses are not replaced, deficiency may result in an increase in stress hormone production. The body's need for vitamin C is higher during times of emotional and physical stress. Two primary storage areas, the adrenal glands and the pituitary gland, may become depleted during prolonged stress response. That is, stress uses up a considerable amount of stored vitamin C, a consequence of which may be a decreased resistance to infection, which, ironically, is likely to increase stress. The mineral iron is needed for certain neurotransmitters to function properly. Iron deficiency may therefore cause decreased work performance.

13.7 SUMMARY

Among specific biofeedback applications are EMG, EEG, cardiovascular feedback, GSR, peripheral skin temperature feedback, and gastrointestinal feedback. All are able to assist performers in their efforts to manage stress and anxiety responses. An important point emphasized repeatedly is that biofeedback training is a learning process, wherein the learner/client is made aware of his internal, physiological activity. Performers are encouraged and taught to use thoughts, images, and other conscious interventions to manipulate physiological reactions that cause discomfort or performance decrement. A biofeedback model is available for use in any and all applications irrespective of the physiological system targeted.

Beta-blocking agents are often employed as a strategy for performance-related stress management, although their use involves considerations of their impact upon human physiology and safety, as well as ethics. A possible stigma is involved for a performer who is known to take a chemical agent.

Biochemical changes at the hormonal level is associated with anxiety and stress.

Nutritional factors may be causally related to stress/anxiety responses.

14

EXERCISE

LEARNING OBJECTIVES

After reading this chapter, you should be able to:

- Define exercise, aerobic exercise, aerobic fitness, and anaerobic exercise
- Describe the physiological changes that accompany exercise
- Discuss the difficulties involved in researching stress modification through exercise
- Expand upon the role of biochemistry in the control of stress via exercise
- Describe exercise as a socially acceptable arena for emotional release and sensation seeking
- Explain how exercise may induce stress and anxiety
- Speculate upon the causes for exercise addiction

IMPORTANT TERMS

- Exercise
- Aerobic exercise
- Anaerobic exercise
- Aerobic fitness

- Neurotransmitter
- Exercise addiction
- Beta-endorphin

14.1 INTRODUCTION

In the section "Performance as a Physical Experience" in Chapter 4, important functional and structural characteristics of the skeletal and muscular systems were described. Comments about the fuel necessary for muscular contraction were also offered, and a few basic physiological concepts relative to exercise were reviewed.

As we proceed to make judgments about the value of exercise in stress management, it becomes necessary to establish an operational understanding of the term *exercise* itself. Exactly what is exercise?

Undoubtedly the term has something to do with physical effort and activity. For our purpose, let us define exercise in the following way: *Exercise* refers to sustained, regularly conducted, rigorous physical activity designed to enhance motor skill and neuromuscular coordination, increase level of fatigue resistance, and improve muscular strength, endurance, power, agility, flexibility and balance (all of the aforementioned are the components of fitness). Discomfort, fatigue, and perhaps joy and satisfaction may also be parts of the definition of exercise, depending upon who you are. Exercise has different meanings for different people (Berger, Pargman, & Weinberg, 2000). Sometimes, its goal is to improve cardiovascular status. Sometimes, its emphasis is upon skill or ability improvement. Sometimes, the aim is stress reduction. It is with this latter objective that we are primarily concerned.

Irrespective of its meaning or purposes, physical exercise, in one way or another, results in certain adaptive physiological responses. These responses may be categorized according to two general kinds of activities: *aerobic* and *anaerobic* exercise. The essential difference between the two lies in the way in which energy for work (muscular contraction) is made available. It is important to note that the term *exercise* should not bring to mind only sportlike activities or experiences taking place in gymnasiums or athletic environments. An hour seated in front of a piano keyboard practicing Chopin etudes or standing in front of an orchestra conducting a major symphonic work is also a rigorous physical challenge that satisfies the definition of exercise. Needless to say, dancers exercise at intense levels, and actors frequently train physically in order to be adequately prepared to meet the fitness demands of certain roles.

14.2 AEROBIC EXERCISE

Technically, *aerobic* means "with oxygen." Oxygen is critical to the metabolic function of your body's cells, and without an adequate supply of oxygen most tissues (particularly brain cells) would die within a few minutes. In aerobic exercise, oxygen from environmental air is readily available. Typically, it enters the lungs during rhythmic breathing cycles, such as during jogging or swimming.

The oxygen (O_2) in the air (about 21 percent of environmental air is oxygen) makes its way to the heart, which then distributes it throughout the body via blood-pumping action. Arteries and arterioles (the smaller blood vessels branching off of arteries) carry oxygenated (rich in O_2) blood to the cells. Ultimately, "used" blood from which oxygen has been taken is carried back to the heart through the veins. This blood is then directed to the lungs for oxygenation (O_2 pickup) and removal of waste gas. This cycle is repeated continually during aerobic exercise.

Regular participation in rigorous physical activity (training) results in a strengthening of your capacity to bring in environmental air and deliver extracted oxygen to body cells. *Fitness,* or more specifically *aerobic fitness*, is the term applied to your ability to do this efficiently. A unit of measurement used to assess your fitness is called *maximal oxygen consumption*. The higher your maximal oxygen consumption, the more oxygen you are able to bring in and use to fuel your metabolic activities within a given interval of time. Your ability to use aerobic processes for satisfying oxygen requirements correlates positively with the duration of your exercise. When anaerobic metabolic waste products accumulate, you are compelled to reduce the rigor with which you exercise or to stop altogether.

When the intensity of your physical work is low, most of your fuel (oxygen) is derived aerobically. Cycling and walking are additional examples of aerobic activities. When you cycle or walk at moderate speeds, your air and oxygen intake should be sufficient to meet the metabolic needs of muscle and other tissues. However, when the rate at which you perform exercise is increased to the extent that your supply is no longer adequate, such as in sprint running or competitive cycling, other fuel-releasing pathways take over.

14.3 ANAEROBIC EXERCISE

When short bouts of high-intensity exercise are performed, such as sprinting free-style for 25 yards in the pool or pressing a very heavy weight, there is insufficient time for the body to implement aerobic processes. The fuel for these kinds of activities must therefore come from chemical actions without oxygen. And that is what the term *anaerobic* means — "without oxygen."

Anaerobic pathways permit a relatively rapid release of energy, but only for very short periods of time, approximately a minute or so. Beyond this time, the performer experiences enough fatigue to cause a slowdown of the activity, or its complete cessation. Lactic acid, a waste product of muscular activity, builds up in the muscle tissue itself and eventually in the blood. It causes a subsequent increase in breathing rate in order to force the body to inspire more air, and it interferes with further muscular contraction.

When you train in order to improve anaerobic fitness, your muscular strength, endurance, and power are increased. *Strength* is defined as the amount of force invested in a maximal muscular contraction. *Muscular endurance* refers to the number of repetitions of a muscular contraction produced within a period of about one to two minutes. The amount of time you are able to sustain a contraction (e.g., hanging from a bar) is also a measure of your endurance.

The individual who is well prepared for physical activity of all sorts, that is, who is said to be in "good shape," has well-developed aerobic as well as anaerobic energy-releasing systems. In order to attain this condition, one must train aerobically and anaerobically, for the two develop independently of each other.

14.4 OTHER PHYSIOLOGICAL DIMENSIONS OF EXERCISE

As we've already acknowledged, the animal cell's need for oxygen is constant and critical. The aroused organism has even greater need for this essential fuel. As the body is exercised, chains of biochemical reactions occur, which result in increased oxygen supplies to the tissues.

However, other demands also arise, and therefore increased oxygen supply is not the exclusive biological imperative of the body during rigorous activity. When you exercise, not only does your breathing rate increase, but body temperature is elevated. The volume of perspiration also increases, and so does the amount of *neurotransmitters*. These are chemicals (such as norepinephrine) that carry messages from nerves to muscles and dictate muscular contraction. Exercise also results in chemical by-products other than lactic acid that make their way to the blood. In sum, exercise is highly activating and results in significant physiological change with which the body is obliged to cope.

The question before us now concerns the relationship between exercise and stress reactivity. More specifically, does sustained and rigorous physical activity inhibit some of the negative consequences of stress? Is exercise somehow capable of helping us manage stress, and if so, why? What are the mechanics, principles, and models that account for this capability?

14.5 EXERCISE AS A STRESS MANAGEMENT TOOL

Physical exercise has many therapeutic objectives: regulation of body weight, neuromuscular rehabilitation, and cardiovascular rejuvenation, to name but a few. Ample research has demonstrated the integrity of each of these applications. Unlike the aforementioned and frequently stated objectives of exercise, a very meager amount of research has been accomplished relative to the effect of exercise on stress reactivity.

Undoubtedly, the kind of research necessary to establish exercise as a control agent for stress reaction is very difficult to implement. First of all, exercise reactions fluctuate very broadly within individuals. Although this would be a problem in research designs that investigate any hypothesized correlate of stress, it is particularly irksome in the case of exercise.

It is often difficult to distinguish between responses due to the stress of exercise and the singular stress reaction toward which the therapeutic exercise is directed. Additionally, fitness levels (readiness to perform fairly rigorous exercise) are difficult to standardize in experimental subjects, even if relevant variables such as age, sex, height, weight, occupation, etc., are controlled. Furthermore, the dose, or exercise prescription (intensity and duration), necessary to evoke a predictable therapeutic effect is not easy to determine. This factor alone merits investigation as an independent research variable. A dependent variable owes its observed change in value to the impact or effectiveness of the independent variable. For example, in a research design that examines the effect of chemical A upon cellular growth, cellular growth would be the dependent variable and chemical A the independent variable. For these reasons, there does indeed exist a lack of available research findings that support a case for exercise being a robust and practical modifier of stress reactivity.

14.6 EXERCISE AND STRESS

Despite the paucity of research, there is some evidence that exercise can be effective in the management of performance-related stress. I will now examine some of the relationships between exercise and stress reactivity. First, general biochemical considerations will be addressed. Then, physical fitness in relation to anxiety will be discussed. Following this,

I will examine an interesting psychological framework that suggests that some performers have particularly high needs for stimulation. In such persons, exercise may be a readily available source of arousal and therefore a form of (needed) stress. Lastly, I will discuss the notion of exercise addiction, which implies that those who regularly exercise may develop a physiological dependency upon the chemical by-products of rigorous exercise.

14.6.1 Physiological Considerations

When exercise is sustained for approximately 35 minutes or more, when it is administered regularly for a minimum of three times per week, and when it is rhythmic (swimming, cycling, rowing), physiological changes may be anticipated. Aerobic energy-releasing mechanisms (release of oxygen) become strengthened. The ability of the lungs to bring in environmental air and expel "waste" air with each breathing cycle is improved through regular aerobic exercise. The heart muscle becomes stronger and more efficient and consequently beats less frequently each minute. Blood pressure is also lowered as a result of training. If caloric intake remains unchanged, stored body fat is likely to diminish, and therefore the circulatory system must service a decreased amount of living tissue. Meaningful long-term effects of exercise are likely to appear between the sixth and the eighth week of training.

But, there are also short-term outcomes of exercise. For instance, even a single bout of rigorous physical activity results in the burning up of products such as catecholamines and other stress hormones; fluctuations in blood glucose (sugar) levels; changes in pituitary, thyroid, and gonadal activity; and increases in salivary, immunoglobulin, and urinary cortisol levels. By assessing the magnitude of these changes, scientists can determine if stress responses are actually occurring. Some of these were also addressed in Chapter 13 as hormonal responses to stress. Here they are discussed as exercise by-products. All of these changes improve general health and result in an improved ability to cope with the biological consequences of stress.

In Chapter 2, we reviewed Selye's well-known three-stage model for human stress response. The general adaptation syndrome (GAS) describes the biological ways in which all of us react to stressors, irrespective of their origin or kind. If persistently offensive, stressors will predictably impose very serious physical consequences such as disease, change in organ size and function, and even death. In particular, the sympathetic nervous system increases its activity when stress occurs. The adrenal glands become activated, both cortically and medullarly.

These glands, which are located just above the kidneys, have two functional parts — an inner medulla and an outer cortex. Each is responsible for dramatic physiological activity. For example, the medulla, when stimulated by a response to stress from the sympathetic nervous system, releases adrenaline. This substance in turn causes an increase in blood pressure and a constriction of blood vessels servicing the skin surface.

Adrenaline (also known as epinephrine, as discussed in Chapter 13) is one of a group of body chemicals known as catecholamines. They are produced in greater quantities during stressful situations. In fact, presence of catecholamines in the urine may be used as a test for stress. Some of these chemicals are believed to be related to the feelings of anxiousness accompanying the stress response (Chapter 6). The adrenal cortex produces other hormones in response to stress that are physiologically critical to well-being.

In essence, what the brain is doing in response to its perception of the presence of a stressor is preparing the body for "action" — that is, in the words of the famous physiologist Walter Cannon, fight or flight. Cannon (1932) coined this phrase in order to depict the stress-induced arousal we have been referring to. His speculation is that humans are genetically programmed to respond this way to perceived stressors for protective purposes.

Environmental stimuli or signals that are interpreted by the organism to be harmful in some way are stressors. In response to this perception, the sympathetic nervous system mobilizes an array of physiological defenses. All sorts of complex biochemical activity occurs, which in turn triggers self-protective changes in organ and system function. Some of these were detailed in Chapters 2 and 13.

The point here is that in the aerobically well conditioned individual, many of these activating physiological responses occur at minimal levels. Elevated aerobic fitness secured through regular exercise may promote a transferable readiness to cope with the physiological correlates of stress reactivity that are problematic. Since regular, sustained rigorous physical activity tends to strengthen physiological mechanisms, regular exercise may be helpful in preparing your body to respond with less severity. By way of analogy, we would expect a trained competitive swimmer to surface and swim to shore after his or her boat had capsized more easily than a person who had never trained as a swimmer. However, this same swimmer may also be able to generalize his physiological fitness to nonexercise stressful situations.

This hypothesized preventative function of exercise is supported by data from investigations by Fusco and Gutin (1974) and Zimkin (1964).

Perhaps a good way to summarize this section is to borrow a statement from Gutin (1983, p. 97). He says:

> Although the physiological mechanisms behind simple resistance and cross-resistance are incompletely understood, their implications for health are enormous. It is partially through this ability to increase general resistance to stress that exercise improves health and longevity.

14.6.2 Exercise and Mood

Exercise interacts with our body's physiological responses to stressors in yet another beneficial way. We have already observed the nature of the involvement of the sympathetic nervous system in stress responsiveness. As Cannon has so unforgettably suggested, evolutionary forces require that humans prepare systemically to run or fight in the face of noxious stimuli. However, many taboos today prevent us from doing either. The result is that we may be temporarily committed to an inoperable state of physiological arousal. Our biochemistry is geared for confrontation and we are ready for attack and parry, yet we have been socialized to swallow hard and count to ten. In the large majority of social situations, we are obliged to avoid fighting (perhaps with the exception of law enforcement and military circumstances). We have been taught that to swat, slam, or slap another is immoral, illegal, or at least improper. Only in competitive sports are these behaviors permissible in highly circumscribed ways. Most of us have been conditioned to consider flight as a cowardly action, so it is an alternative that we find repugnant.

But many of us have learned that fairly rigorous exercise at this time is marvelously helpful in diffusing the emotional upheaval associated with the biochemical activation that typically results in somatic anxiety (and overt physiological discomfort), as compared with cognitive anxiety (which is associated with responses such as worry, insomnia, and difficulty in concentration). A visit to the woodpile where we may chop away with reckless abandon, a vigorous jog, or something similarly physical often helps us blow off steam and feel better, in a rather inexpensive way. An admittedly simplistic explanation is that with exercise we are able to "use up" the available physiological charge that has been primed in readiness for fight or flight. We unload pent-up emotional as well as biochemical ammunition and reduce or diffuse tendencies. Although some researchers (Silva & Schulta, 1984) speculate that vigorous physical activity may actually induce irritability because of lactic acid buildup, most available research findings suggest otherwise. Of course, exercise done in unpleasant surroundings, such as jogging in very heavy traffic, where there is much noise and air pollution, might increase discomfort and foster anxiety.

Bouts of stimulating exercise are often alleged by participants to be stress-reducing experiences. Many exercisers believe that positive mood shifts occur as a consequence of a good workout. For example, a person might think to himself:

> When I'm feeling down or logy I take a workout at the gym and I usually feel better. When I'm frustrated or angry I find that a three-mile jog reins me in. I knock myself out a little — sweat a bit — and then I seem to let loose from my fury. Then I realize that I had no business being mad in the first place. Exercise is really good therapy for me.

Moods are feelings about which we are aware. Although fleeting in nature, they may remain with us for hours at a time. We are perfectly capable of confessing to a friend that we've been upset or nervous all morning. You may feel "blue" or be "down" because a heavy snowfall has prevented you from leaving the house. You may be "on edge" for a full day before an important exam or performance is scheduled. In contrast, *emotions* are more intense and of lesser duration. Emotions are also usually related to specific causal events, such as something that someone said or did. You experience rage when observing some gross miscarriage of justice, but get over it soon. You believe that a competitor has intentionally fouled you. However, the strong anger we feel is soon reduced. You get over it, recapture your equanimity, and resume emotionally controlled play. Your response to what you've seen or experienced doesn't stay with you for an extended period.

The work of a friend and colleague of mine, Dr. Bonnie Berger of Bowling Green University, continues to generate findings that support a relationship between exercise and positive mood change. In a string of publications centered on a wide variety of physical activities, she has examined, among others, swimming, jogging, walking, hatha yoga, and fencing (Berger, 1994; Berger, Butki, & Berwind, 1995; Berger, Friedman, & Eaton, 1988; Berger & Motl, 2000). Invariably her subjects (in many instances, but not always, college-age students) evince significant changes on the Profile of Mood States (POMS) after exercise. What processes underlie these changes? Why do we feel better after exercise? Can these mood shifts be clarified in terms of neuroanatomical factors?

Arne Dietrich proposes a hypothesis based upon principles of cognitive psychology that rely upon brain anatomy. He suggests that exercise induces a *state of transient hypofrontality*. Dietrich (2003) believes that exercise causes activation in all parts of the central nervous system needed to satisfy the demands of motor activity. Depending upon the physical activity, different cognitive emphases are engaged. Some exercise activities require heavy memory functions, as in the case of many sports; others require a good deal of interpretive responses to stimuli (perceptual demands). Many areas of the brain become highly activated, and there is therefore an across-the-board increase in brain function. This is due to the fact that a very substantial portion of the brain is involved in motor and perceptual function. But since we have limited capacities to process information (see Chapter 5) and attend to incoming stimuli, the higher cognitive brain centers (prefrontal cortex) may become somewhat deactivated.

Dietrich suggests that exercise may simply "take the sharp edge off" of higher brain center functions (frontal lobe cortex) and produce "an inability to focus on life's worries" (p. 9). The prefrontal cortex, the brain area involved in analytical, worrisome, or anxiety-producing thinking, is then free to disengage, since it must respond to the demands levied by exercise. Of course, the physical activity must be strenuous for this to occur. When the exercise is extremely challenging and fatiguing, the consequence is a focused awareness of discomfort, and the prefrontal regions of the cortex become engaged in an effort to decipher the degree of alarm and danger to the exerciser. The exercise is then perceived as stressful.

In a number of old studies, anxiety has been shown to be lowered in the face of long-term exercise treatments (Jette, 1969; Layman, 1974; Popjoy, 1967). More recently published findings support this connection (Berger, 1994; Berger et al., 1988, 1995; Berger & Motl, 2000). That is, those who have been engaged regularly in programs of vigorous physical activity for lengthy periods of time seem to score lower on trait anxiety scales than nonexercisers. Exercisers also seem to be more tough-minded than nonexercisers. Perhaps this accounts for their increased stress-coping abilities and their lower inclination toward anxiety. However, no causal relationship between the two variables has been established.

On the other hand, the situation is quite different when it comes to the short-term effects of strenuous exercise upon state anxiety. In a series of studies, William P. Morgan of the University of Wisconsin, Madison (1971, 1973, 1979, 1981), has been able to show that exhaustive exercise (running, walking) causes anxiety to be elevated immediately after, as well as for periods as long as five minutes after termination. But at about five minutes after exercise, anxiety levels return to preexercise levels.

Although the picture is not entirely clear, one possible interpretation of these findings is that biochemical factors need a period of settling down or deactivation before anxiety is lowered. It appears that heart rate is raised during exercise but then comes down gradually and is lower the rest of the day than it was before the exercise. Likewise, intensification of the physiological aspects of anxiety immediately after exercise leads to a consequent reduction in anxiety level.

Perhaps relief from anxiety and stress is forthcoming after exercise because participants are usually obliged to change their physical location in order to exercise. When this is done, the stressors themselves are at least temporarily avoided. For instance, if an argument with another person is causing you to feel stressed and you leave the room in order to exercise, you also have left the primary source of your stress, which is the person with whom you were arguing.

Permit me to speculate upon another dimension of exercise that could conceivably account for an exerciser's "feeling better," i.e., the personal washing and grooming that often follow participation in rigorous physical activity. It is common for those who exercise to shower or bathe after a workout. When we shower or bathe, we are often in a private environment that may be associated with very few stressors of relatively low intensity. Clothing is often changed before or after exercise (or on both occasions). Brushing or combing the hair, putting on clean clothing, and glancing in the mirror may all contribute to improved feelings about the self and consequently a reduction in anxiety. For these incidental reasons as well, exercise is helpful in anxiety control. A graduate student of mine and I recently completed a study whose results show that subjects participating in different types of exercise (treadmill running, elliptical machine, stationary bike/spinning, aerobic dance, kick boxing/martial arts, and weight training) demonstrated postexercise positive changes in mood as long as their physical activity was followed by a shower. The same exercisers, in a no-shower condition, did not (McGinnis, 2004). Raglin and Morgan (1987) discussed a possible *shower effect* in a study that had a different focus but whose results permitted speculation about this phenomenon.

14.6.3 Stimulus Seeking, Stress, and Exercise

There is yet another perspective that may clarify the stress-reducing effect of physical activity. For some persons, the inability to participate in exercise is actually stress inducing. Heretofore, our emphasis has been upon coping with stress through the medium of exercise. Now we shall see that in certain individuals, the need for high stimulation is very strong; so strong that if it remains unsatisfied, the consequences are often feelings of restlessness, unfulfillment, irritability and boredom. The body requires homeostasis or calmness, but also needs stimulation. During distress, its inclination is to be active. People fidget, pace, and demonstrate restlessness when in the grip of stress and/or anxiety. As Seaward (2000) has put it, when the body is inactive during stressful situations, organs go into overdrive akin to flooring the accelerator pedal of a car while it is in "park."

According to Marvin Zuckerman of the University of Delaware, some humans have personality traits that are expressed as needs for high or low stimulation. He believes that the foundation for this trait is largely (but not entirely) biological. High-sensation seekers may encounter social reprisals if and when they pursue certain ways of satisfying their needs for stimulation. Many physical activities, such as those included in sports and the performing arts, are not only socially approved but commonly reinforced. Therefore, such activities may displace drug abuse, some forms of sexual exploration, and risky adventurous behavior in high-sensation seekers. High arousal needs in these individuals may be satisfied through participation in socially sanctioned experiences such as those found in competitive sports, theater, and dance. Thus, exercise may provide opportunity for intense excitement or stress, which in high-sensation seekers represents a very strong need (Figure 14.1).

14.6.4 Exercise as Stress

Exercise may also be considered a stressor for persons who are low in sensation seeking. If you scored from one to three points on the abbreviated form of Zuckerman's sensation-seeking scale, then you are likely to react in a stressed way to the psychological and physiological arousal provoked by vigorous exercise. Even the thought of participating in a bout of exercise may generate heightened activation. If strenuous exercise is expected of you, such as is usually required in military basic training or in rigorous preseason conditioning programs for athletic team participation, you are likely to respond somatically and cognitively in stressed ways.

For example, low-sensation seekers who unwisely make a commitment to prepare for a road race may be inviting an unwelcome dose of anxiety. Each and every training session becomes an emotional tribulation. Only through self-discipline do they force themselves to complete each training workout. The experience is therefore not only undesirable, but in view of their commitment to "see this thing through," actually painful. They anticipate tomorrow's grueling, distasteful training

Following is an abbreviated form of Zuckerman's test for sensation seeking tendencies. "Determine whether you are a high or low sensation seeker.

Circle choice A or B, that best describes your likes or dislikes, or the way you feel.

1. A. I would like a job that requires a lot of traveling.
   B. I would prefer a job in one location.
2. A. I am invigorated by a brisk cold day.
   B. I can't wait to get indoors on a cold day.
3. A. I get bored seeing the same old faces.
   B. I like the comfortable familiarity of everyday friends.
4. A. I would prefer living in an ideal society in which everyone is safe, secure and happy.
   B. I would have preferred living in the unsettled days of our history.
5. A. I sometimes like to do things that are a little frightening.
   B. A sensible person avoids activities that are dangerous.
6. A. I would not like to be hypnotized.
   B. I would like to have the experience of being hypnotized.
7. A. The most important goal in life is to live it to the fullest and experience as much as possible.
   B. The most important goal in life is to find peace and happiness.
8. A. I would like to try parachute-jumping.
   B. I would never want to try jumping out of a plane, with or without a parachute.
9. A. I enter cold water gradually, giving myself time to get used to it.
   B. I like to jump right into the ocean or a cold pool.
10. A. When I go on a vacation, I prefer the comfort of a good room and bed.
    B. When I go on a vacation, I prefer the change of camping out.
11. A. I prefer people who are emotionally expressive even if they are a bit unstable.
    B. I prefer people who are calm and even-tempered.
12. A. A good painting should shock or jolt the senses.
    B. A good painting should give one a feeling of peace and security.
13. A. People who ride motorcycles must have some kind of unconscious need to hurt themselves.
    B. I would like to drive or ride a motorcycle.

Scoring

Count one point for each of the following items that you have circled: 1A, 2A, 3A, 4B, 5A, 6B, 7A, 8A, 9B, 10B, 11A, 12A, 13B. Add up your total and compare it with the norms below:

1–3   Very low on sensation-seeking
4–5   Low
6–9   Average
10–11 High
12–13 Very high

Figure 14.1   Zuckerman's test for sensation-seeking tendencies.

session with dread and will feel guilty if they quit or fail to appear for their workout. Quitting may be interpreted as a breach of intellectual honesty that in and of itself is stressful. People who place themselves on impractical exercise programs for weight regulation purposes may also find themselves in a similar bind.

Even the experienced exerciser, such as the advanced runner, may react stressfully to the prospect of braving inclement weather (such as a dark, cold, rainy early morning) in order to satisfy his or her training schedule. Exercise can be stress inducing!

14.6.5 Exercise Addiction

Considerable speculation has been made about individuals who become addicted to or dependent upon certain activities, such as distance running. I have described some of the consequences and causes of this form of habituation or dependency and have summarized a good deal of the available research in this area in three previously published articles, two done in collaboration with my former graduate student Dr. Michael Sachs (Sachs & Pargman, 1979, 1984) and another written alone (Pargman, 1980). In these materials, psychological and physiological symptoms are described that are associated with running deprivation in subjects with substantial histories of distance running. These symptoms included restlessness, guilt feelings, irritability, tension, bloatedness, muscle twitching, and discomfort. They were reported by subjects (runners we queried) after 24 to 36 hours without activity.

Although the available information is not by any means conclusive, there is some evidence suggesting that the existence of a true physiological addiction to aerobic activities (such as running and swimming) involves certain chemical compounds that are produced by the brain. One of these is *beta-endorphin polypeptide,* which is molecularly very close to opium. It is therefore referred to as the body's own opiate and has been shown to have an analgesic effect. It has also been known to produce euphoria and reduce pain sensation and is believed by some to be instrumental in altering states of consciousness (Colt, Wardlaw, & Frantz, 1981; Markoff, Ryan, & Young, 1982). I was among the first to describe this phenomenon and label it the *runner's high.* In other words, as a result of substantial periods of time in which an individual regularly runs long distances (e.g., six miles a day, six days a week, for a year), increased amounts of endorphins appear in the body. The transient hypofrontality hypothesis promulgated by Dietrich (2003) and discussed earlier in this chapter may also contribute to a clarification of so-called runner's high.

Thus, it may be speculated that a general biochemical tolerance to long-term running, as well as to the elevated levels of endorphins in the body per se, develops. This perhaps explains the stress reaction observed to often follow inactivity. *Withdrawal symptoms* may be an entirely appropriate term to use in describing the subsequent distressful feelings.

14.7 SUMMARY

Aerobic exercise is physical activity done in the presence of adequate supplies of oxygen — jogging or swimming, for example. Anaerobic exercise involves short bursts of energy, wherein inadequate oxygen supplies are present — sprinting, for example.

Fitness level is related to regular participation in rigorous physical activity that strengthens the body's capacity to inhale environmental air and deliver extracted oxygen to body cells. Physically fit individuals may be advantaged in their confrontations with distress. A cathartic effect provided by exercise may enable stressed persons to dissipate some of the body's physiological preparations in anticipation of the fight-or-flight response.

The theoretical framework of Zuckerman recognizes variability in the human need for stimulation in terms of the application of exercise-related arousal. The reported positive changes in mood, or affect, are perceived by two hypotheses: one dealing with the production of the body's so-called opiate (*beta-endorphin polypeptide,* and the other with Dietrich's hypothesis of transient hyperfrontality.

Exercise addiction is a known phenomenon that can involve physical withdrawal symptoms.

REFERENCES

Adler, R. K., MacRitchie, K., & Engel, G. L. (1971). Psychological processes & ischemic stroke (occlusive cerebro vascular disease: Observations on 32 men with 35 strokes). *Psychosomatic Medicine, 33,* 1–29.

Allport, F. H. (1924). *Social psychology.* Boston: Houghton Mifflin.

Baddeley, A. D. (1972). Selective attention and performance in dangerous environments. *British Journal of Psychology, 63,* 537–546.

Bahrke, M. S., Yesalis, C. E., & Wright, J. E. (1990). Psychological and behavioural effects of endogenous testosterone levels and anabolic-androgenic steroids among males. A review. *Sports Medicine, 10,* 303–337.

Baird, C. L., & Sands, L. (2004). A pilot study of the effectiveness of guided imagery with progressive mind relaxation to reduce chronic pain and mobility difficulties of osteoarthritis. *Pain Management Nursing, 5,* 97–104.

Bandler, R., & Grinder, J. (1982). *Reframing: NLP* [neurolinguistic programming] *and the transformation of meaning.* Moab, UT: Real People Press.

Bandura, A. (1965). Behavioral modification through modeling practices. In L. Krasner & I. Ullman (Eds.), *Research in behavior modification* (pp. 310–340). New York: Holt, Rinehart & Winston.

———. (1977). Self-efficacy toward a verifying theory of behavior change. *Psychology Review, 84,* 191–215.

———. (1997). *Self-efficacy: The exercise of control.* New York: Freeman.

———. (2001). Social cognitive theory: An agentive perspective. *Annual Review of Psychology, 52,* 1–26.

Bellisle, F. (2004). Effects of diet on behaviour and cognition in children. *British Journal of Nutrition, 92*(Suppl 2), S227–S232.

Benson, H. (1975). *The Relaxation Response*. New York: Avon Books.

Bera, T. K., Gore, M. M., & Oak, J. P. (1998). Recovery from stress in two different postures and in Shavasana — a yogic relaxation posture. *Indian Journal of Physiology and Pharmacology, 42*, 473–478.

Berger, B. G. (1994). Coping with stress: The effectiveness of exercise and other techniques. *Quest, 46*, 100–119.

Berger, B. G., Butki, B. D., & Berwind, J. S. (1995). Acute mood changes associated with competitive and non-competitive physical activities. *Journal of Applied Sport Psychology, 7*, 541.

Berger, B. G., Friedman, E., & Eaton, M. (1988). Comparison of jogging, the relaxation response, and group interaction for stress reduction. *Journal of Sport and Exercise Psychology, 10*, 431–447.

Berger, B. G., & Motl, R. W. (2000). Exercise and mood: A selective review and synthesis of research employing the profile of mood states. *Journal of Applied Sport Psychology, 12*, 69–92.

Berger, B. G., Pargman, D., & Weinberg, R. S. (2000). *Foundations of Exercise Psychology*. Morgantown, WV: Fitness Information Technology, Inc.

Berkowitz, L. (1989). Frustration-aggression hypothesis: Examination and reformulation. *Psychological Bulletin, 106*, 59–73.

Berkowitz, L., & Hamon-Jones, E. (2004). Toward an understanding of the determinants of anger. *Emotion, 4*, 107–130.

Bernhardt, P. C., Dabbs, J. M., Fielden, J. A., & Lutter, C. D. (1998). Testosterone changes during vicarious experiences of winning and losing among fans at sporting events. *Physiological Behavior, 65*, 59–62.

Bernstein, D. A., & Borkovec, T. D. (1973). *Progressive relaxation training*. Champaign, IL: Research Press.

Bernstein, D. A., Borkovec, T. D., & Hazleh-Stevens, H. (2000). *New directions in progressive relaxation training: A guidebook for helping professionals*. Westport, CT: Praeger.

Bhavanani, A. B., Madanmohan, & Udupa, K. (2003). Acute effect of Mukh bhastrika (a yogic bellows type breathing) on reaction time. *Indian Journal of Physiology and Pharmacology, 47*, 297–300.

Bishop, S. R. (2002). What do we really know about mindfulness-based stress reduction? *Psychosomatic Medicine, 64*, 71–83.

Blumenstein, B. (2002). Biofeedback applications in sport and exercise: Research findings. In B. Blumenstein, M. Bar-Eli, & G. Tenenbaum (Eds.), *Brain and body in sport and exercise* (pp. 37–54). New York: John Wiley & Sons.

Blundell, J., Gumaste, D., Handley, R., & Dye, L. (2003). Diet, behavior and cognitive function: A psychobiological view. *Scandinavian Journal of Nutrition, 47*, 85–91.

Bond, C. F., & Titus, L. J. (1983). Social-Facilitation: A meta-analysis of 241 studies. *Psychological Bulletin, 94,* 265–292.

Booth, A., Shelley, G., Mazur, A., Tharp, G., & Kittok, R. (1989). Testosterone, and winning and losing in human competition. *Hormones and Behavior, 23,* 556–571.

Borden, R. J. (1980). Audience influence. In P. B. Paulus (Ed.), *Psychology of group influence.* Hillsdale, NJ: Erlbaum.

Boutcher, S. H., & Zinsser, N. W. (1990). Cardiac deceleration of elite and beginning golfers during putting. *Journal of Sport and Exercise Psychology, 12,* 37–47.

Boyle, C. A., Savers, S. P., Jensen, B. E., Headly, S. A., & Manos, T. M. (2004). The effects of yoga training and a single bout of yoga on delayed onset muscle soreness in the lower extremity. *Journal of Strength and Conditioning Research, 18,* 723–729.

Brown, B.B. (1977). *Stress and the Art of Biofeedback.* New York: Harper & Row.

Budzynski, T. H. & Peffer, K. E. (1980). Biofeedback training. In I. L. Kutash & L. B. Schlesinger (Eds.), *Handbook on Stress and Anxiety.* San Francisco: Jossey-Bass.

Bunce, D., & Stephenson, K. (2000). Statistical considerations in the interpretation of research on occupational stress management interventions. *Work and Stress, 14,* 197–212.

Bunker, L., & Rotella, R. (1980). Achievement and stress in sport: Research findings and practical suggestions. In W. F. Straub (Ed.), *Sport psychology: An analysis of athlete behavior.* Ithaca, NY: Mouvement.

Burgess, S. (1976). Stimulus-seeking, extraversion and neuroticism in regular occasional and non-exercisers. Unpublished masters thesis, Florida State University.

Cameron, R., & Meicenbaum, D. (1982). The nature of efficient coping and the treatment of stress-related problems: A cognitive behavioral perspective. In L. Goldberger & S. Breznitz (Eds.), *Handbook of Stress, Theoretical and Clinical Aspects.* New York: The Free Press.

Cannon, W. B. (1932). *The wisdom of the body.* New York: W. W. Norton.

Carlson, C. R., & Hoyle, R. H. (1993). Efficacy of abbreviated progressive muscle relaxation training: A quantitative review of behavioural medicine research. *Journal of Consulting and Clinical Psychology, 61,* 1059–1067.

Carron, A. (1980). *Social psychology of sport.* Ithaca, NY: Mouvement Publications.

Carron, A., & Bennett, B. (1976). The effects of initial habit strength differences upon performance in a coaction situation. *Journal of Motor Behavior, 8,* 297–304.

Cartwright, M., Wardle, J., Steggles, N., Simon, A. E., Croker, H., & Jarvis, M. J. (2003). Stress and dietary practices in adolescents. *Health Psychology, 22,* 362–369.

Cherniss, C. (1980). *Professional burnout in human service organizations.* New York: Praeger.

Colt, E., Wardlaw, S., & Frantz, A. (1981). The effects of running on plasma Beta-Endorphins. *Life Sciences, 28,* 1637–1640.

Cooke, L. E. (1982). *Stress and anxiety in sport.* Sports council research project. Sheffield, England: Sheffield City Polytechnic.

Cotrell, N. B. (1972). Social facilitation. In C. G. McClintock (Ed.), *Experimental social psychology* (pp. 185–236). New York: Holt, Rinehart, & Winston.

Cotrell, N. B., Wack, D. L., Sekerak, G. J., & Little, R. H. (1968). Social facilitation of dominant responses by the presence of an audience and the mere presence of others. *Journal of Personality and Social Psychology, 9,* 245–250.

Cox, R. (1993). *Sport psychology: Concepts and applications* (3rd ed). Dubuque, IA: Brown.

Craig, A. (1986). Acute effects of meals on perceptual and cognitive efficiency. *Nutrition Reviews, 44*(Suppl), 163–171.

Cratty, B. J. (1981). *Social psychology in athletics.* Englewood Cliffs, NJ: Prentice-Hall.

Cruess, D. G., Antoni, M. H., Schneiderman, N., Ironson, G., McCabe, P., Fernandez, J. B., Cruess, S. E., Kilmas, N., & Kumar, M. (2000). Cognitive-behavior stress management increases free testosterone and decreases psychological distress in HIV-seropositive men. *Health Psychology, 19,* 12–20.

Csikszentmihalyi, M. (2005). *Beyond boredom and anxiety.* San Francisco, CA: Jossey-Bass.

Csikszentmihalyi, M., & Jackson, S. (1999). *Flow in sports: The keys to optimal experiences and performances.* Champaign, IL: Human Kinetics.

Dale, J., & Weinberg, R. S. (1990). Burnout in sport: A review and critique. *Journal of Applied Sport Psychology, 2,* 67–83.

Daniels, F. S. & Hatfield, B. (1981). Biofeedback. *Motor Skills: Theory into Practice, 5,* 69–72.

Darwin, C. (1859). *The origin of the species.* London: Penguin Books (reprint).

Dietrich, A. (2003). Functional neuroanatomy of altered states of consciousness: The transient hypofrontality hypothesis. *Consciousness and Cognition, 12,* 231–256.

Digman, J. M. (1990). Personality structure: Emergence of the five factor model. *Annual Review of Psychology, 41,* 417–440.

Dobson, C. B. (1982). *Stress, the Hidden Adversary.* Lancaster, England: MTP Press.

Dowhrend, B. S., Krasnoff, L., & Askenasy, A. R. (1978). Exemplification of a method for scaling life events: The PERI life events scale. *The Journal of Health and Social Behavior, 19,* 205–229.

References • 225

Driscoll, M. P. (2005). *Psychology of learning for instruction*, 3rd Ed. Boston: Pearson.

Driskell, J., Salas, E., & Johnston, J. (2000). Does stress lead to a loss of team perspective? *Human Performance in Extreme Environments, 5,* 69–76.

Dugdale, J. R., & Eklund, R. C. (2002). Do not pay any attention to the umpires: Thought suppression and task-relevant focusing strategies. *Journal of Sport and Exercise Psychology, 24,* 306–319.

Easterbrook, J. A. (1959). The effect of emotion on cue utilization and the organization of behavior. *Psychological Reviews, 66,* 183–201

Ekman, P. (1993). Facial expression of emotion. *American Psychologist, 48,* 384–392.

Elkins, J. S. (2003). Hatha yoga as a supplemental discipline for athletes and dancers. *Georgia Association for Health, Physical Education and Dance Journal, 1,* 12–15.

Eppley, K. R., Abrams, A. I., & Shear, J. (1989). Differential effects of relaxation techniques on trait anxiety: A meta-analysis. *Journal of Clinical Psychology, 45,* 957–979.

Erickson, M. H., & Rossi, E. L. (1979). *Hypnotherapy: An exploratory casebook.* New York: Irvington.

Eysenck, H. J. (1998). *Dimensions of personality.* New Brunswick, NJ: Transaction Publishers.

Fazey, J. A., & Hardy, L. (1988). *The inverted-U hypothesis: A catastrophe for sport psychology* (British Association of Sports Sciences Monograph No. 1). Leeds, England: National Coaching Foundation.

Feigley, D. A. (1984). Psychological burnout in high level athletes. *The Physician and Sports Medicine, 12,* 109–112, 115–119.

Feltz, D. L., Landers, D. M., & Becker, B. J. (1988). A revised meta-analysis of the mental practice literature on motor skill learning. In D. Druckman & J. A. Swets (Eds.), *Enhancing human performance: Issues, theories, and techniques* (p. 274). Washington, DC: National Academy Press.

Field, T. (1998). Massage therapy effects. *American Psychologist, 53,* 1270–1281.

———. (2004). Massage and aroma therapy. *International Journal of Cosmetic Science, 26,* 169–170.

Fillingham, R. B., & Fine, M. A. (1986).The effects of internal versus external information processing on symptom perception in an exercise setting. *Health Psychology, 5,* 115–123.

Folkman, S., & Lazarus, R. S. (1980). An analysis of coping in a middle-aged community sample. *Journal of Health and Social Behavior, 21,* 219 – 239.

Freud, S. (1926). Inhibitions, symptoms, and anxiety. In J. Strachey (Trans.), *The standard edition of the complete psychological works of Sigmund Freud* (Vol. 20, pp. 77–174). London: Hogarth Press.

Freudenberger, H. J. (1983). Burnout: Current knowledge and relevance to old age psychiatry. *International Journal of Geriatric Psychiatry, 13,* 520–526.

Friedman, M., & Rosenman, R. (1970). *Type A behavior and your heart.* New York: Alfred A. Knopf.

Friedman, M., & Rosenman, R. H. (1971). Type A behavior pattern: Its association with coronary heart disease. *Annals of Clinical Research, 3,* 300–312.

Friedman, M., & Rosenman, R. H. (1974). *Type A behavior and your heart.* New York: Knopf.

Fusco, R., & Gutin, B. (1974). Effects of exercise training on cardiovascular response of human subjects to a localized stressor. *American Corrective Therapy Journal, 28,* 42–46.

Ghoncheh, S., & Smith, J. C. (2004). Progressive muscle relaxation, yoga stretching, and ABC relaxation theory. *Journal of Clinical Psychology, 60,* 131–136.

Gillespie, A. H., & Devine, M. M. (1982). Nutrition and the management of stress. *Human Ecology Forum, 13,* 14–17.

Goodenough, D. R. (1986). History of the field dependence construct. In M. Bertini, D. Pizzamiglio, & S. Wagner (Eds.), *Field dependence in psychology theory, research and application* (pp. 5–14). London: Erlbaum.

Gould, D. (1993). Intensive sport participation and the prepubescent athlete: Competitive stress and burnout. In B. R. Cahill & A. J. Pearl (Eds.), *Intensive participation in children's sports* (pp. 19–38). Champaign, IL: Human Kinetics.

Gould, D., & Weiss, M. (1981). The effects of model similarity and model talk on self-efficacy and muscular endurance. *Journal of Sport Psychology, 3,* 17–29.

Graves, N., Krepcho, M., Mayo, M. L. S., & Hill, J. (2004). Does yoga speed healing for patients with low back pain? *Journal of Family Practice, 53,* 661–662.

Green, R. G. (1980). The effects of being observed on performance. In P. B. Paulus (Ed.), *Psychology of group influence* (pp. 61–98). Hillsdale, NJ: Erlbaum.

Greenberg, J. S., & Pargman, D. (1989). *Physical fitness: A wellness approach* (2nd ed.). Englewood Cliffs, NJ: Prentice-Hall.

Greene, W. A., & Miller, G. (1958). Psychological factors and reticuloendothelial disease: Observations on a group of children and adolescents with leukemia. An interpretation of disease development in terms of the mother–child unit. *Psychosomatic Medicine, 20,* 124–144.

Greenspan, F. S., & Stewler, G. J. (Eds.). (1997). *Basic and clinical endocrinology.* Stamford, CT: Appelton & Lange.

Gutin, B. (1983). *The High Energy Factor.* New York: Random House.

Haas, J., & Roberts, C. C. (1975). Effect of evaluative others upon learning and performance of a complex motor task. *Journal of Motor Behavior, 7,* 81–90.

Hanin, Y. L. (1989). Intrapersonal and intragroup anxiety in sports. In D. Hackfort & C. D. Spielberger (Eds.), *Anxiety in Sports: An international perspective*. New York: Hemisphere.

———. (1997). Emotions and athletic performance: Individual zones of optimal functioning. *European Yearbook of Sport Psychology, 1*, 29–72.

———. (2003, February). Performance related emotional states in sport: A qualitative analysis [48 paragraphs]. *Forum Qualitative Sozialforschung/ Forum: Qualitative Social Research* [Online journal], 4. Available at: http://www.qualitative-research.net/fqs-texte/1-03/1-03hanin-e.htm. Retrieved December 23, 2005.

Hardy, L., & Parfitt, G. (1991). A catastrophic model of anxiety and performance. *British Journal of Psychology, 82*, 163–178.

Harinath, K., Malhotra, A. S., Pal, K., Prasad, R., Kumet, R., Kain, T. C., Rai, L., & Sawhney, R. C. (2004). Effects of hatha yoga and Omkar meditation on cardiorespiratory performance, psychologic profile and melatonin secretion. *Journal of Alternative and Complementary Medicine, 10*, 261–268.

Hatfield, B. B., Landers, D. M., & Ray, W. J. (1984). Cognitive processes during self-paced motor performance: An electroencephalographic profile of skilled marksmen. *Journal of Sport Psychology, 6*, 42–59.

Heaton, P. (2003). Pitch, labeling and disembedding in autism. *Journal of Child Psychology and Psychiatry, 44*, 543.

Henschen, K. (1998). Athletic staleness and burnout: Diagnosis, prevention and treatment. In J. M. Williams (Ed.), *Applied sport psychology: Personal growth to peak performance* (pp. 398–408). Mountain View, CA: Mayfield.

Hernandez-Reif, M., Field, T., Krasnegor, J., & Theakston, H. (2001). Lower back pain is reduced and range of motion increased after massage therapy. *International Journal of Neuroscience, 106*, 131–145.

Highlen, P. S., & Bennett, B. B. (1979). Psychological characteristics of successful and non-successful wrestlers. *Journal of Sport Psychology, 3*, 123–137.

Hill, P. (1991). It's not what you eat, but how you eat it. *Nutrition, 7*, 385–395.

Holmes, I. H., & Rahe, R. H. (1967). The Social Readjustment Rating Scale. *Journal of Psychosomatic Research, 11*, 213–218.

Ironson, G., Field, T., Scafidi, F., Kumar, M., Kumar, A., Price, A., Goncalves, A., Hashimoto, M., Burman, I., Tetenman, C., Patarca, R., & Fletcher, M. (1996). Massage therapy is associated with enhancement of the immune systems' cytotoxic capacity. *International Journal of Neuroscience, 84*, 205–218.

Iso-Ahola, S. E., & Hatfield, B. (1986). *Psychology of sports: A social psychological approach*. Dubuque, IA: Brown.

Jacobs, S. C., & Meyers, J. K. (1976). Recent life events and acute schizophrenic psychosis: A controlled study. *Journal of Nervous and Mental Disease, 162*, 75–87.

Jayasinghe, S. R. (2004). Yoga in cardiac health (a review). *European Journal of Cardiovascular Prevention and Rehabilitation, 11*, 369–375.

Jensen, P. S., & Kenny, D. T. (2004). The effects of yoga on the attention and behaviour of boys with attention-deficit/hyperactivity disorder (ADHD). *Journal of Attention Disorders, 7*, 205–216.

Jette, M. (1969). *A study of long-term physical activity in sedentary middle-aged men.* Unpublished Ph.D. Dissertation, University of Illinois-Urbana.

Jones, M. (2003). Controlling emotions in sport. *Sport Psychologist, 17*, 447–486.

Kabat-Zinn (2003). Mindfulness-based interventions in context: Past, present and future. *Clinical Psychology: Science and Practice, 10*, 144–156.

Kabat-Zinn, J., Lipworth, L., & Burney, R. (1985). The clinical use of mindfulness meditation for the self-regulation of chronic pain. *Journal of Behavioral Medicine, 8*, 163–190.

Kabat-Zinn, J., Lipworth, L., Burney, R., & Sellers, W. (1987). Four-year follow-up of a meditation-based program for the self-regulation of chronic pain: Treatment outcome and compliance. *Clinical Journal of Pain, 2*, 150–173.

Kabat-Zinn, J., Massion, A. O., Kristeller, J., Peterson, L. G. Fletcher, K. E., Pbert, L., Lenderking, W. R., & Santorelli, S. F. (1992). Effectiveness of a meditation-based stress reduction program in the treatment of anxiety disorders. *American Journal of Psychiatry, 19*, 936–943.

Kaplan, R. J., Greenwood, C. E., Winocur, G., & Thomas, M. (2001). Dietary protein, carbohydrate, and fat enhance memory performance in healthy elderly. *American Journal of Clinical Nutrition, 74*, 687–693.

Kaplan, R. J., Greenwood, C. E., Winocur, G., & Wolever, T. (2000). Cognitive performance is associated with glucose regulation in healthy elderly persons and can be enhanced with glucose and dietary carbohydrates. *American Journal of Clinical Nutrition, 72*, 825–836.

Kelley, B. C. (1994). A model of stress and burnout in college coaches: Effects of gender and time of season. *Research Quarterly for Exercise and Sport, 65*, 48–58.

Kelley, B. C., & Gill, D. L. (1993). An examination of personal/situational variables, stress appraisal and burnout in collegiate teacher-coaches. *Research Quarterly for Exercise and Sport, 64*, 94–102.

Knipe, J. (2005). How we can cope with a tough loss. Philadelphia *Daily News,* February 8.

Kyllo, L. B., & Landers, D. M. (1995). Goal setting in sport and exercise: A research synthesis to resolve the controversy. *Journal of Sport and Exercise Psychology, 17*, 117–137.

Landers, D. (1980). The arousal-performance relationship revisited. *Research Quarterly for Exercise and Sport, 51*, 77–90.

Landers, D. M., & McCullagh, P. D. (1976). Social facilitation of motor performance. *Exercise and Sport Science Reviews, 4*, 125–126.

Layman, E. (1974). Psychological effects of physical activity. In J. Wilmore (Ed.), *Exercise and Sports Science Review*. New York: Academic Press.

Lazarus, R. S. (1993). From psychological stress to the emotions: A history of changing outlooks. *Annual Review of Psychology, 44*, 1–21.

Lehrer, P. M. (1982). How to relax and how to not relax: A re-evaluation of the work of Edmund Jacobson. *Behavior Research and Therapy, 20*, 417–428.

Lehrer, P. M., Rosen, R. C., Kostis, J. B., & Greenfield, D. (1987). Treating stage fright in musicians: The use of beta-blockers. *New Jersey Medicine, 84*, 27–33.

Lieberman, H. R. (2003). Nutrition, brain function and cognitive performance. *Appetite, 40*, 245–254.

Lieberman, H. R., Falco, C. M., & Slade, S. S. (2002). Carbohydrate administration during a day of sustained aerobic activity improves vigilance as assessed by a novel ambulatory monitoring device and mood. *American Journal of Clinical Nutrition, 76*, 120–127.

Liu, W. (2003). Field dependence-independence and sports with a preponderance of closed or open skill. *Journal of Sports Behavior, 26*, 285–297.

Locke, E. A., & Lathham, G. P. (2002). Building a practically useful theory of goal setting and task motivation: A 35-year odyssey. *American Psychologist, 57*, 705–715.

Londsale, D. (1986). Three circles of health: Application of Boolean algebra in health assessment. *International Journal of Biosocial Research, 8*, 80–83.

MacCracken, M. J., & Stadulis, R. E. (1985). Social facilitation of young children's dynamic balance performance. *Journal of Sport Psychology, 7*, 150–165.

Macleod, J., Smith, G. D., Heslop, P., Metcalfe, C., Carroll, D., & Hart, C. (2002). Psychological stress and cardiovascular disease: Empirical demonstration of bias in a prospective observational study of Scottish men. *British Medical Journal, 324*, 1247.

Magill, R. A. (2003). *Motor learning and control: Concepts and applications* (7th ed.). Boston: McGraw-Hill.

Mahoney, M. J., & Avener, M. (1977). Psychology of elite athletes. *Cognitive Therapy and Research, 1*, 135–141.

Manchanda, S. C., Narang, R., Reddy, K. S., Sachdeva, V., Prabhakaran, D., Rajani, M., & Bajlani, R. (2000). Retardation of coronary atheroscherosis with yoga lifestyle intervention. *Journal of the Association of Physicians of India, 48*, 687–694.

Mangum, M., Hall, E. L., Pargman, D., & Sylva, M. (1986). Relationship between perceptual style and ability to reproduce a standard work task. *Perceptual and Motor Skills, 62*, 543–547.

Marbeto, J. A. (1967). The incidence of prayer in athletics as indicated by selected California collegiate athletes and coaches. Masters thesis, Universtity of California, Santa Barbara.

Markoff, R., Ryan, P., & Young, T. (1982). Endorphins and mood changes in long-distance running. *Medicine & Science in Sports, 14,* 11–14.

Martens, R. (1974). Arousal and motor performance. *Exercise and Sport Sciences Reviews, 2,* 155–188.

———. (1977). *Sport Competition Anxiety Test.* Champaign, IL; Human Kinetics.

Martens, R., Vealey, R. S., & Burton, D. (Eds.). (1990). *Competitive anxiety in sport.* Champaign, IL: Human Kinetics.

Martin, J. J., Kelley, B. C., Eklund, R. C. (1999). A model of stress and burnout in male high school athletic directors. *Journal of Sport and Exercise Psychology, 21,* 280–294.

Martin, L., Lane, A. M., Dowen, C. J., Homer, M. R., & Milton, K. E. (2004). Effect of water pressure on heart rate and mood state responses after aquamassage. *Journal of Sports Sciences, 22,* 249.

Maslach, C., & Jackson, S. E. (1981). The measurement of experienced burnout. *Journal of Occupational Behavior, 2,* 99–113.

Maslach, C., Schaufeli, W. B., & Leiter, M. P. (2002). Job burnout. *Annual Review of Psychiatry, 52,* 397–422.

Maslow, A. (1971). *The farther reaches of human nature.* New York: Viking Press.

Masuda, A., Hayes, S., Sackett, C., & Twohig, M. P. (2004). Cognitive diffusion and self-relevant negative thoughts: Examining the impact of a ninety-year-old technique. *Behavior Research and Therapy, 42,* 477–485.

Matsui, T., Okada, A., Inoshita, O. (1983). Mechanism of feedback affecting task performance. *Organizational Behavior and Human Performance, 31,* 114–122.

McComb, R., Tacon, A., Randolph, P., & Caldera, Y. (2004). A pilot study to examine the effects of a mindfulness-based stress-reduction and relaxation program on levels of stress hormones, physical functioning, and submaximal exercise responses. *Journal of Alternative and Complementary Medicine, 10,* 819–827.

McCrae, R. R., & Costa, P. T., Jr. (1997). Personality trait structure as a human universal. *American Psychologist, 52,* 509–556.

McCullagh, P. D., & Landers, D. M. (1975). A comparison of the audience and coaction paradigms. In D. M. Landers (Ed.), *Psychology of sport and motor behavior 2* (pp. 209–220). University Park: Pennsylvania State University Press.

McGinnis, J. (2004). *The after-exercise shower: Its effect upon mood.* Unpublished Master's Thesis, Florida State University.

McNally, R., & Ricciardi, J. (1996). Suppression of negative natural thoughts. *Behavioral and Cognitive Psychotherapy, 24,* 17–25.

Melzack, R., & Wall, P. D. (1965). Pain mechanisms: A new theory. *Science, 150,* 971–979.

Meyers, A. W., Cooke, C. J., Cullen, J., & Liles, L. (1979). Psychological aspects of athletic competitors: A replication across sports. *Cognitive Therapy and Research, 3,* 361–366.

Miller, N. (1980). Effects of learning on physical symptoms produced by psychological stress. In H. Selye (Ed.). *Selye's guide to stress research, vol. 1.* New York: Van Nostrand.

Miyake, A., Witzki, A. H., & Emerson, M. J. (2001). Field dependence–independence for a working memory perspective: A dual-task investigation of the Hidden Figures Test. *Memory, 9,* 445–457.

Morgan, W. P. (1973). Influence of acute physical activity on state anxiety. Proceedings of the National College Physical Education Meeting, 113–121.

Morgan, W. P. (1979). Anxiety reduction following acute exercise. *Psychiatric Annals, 9,* 34–45.

Morgan, W. P. (1981). Psychological benefits of physical activity. In F. Nagle & H. Montoye (Eds.), *Exercise in health and disease.* Springfield, IL: Thomas.

Morgan, W. P. (1993). Hypnosis and sport psychology. In J. Rue, S. J. Lynn, & I. Kirsch (Eds.), *Handbook of clinical hypnosis* (pp. 649–670). Washington, DC: American Psychological Association.

———. (2002). Hypnosis in sport and exercise psychology. In J. L.Van Raalte, & B. W. Brewer (Eds.), *Exploring sport and exercise psychology* (2nd ed., pp. 151–181). Washington, DC: American Psychological Association.

Morgan, W. P., Roberts, J., & Feinerman, A. (1971). Psychologic effect of acute physical activity. *Archives of Physical Medicine and Rehabilitation, 52,* 422–425.

Morley, S., Eccleston, C., & Williams, A. (1999). A systematic review and meta-analysis of randomized controlled trials of cognitive behaviour therapy and behavior therapy for chronic pain in adults, excluding headache. *Pain, 80,* 1–13.

Muchenbaum, D. Stress inoculation training for coping with stressors. *The Clinical Psychologist, 49,* 4–7.

Murata, T., Takahashi, T., Hamada, T., Omori, M., Kosaka, H., & Wada, Y. (2004). Individual trait anxiety levels characterizing the properties of Zen meditation. *Neuropsychology, 50,* 189–194.

Murray, H. A. (1943). *Thematic Apperception Test.* Cambridge, MA: Harvard University Press.

Naatanen, R. (1969). Anticipation of relevant stimuli and evoked potentials: A comment on Donchin's and Cohen's averaged evoked potentials and intramodalilty selective attention. *Perceptual and Motor Skills, 28,* 639–646.

Nagel, J. J. (1993). Stage fright in musicians: A psychodynamic perspective. *Bulletin of the Menninger Clinic, 57,* 492–503.

Nash, H. L. (1987). Elite child-athletes: How much does victory cost? *The Physician and Sports Medicine, 15,* 128–133.

Neftel, K. A., Adler, R. H., Kappeli, L., Rossi, M., Dolder, M., Kaser, H. E., Bruggesser, H. H., & Vorkauf, H. (1982). Stage fright in musicians: A model illustrating the effect of beta blockers. *Psychosomatic Medicine, 44,* 461–469.

Neiss, R. (1988). Reconceptualizing arousal: Psychobiological states in motor performance. *Psychological Bulletin, 103,* 345–366.

Nideffer, R. M. (1976). Test of attentional and interpersonal style. *Journal of Personality and Social Psychology, 39,* 314–404.

———. (1981). *The ethics and practice of applied sport psychology.* Ithaca, NY: Mouvement Publications.

Nideffer, R. M., & Sagal, M. S. (2001a). *Assessment in sport psychology.* Morgantown, WV: Fitness Information Technology.

Nideffer, R. M., & Sagal, M. (2001b). Concentration and attentional control training. In J. M. Williams (Ed.), *Applied sport psychology: Personal growth to peak performance* (4th ed, pp. 312–332). Mountain View, CA: Mayfield.

Obermeier, G. E., Landers, D. M., & Easter, M. A. (1983). Social facilitation on speed events: The coaction effect on racing dogs. In W. N. Widmeyer (Ed.), *Physical activity and the social sciences* (pp. 418–430). Ithaca, NY: Mouvement Publications.

Okwumabua, T. M., Meyers, A. W., Schlesser, R., & Cooke, C. J. (1983). Cognitive strategies and running performance: An exploratory study. *Cognitive Therapy and Research, 7,* 363–370.

Oltman, P. K., Goodenough, D. R., Witkin, H. A., Freedman, N., & Friedman, F. (1975). Psychological differentiation as a factor in conflict resolution. *Journal of Personality and Social Psychology, 32,* 730–736.

Osipenko, M. F., Pankova, L. F., & Vergazov, V. M. (2004). Mycotic infection in gastric peptic ulcer. *Klincheskaia Meditsina, 11,* 35–38.

Pargman, D. (1976). Visual disembedding and injury in college football players. *Perceptual and Motor Skills, 42,* 762.

———. (1980). The way of the runner: An examination of motives for running. In R. M. Suinn (Ed.), *Psychology in sports: Methods and applications,* (pp. 90–98). Minneapolis: Burgess.

Pargman, D., Bender, P., & Deshaies, P. (1975). Correlation between visual disembedding and basketball shooting by male and female varsity college athletes. *Perceptual and Motor Skills, 4,* 956.

Pargman, D., & Burgess, S. (1979). Hooked on exercise: A psychobiological explanation. *Motor Skills: Theory Into Practice, 3,* 115–122.

Pargman, D., Sachs, M. L., & Deshaies, P. (1976). Field dependence–independence and injury in college football players. *American Corrective Therapy Journal, 30,* 174–176.

Pargman, D., Schreiber, L. E., & Stein, F. (1974). Field dependence of selected athletic sub-groups. *Medicine and Science in Sports, 6,* 283–286.

Pargman, D., & Ward, T. (1976). Biomechanical correlates of psychological differentiation in female athletes. *Research Quarterly, 47,* 750–755.

Parshad, D. (2004). Role of yoga in stress management. *West Indian Medical Journal, 53,* 191–194.

Paulus, P. B., & Cornelius, W. L. (1974). An analysis of gymnastic performance under conditions of practice and spectator observations. *Research Quarterly for Exercise and Sport, 45,* 56–63.

Paulus, P. B., Shannon, J. C., Wilson, D. L., & Boone, T. D. (1972). The effect of spectator presence on gymnastics performance in a field situation. *Psychonomic Science, 29,* 88–90.

Pavlov, I. P. (1927). *Conditioned reflexes.* London: Oxford University Press.

Pearson, P. H. (1970). Relationships between global and specified measures of novelty seeking. *Journal of Consulting and Clinical Psychology, 34,* 199–204.

Pennebaker, J. W., & Lightner, J. M. (1980). Competition of internal and external information in an exercise setting. *Journal of Personality and Social Psychology, 39,* 115–174.

Perlin, L. I., & Leiberman, M. A. (1979). Social sources of emotional distress. In R. G. Simmons (Ed.), *Research in community health.* Greenwich, CT: JAI Press.

Perlin, L. I., Menaghan, E. G., Lieberman, M. A., & Mullan, J. T. (1981). The stress process. *Journal of Health and Social Behavior, 22,* 337–356.

Petrie, A. (1967). *Individuality in pain and suffering.* Chicago: University of Chicago Press.

Popjoy, D. (1967). The effects of a physical fitness program on selected psychological and physiological measures of anxiety. Unpublished Ph.D. Dissertation, University of Illinois.

Posen, D. (2004). *Always change a losing game.* Toronto: Kay Porter, Inc.

Powers, S. K., & Howley, E. T. (2001). *Exercise physiology: Theory and application to fitness and performance.* Boston: McGraw-Hill.

Raglin, J. S., & Morgan, W. P. (1987). Influence of exercise and quiet rest on state-anxiety and blood pressure. *Medicine and Science in Sports and Exercise, 19,* 456–463.

Raju, P. S., Prasad, K. V., Venkata, R. Y., Murthy, K. J., & Reddy, M. V. (1997). Influence of intensive yoga training on physiological changes in 6 adult women: A case report. *Journal of Alternative and Complementary Medicine, 3,* 291–295.

Rassin, E., Diepstraten, P., Merchelbach, H., & Muris, P. (2001). Thought–action fusion and thoughts suppression in obsessive disorder. *Behavior Research and Therapy, 39,* 747–764.

Raub, J. S. (2002). Psychophysiologic effects of hatha yoga on musculoskeletal and cardiopulmonary function. A literature review. *Journal of Alternative and Complementary Medicine, 8,* 797–812.

Ravnskov, U. (1992). Cholesterol lowering trials in coronary heart disease: Frequency of citation and outcome. *British Medical Journal, 4,* 15–19.

Rejeski, W. J. (1985). Perceived exertion: An active or passive process? *Journal of Sport Psychology, 7,* 371–378.

Riding, R. J., & al-Salih, N. (2000). Cognitive style and motor skill and sports performance. *Educational Studies, 26,* 19–32.

Rushall, B. S., & Siedentop, D. (1972). *The development and control of behavior in sport and physical education.* Philadelphia: Lea & Febiger.

Russell, W. D., & Weeks, D. L. (1994). Attentional style in ratings of perceived exertion during physical exercise. *Perceptual and Motor Skills, 78,* 779–783.

Rutledge, P. (1998). Obsessionality and the attempted suppression of unpleasant personal intrusive thoughts. *Behavior Research and Therapy, 36,* 403–416.

Ryan, D., & Simons, J. (1983). What is learned in mental practice of motor skills: A test of the cognitive-motor hypothesis. *Journal of Sport Psychology, 5,* 419 – 426.

Ryan, E. D. (1969). Perceptual characteristics of vigorous people. In R. C. Brown & B. J. Cralty (Eds.), *New perspectives of man in action.* Englewood Cliffs, NJ: Prentice-Hall.

Ryan, T. A. (1970). *Intentional behavior.* New York: Ronald Press.

Sachs, M. L., & Pargman, D. (1979). Running addiction: A depth interview examination. *Journal of Sport Behavior, 2,* 143–155.

Sachs, M. L. & Pargman, D. (1984). Running addiction. In M. Sachs & G. Buffone (Eds.), *Running as Therapy an Integrated Approach.* Lincoln: University of Nebraska Press.

Saintsing, E. E., Richman, C. L., & Bergey, D. B. (1988). Effects of three cognitive strategies on long-distance running. *Bulletin of the Psychonomic Society, 26,* 34–36.

Salazar, W., Landers, D. M., Petruzello, S. J., Crews, D. J., Han, M., & Kubitz, K. A. (1990). Hemispheric asymmetry, cardiac response, and performance in elite archers. *Research Quarterly for Exercise and Sport, 61,* 351–359.

Schachter, S., & Singer, J. (1962). Cognitive, social and physiological determinants of emotional state. *Psychological Review, 69,* 379–397.

Schmidt, R. A., & Lee, T. D. (1999). *Motor control and learning: A behavioral emphasis.* Champaign, IL: Human Kinetics.

Scholz, O. B. (2001). Short- and medium-term effects of hypnotic mood induction. *Zeitschrift fur Psychologie, 209,* 118–136.

Schomer, H. H. (1987). Mental strategy programme for marathon runners. *International Journal of Sport Psychology, 18,* 133–151.

Seaward, B. L. (2002). *Managing stress: Principles and strategies for health and well-being, 3rd Ed.* Boston: Jones and Bartlett.

Seijts, G. H., & Latham, G. E. (2001). The effect of distal learning, outcome, and proximal goals on a moderately complex task. *Journal of Organizational Behavior, 22,* 291–307.

Selye, H. (1976). *The stress of life.* New York: McGraw-Hill.

———. (1982). History and present status of the stress concept. In S. Breznitz & I. Goldberger (Eds.), *Handbook of stress, theoretical and clinical aspects* (pp. 7–17). New York: The Free Press.

Shapiro, F. (2001). *Eye movement desensitization and reprocessing: Basic principles, protocols, and procedures* (2nd ed.). New York: Guilford Press.

Shapiro, S. L., Schwartz, G. E., & Bonner, G. (1998). Effects of mindfulness-based stress reduction on medical and premedical students. *Journal of Behavioral Medicine, 21,* 581–589.

Short, N. P., & Curran, J. (2004). Unreliable evidence. *Journal of Psychiatric and Mental Health Nursing, 11,* 106–115.

Shultz, J. H., & Luthe, W. (1969). *Autogenic therapy, Vol. 1: Autogenic methods.* New York: Grane and Stratton.

Silva, J. M. & Shultz, B.B. (1984). Research in the psychology and therapeutics of running: A methodological and interpretive review. In M. Sachs & G. W. Buffone (Eds.), *Running as therapy an integrated approach.* Lincoln: University of Nebraska Press.

Simpson, G. C., Mackay, C. J., & Cox, T. (1974). Blood sugar levels in response to stress. *Ergonomics, 17,* 481.

Singer, R. N. (1965). Effects of spectators on athletes and nonathletes performing a gross motor task. *Research Quarterly for Exercise and Sport, 36,* 473–482.

Skinner, B. F. (1963). Behaviorism at fifty. *Science, 140,* 951–958.

Smith, R. E. (1986). Toward a cognitive-affective model of athletic burnout. *Journal of Sport Psychology, 8,* 36–50.

Smith, T. W., & Williams, P. G. (1992). Personality and health: Advantages and limitations of the five-factor model. *Journal of Personality, 60,* 395–423.

Solomon, R., & Corbit, J. (1974). An opponent-process theory of motivation: Temporal dynamics of affect. *Psychological Review, 81,* 119–145.

Sorrell, W. (1965). To be a critic. *Dance Scope, 1,* 3–9.

Spence, D. P. (1982). Verbal indicators of stress. In L. Goldberger & S. Breznitz (Eds.), *Handbook of stress: Theoretical and clinical aspects* (pp. 295–305). New York: Free Press.

Spielberger, C. D., Gorsuch, R. I., & Lushene, R. E. (1970). *Manual for the state-trait anxiety inventory.* Palo Alto, CA: Consulting Psychologist Press.

Stanton, H. E. (1994). Reduction of performance anxiety in music students. *Australian Psychologist, 29,* 124–127.

Sunshine, W., Field, T., Schanberg, S., Quintino, O., Fierro, K., Kuhn, C., Burman, I., & Schanberg, S. (1996). Fibromyalgia benefits from massage therapy and transcutaneous electrical stimulation. *Journal of Clinical Rheumatology, 2,* 18–22.

Takahashi, T., Murata, T., Hamada, T., Omori, M., Kosaka, H., Yoshida, H., & Wadi, Y. (2005). Changes in EEG and autonomic nervous activity during meditation in association with personality traits. *International Journal of Psychophysiology, 55,* 199–207.

Taylor, B. (1983, April). Dancers world: Performance butterflies. *Dance Magazine.*

Taylor, J. A. (1953). A personality scale of manifest anxiety. *Journal of Abnormal and Social Psychology, 48,* 285–290.

Tenenbaum, G. (2004). A social cognitive perspective of perceived exertion and exertion tolerance. In R. Singer, C. Janelle, & H. Hasenblas (Eds.), *Handbook of sport psychology* (pp. 810–820). New York: Wiley & Sons.

Tindall, B. (2004). Better playing through chemistry. *New York Times,* October 17. Available at: http://www.mozartinthejungle.com/work4.htm. Retrieved January 3, 2006.

Triplett, N. (1897). The dynamogenic factors in pacemaking and competition. *American Journal of Psychology, 9,* 507–553.

Vandenbergh, R. L., & Sussman, R. E. (1967). Alterations of blood glucose levels with chemical stress: The effect of final examinations in university students with insulin-requiring diabetes mellitus (paper presented at the 27th annual meeting of the American Diabetic Association, Atlantic City, New Jersey). *Diabetes, 16,* 537.

Vijayalakshmi, P., Madanmohan, Bhavanani, A. B., Patil, A., & Babu, K. (2004). Modulation of stress induced by isometric handgrip test in hypertensive patients following yogic relaxation training. *Indian Journal of Physiology and Pharmacology, 48,* 59–64.

Wankel, L. M. (1972). Competition in motor performance: An experimental analysis of motivational components. *Journal of Experimental Social Psychology, 8,* 427–437.

———. (1975). The effects of social reinforcement and audience presence upon the motor performance of boys with different levels of initial ability. *Journal of Motor Behavior, 7,* 207–216.

———. (1984). Audience effects in sport. In J. M. Sylva & R. S. Weinberg (Eds.), *Psychological foundations of sport* (pp. 293–314). Champaign, IL: Human Kinetics.

Weinberg, R. R. (1990). Anxiety and motor performance: Where do we go from here? *Anxiety Research, 2,* 227–242.

Weiss, R. F., & Miller, F. G. (1971). The drive theory of social facilitation. *Psychological Review, 78*, 48–57.

Welford, A. T. (1973). Stress and performance. *Ergonomics, 16*, 567–580.

Wenzlaff, R. M., & Wegner, D. M. (2000). Thought suppression. *Annual Review of Psychology, 51*, 59–91.

West, J., Otte, C., Gehr, K., Johnson, J., & Mohr, D. (2004). Effects of hatha yoga and African dance on perceived stress, affect and stationary cortisol. *Annals of Behavioral Medicine, 28*, 114–118.

Willoughby, W. (1973). Questionnaire for self-administration. In J. Wolpe (Ed.), *The practice of behavior therapy* (2nd ed.). New York: Pergamon Press.

Witkin, H. A. (1964). Origins of cognitive style. In C. Sheer (Ed.), *Cognition: Theory, research, and promise* (pp. 172–205. New York: Harper & Row.

Witkin, H. A. (1977). *Cognitive Styles in Personal and Cultural Adaptation.* Worcester, MA: Clark University Press.

Witkin, H. A., Dyke, R., Faterson, H. F., Goodenough, D. R., & Karp, S. A. (1962). *Psychological differentiation.* New York: Wiley.

Witkin, H. A., Oltman, P. T., Rasking, E., & Karp, S. P. (1971). *A group embedded figures test manual.* Palo Alto, CA: Consulting Psychologists Press.

Wolpe, J. (1958). *Psychotherapy by reciprocal inhibition.* Stanford, CA: Stanford University Press.

Wolpe, J. (1973). *The practice of behavior therapy* (2nd ed.). New York: Pergamon Press.

Wood, R. E., & Locke, E. A. (1990). Goal setting and strategy effects on complex tasks. *Research in Organizational Behavior, 12*, 73–109.

Woolery, A., Myers, H., Sternlieb, B., & Zeltzer, L. (2004). A yoga intervention for young adults with elevated symptoms of depression. *Alternative Therapies in Health and Medicine, 10*, 60–63.

Wrisberg, C., & Pein, R. (1990). Past running experience as a mediator of the attentional focus of male and female recreational runners. *Perceptual and Motor Skills, 70*, 427–432.

Yerkes, R. M., & Dodson, J. D. (1908). The relation of strength of stimulus to rapidity of habit-formation. *Journal of Comparative and Neurological Psychology, 18*, 459–482.

Zaichkowsky, L. D. (1982). Biofeedback for self-regulation of competitive stress. In L. D. Zaichkowsky & W.E. Sime (Eds.), *Stress Management for Sport* (p. 62). Reston, VA: American Alliance for Health, Physical Education, Recreation, & Dance.

Zajonc, R. B. (1965). Social facilitation. *Science, 149*, 269–274.

———. (1980). Copresence. In P. B. Paulus (Ed.), *Psychology of group influence* (pp. 35–60). Hillsdale, NJ: Erlbaum.

Zegans, L. S. (1982). Stress and the development of somatic clinical aspects. In L. Goldberger & S. Breznitz (Eds.), *Handbook of stress: Theoretical and clinical aspects*. New York: Free Press.

Zeitlin, D., Keller, S., Shiflett, S., Schleifer, S., & Bartlett, J. (2000). Immunological effects of massage therapy during acute academic stress. *Psychosomatic Medicine, 62,* 83–84.

Zimkin, N. (1964). Stress during muscular exercises and the state of non-specifically increased resistance. In E. Jokl & E. Simon (Eds.), *International Research in Physical Education*. Springfield, IL: Thomas.

Zuckerman, M. (1960). The development of an affect adjective checklist for the measurement of anxiety. *Journal of Consulting Psychology, 24,* 457–462.

———. (1971). Dimensions of sensation-seeking. *Journal of Counseling and Clinical Psychology, 36,* 41–52.

———. (1990). The psychophysiology of sensation seeking. *Journal of Personality, 58,* 313–345.

———. (1996). The psychobiological model for impulsive unsocialized sensation seeking: A comparative approach. *Neuropsychobiology, 34,* 125–129.

———. (2004). The shaping of personality: Genes, environments, and chance encounters. *Journal of Personality Assessment, 82,* 11–22.

Zuckerman, M., Bone, R. N., Neary, R., Mangelsdorff, B., & Brustman, B. (1972). What is the sensation seeker? Personality trait and experience correlates of the sensation-seeking scales. *Journal of Consulting and Clinical Psychology, 39,* 308–321.

Zung, W. W. K. (1971). A rating instrument for anxiety disorders. *Psychosomatics, 12,* 371–379.

Zung, W. W. K., & Cavenar, O., Jr. (1980). Assessment scales and techniques. In I. L. Kutash & L. B. Schlesinger (Eds.), *Handbook on stress and anxiety*. San Francisco: Jossey-Bass.

INDEX

M